Postfeminist News

SUNY series

———————————

COMMUNICATION
STUDIES

———————————

Dudley D. Cahn, editor

POSTFEMINIST NEWS

Political Women in Media Culture

MARY DOUGLAS VAVRUS

STATE UNIVERSITY OF NEW YORK PRESS

Published by
STATE UNIVERSITY OF NEW YORK PRESS, ALBANY

© 2002   State University of New York

For information, address State University of New York Press,
90 State Street, Suite 700, Albany, NY 12207

Production, Laurie Searl
Marketing, Jennifer Giovani-Giovani

Library of Congress Cataloging-in-Publication Data

Vavrus, Mary Douglas.
  Postfeminist news : political women in media culture / Mary Douglas Vavrus.
    p. cm. — (SUNY series in communication studies)
  Includes bibliographical references and index.
  ISBN 0-7914-5445-2 (alk. paper) — ISBN 0-7914-5446-0 (pbk. : alk. paper)
    1. Mass media and women—United States. 2. Women politicians—United States. 3.
  Feminism and mass media—United States. 4. United States—Politics and
  government—1989– I. Title. II. Series.

P94.5.W652 U68 2002
302.23'082'0973—dc21
                                                                    2002017735

10   9   8   7   6   5   4   3   2   1

This book is dedicated to August and Hallie Vavrus,
for all of their optimism about the future of politics.

Contents

ACKNOWLEDGMENTS

This book started as my dissertation in the Institute of Communications Research at the University of Illinois, so I want to thank my advisor, Paula Treichler, and committee members Cliff Christians, Norman Denzin, and Andrea Press for their intellectual guidance and helpful comments from start to finish. I would not have been able to do much of anything without them or without the wisdom and institutional memory of Diane Tipps, administrative secretary of the Institute of Communications Research. Colleagues at the University of Minnesota, my current institution, also have given me valuable feedback on this project. I want to thank Karlyn Kohrs Campbell and Edward Schiappa in particular for reading drafts of chapters and providing comments that have made this book stronger. The students I have known at the "U" helped me clarify my thoughts on this project; they also provided articles and references, many of which made their way into these chapters. I feel fortunate to have been surrounded by insightful colleagues since the beginning of this project.

The ideas in this book were nurtured by my family members all along. I want to thank my parents, Hallie and Gus, for making me appreciate the importance of political engagement and discussion, and for encouraging me during this project—what has turned out to be a very long political discussion! My sister, Fran, and brother, Steve, have been kindred spirits, both in politics and circumstance: although they were doctoral students at the same time I was, they always made time for me to talk about my project—and they always offered their own interesting and useful commentary. My family has been only generous in providing both intellectual and emotional support.

Although they are not related by blood, the friends I made while in graduate school were indispensable and influenced my thinking and writing with input from their respective disciplines. Stacie Colwell, Agnes Loeffler, Christine Marsick, Deborah Kern, Laurie Blakely, and Maureen Hogan in the Big Yellow House nourished me intellectually and socially; Shawny Anderson, Cat Warren, Lori Reed, Ginna Husting, Mike Greco, Steve Wiley, and Gil Rodman made valuable contributions to all of these chapters as well. Steve Jahn provided me with encouragement and space to write and think, and an insistence on laughter when I could do no more of either.

Finally, I want to note that the National Communication Association gave permission for me to reprint portions of chapter 3, which first appeared in 1998 in *Critical Studies in Mass Communication* 15:3:213–35, as "Working the Senate from the Outside in: The Mediated Construction of a Feminist Political Campaign." Taylor & Francis allowed me to reprint portions of chapter 4, originally published in 2000 in *Political Communication* 17:2:193–213, as "From Women of the Year to 'Soccer Moms': The Case of the Incredible Shrinking Women." The Organization for Research on Women and Communication has permitted me to reprint portions of the afterword, which was first published in 2000 as "Putting Ally on Trial: Contesting Postfeminism in Popular Culture," in *Women's Studies in Communication* 23:3:413–28.

Introduction

The news that just cries out from this welter and mass of information about women's attitudes and condition in 1972 is that women have sprung loose as an independent political force. . . . And once you let a force like that loose, I would suggest that it can never be bottled up again.

—Louis Harris and Associates
pollster Louis Harris in Klemesrud,
"Do Women Want Equality?"

The truth is, except on a few high profile issues—abortion rights, sexual harassment, violence against women—electoral feminism is a pretty pallid affair: a little more money for breast cancer research here, a boost for women business owners there. The main job of the women is the same as that of the men: playing toward the center, amassing campaign funds, keeping business and big donors happy, and currying favor with the leadership in hopes of receiving plums. . . . It would be more accurate to say that, like other social-justice movements, organized feminism is caught in a co-dependent relationship with electoral politics: No matter how often and how blatantly our hopes are betrayed, we keep coming back, begging to have our illusions rewoven for another bout at the polls.

—*The Nation* columnist Katha Pollitt,
"Subject to Debate"

The statements above represent clearly contrasting views on the relationship between women and politics. Louis Harris expressed his optimistic view in 1972, one of the most important years for the second-wave women's movement's push to influence electoral politics. In 1972, after polling 3,000 women and 1,000 men for their opinions on women's equality (Klemesrud 1972, 36), Harris may indeed have felt that he was observing a juggernaut in the making. Katha Pollitt's view, twenty-three years later, is less optimistic, instead expressing disillusionment with the outcomes of feminism's forays into electoral politics.

1

Both Harris's and Pollitt's perspectives on feminism and electoral politics are representative of the way in which mainstream media construct this relationship: in mainstream media narratives, hope springs eternal that women can transform politics in a positive fashion. But the subtext of many of these narratives is a story about the difficulties feminists face when they try to coexist with the institutions of electoral politics, what Pollitt refers to above as a "codependent relationship." It is the tension between these two views that structures media narratives about women in electoral politics in the 1990s, and it is this tension that informs my analysis of the representation of feminism in electoral politics in the 1990s.

More specifically, this book's central thesis is that media representation of political women in the 1990s promotes a form of postfeminism: a revision of feminism that encourages women's private, consumer lifestyles rather than cultivating a desire for public life and political activism. My argument is not about electoral politics as much as it is about representational politics—the politics that govern how discourses about particular women are constituted on television and in the pages of newspapers, magazines, and books. Electoral politics is simply a cultural arena, a site on which struggles for meaning about the appropriateness of women's relationships to socioeconomic power take place. Of course, the realm of electoral politics is not restricted to struggles about women; in fact, until fairly recently, women were hardly part of the picture of electoral politics at all. Since the women's movement of the 1970s, though, women's presence in electoral politics as voters, politicos, and politicians has become much more common and even high profile at times. It thus follows that media coverage of women in electoral politics is significant for the commentary that it provides media audiences about feminism and femininity at particular junctures; about idealized gender roles and transgressions from these; about the media's investments in particular constructions of femininity and feminism; and about the representational process itself—a process that has, historically, generated both progressive and hidebound models of gender. This process has become particularly important, I argue, in the media-saturated era of the 1990s to the present, the period on which this book's analysis is focused.

It is a truism by now in media studies that the mainstream media of the United States play an increasingly significant role in shaping public knowledge about all manner of things, but this is not to say that the media operate as propaganda machines, coercing *tabula rasa* audiences into accepting a party line. Rather, the media (and my book is focused on print and television in particular) create, maintain, extend, and delimit the content and boundaries of the symbolic environment of our lives—and certainly our lives as of the final decade of the twentieth century. The media construct particular views of the world, and through continuous interactions with these views, we mold and shape our own perspectives and orientations toward reality. Communication, particularly mass mediated communication today, in effect creates our realities; through communicative practices, we ritualistically negotiate with and ascribe meaning and value to experiences (Carey 1989). This "reality effect" is what Stuart Hall (1982, 74) argues is *the* media effect to be examined in media scholarship for its potentially far-reaching consequences, both public and private. This process of representation demands that media texts, and news texts are no exception, both generate and respond to the myriad material and symbolic dimensions of the "real world."[1] In other words, the material and the symbolic are mutually constitutive.

The media's contribution to this process, however, is not especially comprehensive or inclusive of a diversity of views and voices—this point, too, is widely accepted by many academics and news workers. It is a point that is hardly debatable now—particularly since the 1980s, for example, when media moguls began to give up any pretense of neutrality (their own or their media organizations') and sometimes voiced their biases loudly and unapologetically and imposed their politics on the multitude of outlets they acquired (see, e.g., Aufderheide 2000; Bagdikian 2000; McChesney 1999; Vavrus, forthcoming).

Even if arguments for media impartiality have become indefensible, the nature of the partiality of different media representations is not always readily apparent. This is particularly so during a historical moment in which the logic of advertising has found its way into all genres of media texts, including news stories (Andersen 1995; McChesney 1999). That is, the creep of advertising using new and innovative means of circulation necessitates a kind of literacy: that ability to read media texts critically and closely to discern not only their manifest messages but their latent appeals. It is the latter appeal that is insidious with its call to join the rituals of a commodity culture, to celebrate individualism, to supplant substance with "lifestyle," and to think in terms of individual gratification rather than public good. In a broad fashion, Robert McChesney (1999, 2) proves this contention, and, further, that the "media have become a significant *anti-democratic* force in the United States" (emphasis in original). Like many political economists, however, his analysis does not focus on how gender figures in this force, and how, in turn, it might be shaped by it. My analysis addresses this issue, and while my argument accords with McChesney's assessment of this anti-democratic terrain, it also departs from his and moves toward rather uncharted territory, specifically, the representational politics around women and how they may play a role in the anti-democratic nature of this force, particularly that component that spins messages about feminism to various media audiences.

With this in mind, the analysis I undertake is specific to media represen-tations of women, however I am acutely aware that the corporate and often anti-democratic tone of mainstream media offerings and policy (described thoroughly by McChesney 1999 and Bagdikian 2000) is used in relation to men as well as women, to children and to teens. For media corporations, the body politic is little more than a collection of target markets whose primary function is to generate advertising revenue, the lifeblood of a commercial media system (McChesney 1997). Some of us are more attractive target markets than others; as I will show in subsequent chapters, women (a particular group of women, that is) constitute an extremely valuable market for advertisers. It is this relationship between advertising and media content that is crucial to bear in mind when examining media texts about women, whether these texts are con-sidered individually or together as particular discursive formations. But it is not the case that advertising and marketing techniques always call attention to themselves (McAllister 1999). Those that do not are more troubling—and ubiquitous. These techniques are sometimes subtle, often seamless promotions for various products, for corporations, for TV and film characters and products, and for lifestyles that appeal to specific demographic groups (often white and middle- to upper-middle class). They are not strictly limited to the ad spaces between media texts; they are woven into news stories, for example, and thus they do double duty as informational and promotional messages (see Andersen 1995 for a discussion of examples and tactics used to dissolve the boundaries between ads and the traditionally separate realms of news and entertainment).

These are the general conclusions that I have reached after spending most of the last decade engaged with some part of this project. In 1992, when I began to examine the subject of political women in the news, I thought that this would be a small news analysis project that might fulfill a graduate seminar requirement. I did not expect it to expand to include media events that spanned the 1990s, nor did I expect that I would see so many clear patterns in the media texts I analyzed for the chapters following this one. However, after poring over several hundred news stories, videos, and transcripts, my interest in discerning longitudinal patterns grew, as did the project's boundaries. I found the homo-geneity and consensus of perspective among these texts startling—even to a media critic such as myself. In retrospect, I can say that I should not have been so surprised; after all, I had been studying critical media theories and had con-sidered at length the abstract issues associated with the commodification of the news. However, seeing concrete and overwhelming evidence of news commodification convinced me that something more than simple event description was occurring in these texts. I pushed on to satisfy my intellectual curiosity and to test theory. What has resulted from this work is a broad argument about media representation and feminism.

Originally, I conceived of this project as an analysis of one phenomenon I read and heard much about in the mainstream media in 1992: the Year of the Woman, the thirteen months preceding the 1992 election. The phrase, "Year of the Woman," appeared regularly in mainstream news to herald a purportedly pro-woman political climate, but the great dissonance between the "year's" women and what seemed to be the material conditions of average women's lives in the United States prompted me to look more closely at the Year of the Woman. Yet, invariably, when I discussed this phenomenon with friends, family, and colleagues, I got one of two responses: a confession of ignorance ("I have no idea what you're talking about"), or an enthusiastic show of support. Those unfamiliar with the Year of the Woman, despite its wide media use, were baffled by my decision to devote time and energy to examining something so "obscure." The others, aware of the thirteen-month phenomenon from the time Anita Hill's name appeared in public discourse (October 6, 1991) to the presidential election of 1992 (November 6), when Barbara Boxer, Carol Moseley Braun, Dianne Feinstein, Patty Murray,[2] and Lynn Yeakel[3] ran for U.S. Senate seats, were enthusiastic about my interest, echoed its possibilities and complications, and were eager to share their observations. This dichotomous response captured some of the fundamental ironies and problems of the concept and spoke volumes about the ways in which media constructions are taken up (or not) at a personal level.

Inevitably, this project grew to encompass other media events concerning women in politics as well. Consequently, my approach to it shifted to reflect both a more formal, systematic investigation and my own commitments to or reservations about particular aspects of theory, feminism, and electoral politics. In my mind, a feminist media studies approach is that which offers the best tools for understanding and intervening into the nexus of media representational practices and lived experience. Feminist media research yields insights about how gender is constructed in and lived through the symbolic environment of popular culture to account not only for media texts but material practices around them, such as voting and issue activism. When a political economy critique is included, such research provides a three-pronged form of analysis that broadens *and* deepens explanations for why we get the representations we do, and how we might read them more critically; to riff Marshall McLuhan, I argue not that the medium is the message, but that the business of media is now the message. In a literal sense, the facts of media mergers and acquisitions are the stuff of breaking news stories (although political economists argue that news organizations do not and because of corporate dictates cannot undertake critical analyses of this trend). In a less obvious sense, though, the business trends among media corporations are ultimately responsible for shaping the products they produce: mass media texts. To understand why these messages are what they are, one must look to the corporations that produce them and how these corporations finance themselves.

This book thus discusses women and these dimensions of the representational politics of media, most particularly the media's construction of feminism in the coverage of electoral politics. Most of the book's chapters concern electoral politics, broadly construed. The afterword focuses on feminist politics in popular culture generally. My guiding question asks whether news coverage of women in politics is culturally significant; my conclusion is that such coverage is clearly significant for several reasons, not the least of which is because print and television news texts illuminate the relationships that women have to socioeconomic power. These texts are woven through with both approving and disparaging intimations about the women they feature, about how much and what kinds of power women can wield most appropriately. In this sense, such texts are always already commenting on feminism, informed as they are by one of the main goals of feminism: to improve the conditions of women's lives by revealing and then subverting the reproduction of patriarchal power.[4]

At a more concrete level, news texts tell stories of challenges to the patriarchal power embodied in political institutions. For example, Year of the Woman stories, such as the *New York Times'* glowing accounts of Year of the Woman candidates (discussed in Chapter 3), coursed with admiration as the candidates and their supporters took on the male-dominated Congress. The way in which women—or any group of candidates and voters—are positioned in the public discourse of news is significant, yet women's constructed relationship to electoral politics is seldom explored in media studies research. This absence is notable if for no other reason than news reports—and the tropes on which they rely—are the only sources most citizens have available for learning about political candidates, their platforms, and the possible future consequences of voting for one or another candidate (stump speeches, to name one example, are rarely experienced firsthand, without broadcast or print mediation). What is more, most voters have no firsthand contact with a corpus of campaign rhetoric; even if a voter happens to be in attendance at one or even a handful of stump speeches, it is virtually impossible for her to attend all of the campaign speeches that a slate of candidates gives in any election year. To expose themselves to candidates' campaign messages, voters must turn to mass media. For women, this coverage simultaneously constructs a perspective on feminist politics as it comments on electoral politics.

What emerges in the following chapters is the gendered logic that undergirds mainstream news narratives about political women and women's issues. I argue that the ways in which political women were discursively framed had significant consequences for public understandings of gender and its relationship to institutional power, race, and socioeconomic class. Dominant public meanings around these resulted from struggles between feminist and nonfeminist or antifeminist groups, each of which stood to gain or lose ideological ground.

OVERVIEW

To contextualize contemporary accounts of political women in mainstream media, the first chapter of this book sets up the theoretical framework for the analysis in the following chapters. This chapter provides a fuller explanation of the way in which media hegemony theory and articulation work together to construct postfeminist notions about women. For this reason, it also is a chapter about reading media texts critically. As a media critic by trade, I evaluate media texts—TV news, newspapers, radio news, and entertainment media—carefully for their ideological suggestions, even when I am technically "off the clock," but this does not dampen my enthusiasm or prevent my enjoyment of media. On the contrary, I am an avid fan of a number of TV programs, newspapers, and local news programming—both TV and radio. I find that I enjoy these offerings both because I enjoy the sense of belonging to an imagined community of viewers and readers and because I enjoy the critical perspective that I reflexively move to when I become a media consumer. This informal critical practice, falsely perhaps, makes me believe that I am not falling prey to the media maw.

All of this is to say that despite my critique of the mainstream texts that I analyze, I still very much enjoy various media offerings. Both news and entertainment media show great potential for fostering civic-mindedness and community accountability—however one defines the community that she or he calls primary. In their coverage of women, particularly political women, however, the television and print media seem mostly accountable to a very small and exclusive group of women; this surely has consequences for democratic practice, whether in the electoral realm or elsewhere. My intention in chapter 1, then, is to construct a theoretical guide with which readers might navigate the discursive terrain of news coverage.

The chapters subsequent to the first are case studies in what Robert Goldman and Arvind Rajagopal (1991) have termed "mapping hegemony." That is, each of these chapters demonstrates a different fragment of postfeminist ideology; each fragment arises out of the recurrent patterns, tropes, and themes that news texts use in their narratives about four distinct but very much related media events involving women and electoral politics: the Anita Hill–Clarence Thomas hearings of 1991; the Year of the Woman of 1992; the "soccer moms" of 1996; and the Senate campaign of Hillary Rodham Clinton of 2000. Media narratives about each of these events were sometimes ideologically complex and in no way represent a monolithic ideological bloc, but taken together, they reveal a great number of similarities in language and in bias. They are, in fact, more similar than they are different—owing, in large part, to pack journalism tendencies, the influence of corporate owners, and an urgent need for media parent companies to turn a profit. Whatever the motivation, though, the fact of overriding homogeneity remains. These case studies thus work as stand-alone illustrations of tactics used to create and sustain a media event. Together they provide a longitudinal example of the way in which these events function together as a discursive formation with a historically specific hegemony.

Chapter 2 discusses the Anita Hill–Clarence Thomas hearings, their tone of crisis, and how this crisis set up the originary narrative of the Year of the Woman. Mainstream print and television accounts of the hearings permitted more feminist commentary than is usual in news coverage; these also expanded explanations of sexual harassment and its roots in social and professional power disparities. The crisis of white patriarchal authority that I argue emerged in media coverage of the hearings opened a space for feminists to work the media and the political system. Feminist messages generated in the hearings moved from the context of the hearings to the realm of electoral politics in the form of the political campaigns of the Year of the Woman candidates, the media coverage on which chapter 3 is focused. The discursive construction of these candidates' campaigns points to pervasive neoliberalism, a politics that conflates the practices of democracy with the economic policies of capitalism. As McChesney notes, "neoliberal democracy is one where the political sector controls little and debates even less" (1999, 6). Political debates within a neoliberal democracy are "trivial" affairs that cover "minor issues by parties that basically pursue the same probusiness policies regardless of formal differences and campaign debate" (1999, 111). Neoliberalism thus privileges private, corporate solutions to social problems and tends to marginalize critiques of racism and classism as potentially subordinating practices.

Chapter 4 moves from 1992 to 1996 to examine print and television narratives about women during the 1996 presidential campaign. A mere four years after the Year of the Woman's hosannas for female politicians, 1996 election news reports relied upon a very different tone when describing the dominant image of women in electoral politics, the "soccer mom." The soccer mom is a constructed figure that initially serves as a label for a swing voting bloc, but which becomes articulated to a more profitable realm than that of electoral politics: that of consumer. This chapter explicates the emphasis on soccer moms' consumer habits, how it contributes to a postfeminist logic of gender, and how this logic influences the commonsense beliefs of news workers.

Hillary Rodham Clinton's campaign for a U.S. Senate seat is the subject of chapter 5. The years between 1996 and 2000, the latter the year of Hillary's run, were rich with events and policies that had the potential to make a significant impact on the representational politics of feminism: the 1996 Federal Telecommunications Act and the impeachment of President Bill Clinton, a sitting president, for perjuring himself in sexual harassment testimony. Repercussions from both of these shaped and informed media discourse about Hillary Clinton's Senate campaign, and, I argue, influenced news outlets to overlook what could have been another Year of the Woman based on the large numbers of women running for the House of Representatives and the Senate simultaneously with Hillary's run. Chapter 5 discusses the patterns that television news stories displayed in their star-struck commentary on Hillary Rodham Clinton in this context.

The afterword represents a shift in critical object; that is, rather than examining other events in electoral politics, I turn to popular accounts (fictionalized as well as nonfiction) of women's lives from the late 1990s, particularly those accounts that invoke feminism either implicitly or explicitly. I argue that the character of these accounts leads to "postfeminist solipsism" in imagining the whole of flesh-and-blood women's experiences. Postfeminism's influence on political coverage of women suggests that the electoral arena is appropriate for one very specific type of woman: white, straight, and middle class to elite. Popular media examinations of women's lives further restrict the field of possibilities for women by blaming feminism for problems that women experience when they try to achieve professional, parental, and domestic success and satisfaction. Thus not only is it the case that electoral politics appears to be off limits to all but an exclusive club of particular women, but the only politics whose primary goal is specific to improving women's lives—feminism—also appears as an unattractive option. The position that results is postfeminist, and solipsistic at that. The mainstream media's perspective on women's lives is informed by postfeminism to such an extent that it virtually omits even a brief consideration of the possible benefits of feminism. I conclude the afterword with an exploration of one possible intervention into news production about women and feminism, that found in the principles of public journalism.

The purpose of this book is twofold: to encourage media literacy informed by feminist media studies and political economy, and to suggest strategies that offer an activist-oriented approach to media production. The media system, while moving to a fortress-like state, is not impenetrable yet; that is, it has vulnerable spots that activists and media critics can exploit through informed action. It is my hope that this book can contribute to such an effort.

CHAPTER ONE

THEORIZING MEDIA REPRESENTATION
OF ELECTORAL FEMINISM

Since the early 1970s, feminists' substantial battles about gender, race, and class have attracted media attention; the lessons from these have been incorporated thoroughly into some genres (such as TV soap operas). The media's representational practices are considered largely responsible for producing and privileging the meanings associated with feminist politics today (Douglas 1994; Rapping 1994), yet some media representations still construct women as Other: to politics, to finance, to the corporate world, and so on. Thus, even in the 1990s,

> [i]t is still news when women are running for office and taking charge of
> big cities, governors' mansions, and congressional districts in the same
> way it is still news when infants' mothers are called up and shipped off to
> war, and other women are flying helicopters into battle and coming home
> in body bags. In short: It is still news whenever women tackle any job
> American society traditionally has seen as male. What constitutes "news"
> is partly whatever editors or news directors decide and partly a hundred
> years of a tradition that has defined women and their issues as "soft" news,
> while politics is "hard" news and a man's domain. (Witt, Paget, and
> Matthews 1994, 182–83)

The relationship between feminism, female politicians, and the news is still a problematic one, and its troubles are long-standing—well over a century and a half long. Historically, feminists have turned to electoral politics when their struggles needed support from government offices or sympathetic legislators. The 1991–1992 election season was an example of just such a turn. Although it was unique in many ways, it was for female politicians another battle in a century-long-plus war of position to increase their numbers, and thus to increase their power and influence in local, state, and national offices. Unlike past battles with the same objective, however, these were high-profile, mass-mediated events that resulted in much positive publicity for these politicians and the issues they raised. Of course, some of these issues, such as sexual harassment, were made especially vivid and salient by their having been raised in the context of the Anita Hill–Clarence Thomas Senate hearings. The experiences recounted and experienced by Anita Hill as she testified before the Senate Judiciary Committee personalized the politics of the hearings; they contributed to their affective context and to the way such affect was diffused among the women who then ran for political office as a result of Hill's experiences.

The Hill–Thomas hearings and the coverage of political women in the 1990s and 2000 were vitally important for legitimating feminism and reconstituting its public face, yet inevitably feminism also was constrained in its construction in mainstream media. This tension exemplifies the ongoing dialectic by which latter-day social movements are represented to the public and how these representations, in turn, constitute an ideological field. One of the standard methods for analyzing this ideological field consists of mapping recurrent appearances, omissions, and contradictions in reports about a public issue, for example, to see the messages in these patterns and to illuminate the power relations they obscure, but this should not suggest that media texts are semiotically monolithic; they are instead polysemic. Capable of generating multiple interpretations, meanings in media texts are contingent and never guaranteed. For media representation, this ensures that even at the level of production and distribution the most carefully controlled events may take on quite unforeseen lives of their own at the level of reception (Hall 1993). In the events I examine in subsequent chapters, both feminist and antifeminist political blocs work to signify feminism (i.e., fix its meanings) so that it will be advantageous for each group's own purposes. In the process of representing these struggles, media texts foreground some of these meanings while they dismiss, devalue, and even omit others. The resulting ideology reveals as much about the representational politics of media as it does about the role of women and feminism in electoral politics. An examination of feminism in electoral politics at the end of the twentieth century thus necessitates a simultaneous examination of the media processes that construct women's relationship to electoral politics.

The Politics of Representing Feminism

One of the foundational beliefs of feminism is that gender is a culturally constructed, ideological category, the meanings and artifacts of which change over time as a result of historical conditions, thus far resulting in inequitable material conditions for women. Gender also is a naturalized category—something that has allowed its exploitation in the service of patriarchal interests for centuries. The various cultural meanings associated with gender, and the power differential that has resulted from these, have been justified by arguments about biology and gender-appropriate behavior. Social institutions have played different roles in promoting specific ideas about gender; some, for example, fundamentalist churches and conservative organizations such as the Family Research Council, are quite public and strident in their defense of a biologically determined gender hierarchy in which men are genetically programmed to dominate women. Other institutions, for instance, those of mainstream journalism, tend to associate themselves with a liberal philosophy of gender relations and to state their support for equality between women and men in public and private realms. Representations of gender are dynamic and subject to revision, most often (but not necessarily) as the result of struggles between women and social and political institutions.

Contemporary feminist theory also, and importantly, insists upon seeing gender as inextricably tied to race, class, and sexual orientation. In other words, because none of us experiences gender apart from these other forms of identity, feminist analysis must examine how these work together to produce cultural hierarchies (Spelman 1988). As bell hooks is now well known for pointing out, race, class, gender, and sexual orientation work together in different ways for different people; particular identity traits work as "interlocking systems of domination" (1990, 62) that permit some people to dominate while they push others to be dominated. This way of conceptualizing power differentials is a move spurred by poststructuralism and its theorizing around identity construction. It also is a move supported by a socialist or materialist perspective that considers differentially allocated material and symbolic wealth and how they are related to the nexus of gender–race–class (Steeves 1997). A socialist or materialist feminist analysis, such as that employed in these pages, necessitates a focus on critical objects that figure significantly into everyday life practices and reproduce patriarchal domination. Media texts, particularly news texts, are just such objects.

Although conclusions of media studies research support this idea, little research has been done in the area of feminist analysis of news. Those few

studies in this area point to a dearth of research on the ways in which political women and so-called "women's issues" are covered in the news. Margaret
Gallagher's (1992) far-reaching review of trends in feminist media research
notes that a "feminist perspective of the crucially important genres of news,
current affairs and other factual media content is well-nigh absent . . . and long
overdue" (14). In part, the paucity of research in this area results from the news
having long been considered a male domain from production to reception.
That the news industry is male dominated is a claim that has been substanti-
ated often and across various media (see, for instance, chapters by Sue A. Lafky,
Maurine H. Beasley, and Sammye Johnson in Creedon 1993). Public women
and women's issues were, and often still are, considered not worthy of hard
news space, coded instead as more appropriately the subject of human interest stories. This virtual erasure is particularly acute in coverage of women of
color (Gist 1993; Rhodes 1993).

Coverage that marginalizes women as news makers is cause for concern:
News accounts contribute decisively to the discursive construction of reality by
creating, supporting, or refuting cultural beliefs and practices (Rakow and
Kranich 1991; Rivers 1996), but simply adding women to the mix of news
makers is not an adequate response, nor is adding more women to the mix of
news workers. While both of these are necessary, they are not sufficient. As Lies-
bet van Zoonen (1994) points out, expecting drastic changes in media production as a result of placing more women in producer (or encoder) roles rests on
two erroneous notions: that women share a common perspective that will be
translated into the texts they create, and that the culture of media organizations
permits enough autonomy for individual employees' decisions and preferences
to be implemented as conceived (64). To overcome these problematic concep-
tualizations, van Zoonen argues that the media

> can thus be seen as (social) technologies of gender, accommodating, mod-
> ifying, reconstructing and producing contradictory cultural outlooks of
> sexual difference. The relation between gender and communication is
> therefore primarily a cultural one, a negotiation over meanings and values
> that inform whole ways of life. (van Zoonen 1994, 41)

Following van Zoonen, I argue that news texts about political women in the
1990s act as "technologies of gender" by privileging a particular perspective on
women and power while overlooking others. These stories overlap and enhance
one another at times, and at times they are contradictory, but by publicly commenting on women's relationships to power, they always suggest what is and
what is not appropriate for women in the last decade of the twentieth century.

The Year of the Woman is an excellent example of this "technology's" complexity: at times, news accounts challenged some of the more intractable gendered myths with which U.S. society is suffused (e.g., that sexual harassment was a trivial issue, of concern to only a handful of radical feminists) and upheld others (e.g., smart and powerful women, such as Hillary Rodham Clinton, were necessarily manipulative and "bitchy"). Thus news narratives about "political women"[1] are rich, polysemic texts composed of contests for meaning around definitions of womanhood, feminist politics, race, and power; they are texts that can reveal much about the dynamics of these contests and how they function with and in the mediated public sphere. Although the concept of a public sphere has been explicated at length by Jürgen Habermas (1989) and enriched by feminist Nancy Fraser (1990), even these very thoughtful accounts ignore what McLaughlin (1995) refers to as the "mass mediation of public spheres" (155). That the institutions and texts of mass media largely structure public life and suffuse it with meaning is crucial to understanding politics and political campaigns in the contemporary United States. News media are integral to the process of initiating, perpetuating, and even expanding identities of persons associated with or thrust into the political–public realm.

Political campaigns, particularly presidential campaigns, have become ritualistically performed media events, events that gain importance and cultural currency, as John Fiske notes, "in the way that they give a visible and material presence to deep and persistent currents of meaning by which American society and American consciousness shape themselves" (1994, xv). In the two presidential campaign seasons of the 1990s and that of 2000, the political practices of women came to be media events—either as candidates running for office (Year of the Woman candidates and Hillary Rodham Clinton) or as a swing voting bloc ("soccer moms"), but their "persistent currents of meaning" were surely informed by inequities between women and men. For example, although women outnumbered men in the United States in 1991 (51 percent [U.S. Bureau of the Census 1992, 15]) and have been consistently outnumbering men in voting booths since 1980, as of 1992 the composition of most formal political bodies, such as legislatures, was predominantly male. In 1991, of 435 members of the 102nd Congress, twenty-eight were women, and in the Senate only two members were women (U.S. Bureau of the Census 1992, 264). At the state level, women appear to be somewhat better represented: from 1970 to 1990, the percentage of women in state legislatures increased from 4.6 percent to 18.2 percent (Women's Action Coalition 1993, 22). The enthusiasm surrounding 1992's Year of the Woman may have had an impact on encouraging women to redress these gender imbalances: in 1990, the year prior to the beginning of the

Year of the Woman, seventy-eight women ran for congressional office; in 1992, more than twice as many women, 159, ran for congressional office (Women's Action Coalition 1993, 22). This sequence of events suggests the relationship Fiske describes above between media coverage of political women, particularly Anita Hill's experiences, and women's involvement in electoral politics.[2]

The material conditions of the late 1980s and early 1990s were coextensive with the end of Ronald Reagan's second term and with George Bush Sr.'s only term as president of the United States. Bush carried the Reagan legacy through his presidency by relying upon many of the same advisors as and espousing a political philosophy very close to Reagan's. The policies and legislation produced during each administration's reign influenced a wide variety of social and economic practices; these administrations were especially influential in legitimating and normalizing right-wing rhetoric: a combination of a *laissez faire* economic philosophy, conservative social policies, and fundamentalist Christianity. The New Right reframed issues and even dismantled policies that second-wave feminists had fought to create and manage. For example, as president, George Bush Sr. approved a ruling that was known informally as "The Gag Rule"—a ruling that prohibited Title X-funded women's health clinics from mentioning abortion if these clinics were to retain their federal funding.[3] Many feminists viewed this as an alarming attack on abortion rights and free-speech rights, both considered sacrosanct among feminists and free-speech activists. This was not the only manifestation of New Right principles during the 1980s and 1990s. Others are documented in, for example, Lawrence Grossberg's (1992) *We Gotta Get Out of This Place.* This is, among other things, a sweeping analysis of the sociopolitical landscape and climate of the 1980s and early 1990s that documents this rise of the New Right and its profound effect on culture. The rise to prominence of the New Right encompassed both the realms of formal policies and popular discourse and was "put into place through cultural rather than political strategies" (Grossberg 1992, 15), such as defining "family" in a manner that made it seem like the exclusive domain of conservatives—particularly those who claimed to espouse what they called "family values."

Both Susan Faludi (1991) and Elayne Rapping (1994) have discussed cultural strategies crucial to the New Right's opposition to feminism in the 1980s and early 1990s: media representations that derogated feminism as harmful to women and dangerous to sacred social institutions such as motherhood. Some cultural strategies, such as the "New Traditionalist" advertising campaign of the 1980s, blended features from both feminist and antifeminist rhetoric implicitly to condemn feminism. The New Traditionalist campaign consisted of a series of advertisements that glorified domesticity and vilified feminism for failing women. The campaign did not advertise a product but a lifestyle: that of a group of women who had proudly jettisoned their careers to stay home with their children and attend to their home lives. Cultural anxieties about family, work, and domesticity were played out in this campaign that commodified femininity. It is worth mentioning here because of its similarities to postfeminism. In its rendering of sex-appropriate behavior, the New Traditionalist women's stories that appear in each of these advertisements implicitly blame feminism for making them and other women dissatisfied—a condition that they imply can only be addressed through domestic consumerism (Darnovsky 1991).

However, whereas the New Traditionalist blamed feminism, descriptive demographic information about U.S. women from the late 1980s to the early 1990s suggests that structural inequities—and not feminism—were likely as not at the root of any widespread dissatisfaction among women. These data suggest that women, particularly women of color, experienced everyday life in ways that may have primed them to desire change: change in their own life conditions and change in the ranks of the powers that governed them. For example, although the majority of women were married and running households with their spouses in 1991,[4] many women were solely responsible for sustaining their families. In 1989, a woman headed 1 in 5 families—up from 1 in 10 in 1970. Of these 1 in 5 families led by single women, one-third were living below the poverty line (Women's Action Coalition 1993, 40). Between 1979 and 1993, the number of female-led single households living below the poverty level increased from 49.4 percent to 49.9 percent for African-American women, and from 22.3 percent to 29.2 percent for white women (Taeuber 1996, 146). Part of this problem can probably be traced to the absence of child support payments coming into these households: in 1989, 57 percent of women living below the poverty level did not receive the child support that they were legally entitled to, while 42 percent of all women who were entitled to them did not receive child support payments (U.S. Bureau of the Census 1992, 372). Clearly these child support payments were desperately needed in many cases: in 1991, 57 percent of all children living in families headed by women lived below the poverty line. Of the African-American children living in female-headed households, 79 percent lived in poverty (Women's Action Coalition 1993, 40).

Closely related to the poverty level of women in the late 1980s and early 1990s was women's income and employment. By 1992, 58 percent of women ages sixteen and over worked in the U.S. labor force; many of these were mothers (Taeuber 1996, 89). In 1992, 80 percent of African-American women and

73 percent of white women in the labor force had children under age eighteen (Taeuber 1996, 105). As more women than ever worked in the labor force, their median incomes decreased. Between 1989 and 1993, African-American women suffered a particularly large decrease of $448 per year overall, while white women saw their median earnings decrease by $17. White men were still the biggest earners of any workers, followed by white women, African-American women, and African-American men (Taeuber 1996, 89). The median earnings of both married-couple families and families headed by a single woman or man, of any race, experienced decreases between 1989 and 1993, but of all these groups, African-American women fared the worst, as their annual median incomes dropped from $13,553 to $11,905 (Taeuber 1996, 131).

Income patterns of women during the 1980s point to a rather large, class-differentiated wage gap. That is, by the mid-1980s, 10.3 percent of women earned more than $30,000 annually (up from 6.85 percent at the end of the 1970s), but the percentage of women making less than $10,000 in the mid-1980s stood at 18 percent—about the same percentage as at the end of the 1970s (Brenner 1993, 115). Brenner (1993) notes that these circumstances can create class and race conflicts among women:

> [W]omen of colour are over-represented among the low-paid workers who fill the service and retail sales jobs which have expanded in the 1980s to meet new needs generated by women's increased participation in paid labour (e.g., supermarkets and department stores open seven nights a week, fast-food outlets, childcare, nursing homes). (115)

Although some women have experienced economic benefits from feminism, not all have, and in this sense the divisions are very traditional in their race and class composition.

Despite their increased numbers in employment figures, women managed to have families along with working for pay. In terms of reproductive health, women had babies later in life than women before them, while their fertility rates remained at a fairly stable level (with some minor fluctuations occurring). Between 1976 and 1987, birth rates for women ages thirty to thirty-nine increased by more than 33 percent, while the 1980s saw a decrease in teen pregnancy across all ethnic and racial groups surveyed. (The latter is true of the 1990s as well.) Overall, the great majority of pregnant women (76 percent) started prenatal care during the first three months of their pregnancies; however, disparities appear when this figure is broken down to consider race. That is, while a majority of all pregnant women still got prenatal care within the first three months of their pregnancies, a smaller percentage of women of Hispanic origin, Native American women, and African-American women received this early prenatal care (Department of Health and Human Services 1990, 1).[5]

The demographic picture that emerges from the figures above is that of a nation of women who differ significantly from one another along race and class lines, and who, together, exhibit a standard of living significantly lower than that of most white men. These sorts of differences hold true for legislative and electoral practices as well. According to Taeuber (1996, 319–21) and Costello and Stone (2001, 323), more women than men in all three major racial/ethnic groups in the United States voted in the 1992 election, and this has been the case in every presidential election year since 1980. Education level and employment circumstances both affect the propensity to vote: the more formal education a person has completed, the more likely she or he is to vote. Similarly, employed people are more likely to vote in presidential and congressional elections than are unemployed people (U.S. Bureau of the Census 1992, 269).

These data describe the material, structural conditions of women in the United States during the years immediately preceding the 1990s, a field divided along gender, race, and class lines. Occurring concurrently with these deepening divisions was a shift toward conservatism in both politics and culture. Behemoth—and growing—media corporations helped facilitate this trend in many ways, making them, together, one of the most significant cultural sites for the circulation, naturalization, and legitimation of conservative politics (Aufderheide 2000; McChesney 1999; Scheuer 1999; Bagdikian 2000). Conservative commentators such as Rush Limbaugh and Pat Robertson, along with groups such as the Family Research Council, the Christian Coalition, and the Moral Majority, helped shape the terms of political debate and determine the vocabulary and boundaries used with complex issues, such as AIDS policy, abortion, and affirmative action in public discourse (Scheuer 1999; Treichler 1999).

Trends within media industries up to the early 1990s mirrored those in the larger context in terms of gender and the balance of power. As of 1992, according to Lafky (1993), most journalists were of "white male Protestant" stock (89), with 92 percent white, and 66 percent male (91). What is more, in a decade's time (1982–1993) the numbers of women in journalism did not increase significantly, and only a small percentage of these held supervisory or management positions: 17 percent of television news directors; 6 percent of "top" newspaper jobs; and 25 percent of middle-management jobs at newspapers (90). Many women reported sexual harassment on the job: 50 percent of female journalists polled in 1991 reported having been sexually harassed at least one time in their careers (99–100). Lafky (1993) adds that both television and print news organizations are rife with reports and other signs of sex discrimination. Television news correspondent Marlene Sanders (1993) argues that this is due, in part, to a lack of power among female journalists: "We are too few in number. We do not hire and fire. We do not make the story assignments unfettered. We do not have the proportion of top jobs that our numbers in the population or the audience justify" (171). This problem has been documented in entertainment television as well (Lauzen & Dozier 1999a); it is one of the organizational practices that encodes gender into the structures of media texts (van Zoonen 1994) and thus influences the media's technologies of gender.

Enter Postfeminism

The persistent underrepresentation of women in media institutions, as well as in important roles in other significant social and political institutions, was just one part of the picture for women in the 1990s; equal in importance, if less visible, was the widespread attribution of this underrepresentation and gendered power differential to the individual weaknesses of women rather than to the centuries of discriminatory patterns against women (Coppock, Haydon, and Richter 1995). When sex discrimination persists with little or no public contestation, as Brenner documents in her sweeping analysis of women's lives in the 1980s and early 1990s, its continuation may suggest that the resulting organization of labor must somehow reflect women's own choices in the labor market and not structural imbalances and obstacles (1993, 106). This is the flip side of meritocracy: the notion that the few women who have succeeded and who hold powerful positions did it strictly as a result of individual talent and mettle rather than through a combination of struggles (largely feminist) to elevate women's status and opportunities as a class. (This also is related to what Marjorie Ferguson calls the "feminist fallacy." See afterword.) This attribution has been crucial to the emergence of a *postfeminist* ideology and has been documented by feminist scholars whose concerns focus on the nature of postfeminism: where it is found, and what it means to the future of democratic institutions and politics (Dow 1996; Modleski 1991; Stacey 1993; Rapp 1987). These researchers have registered alarms about postfeminist ideology, the presence of which, they contend, undercuts political and cultural progress for all but a select, elite group of women who have benefited from feminism yet dismiss it as no longer being useful to their lives.

For example, Judith Stacey's (1991) ethnographic study of a group of women in the Silicon Valley identified a pervasive postfeminist mentality among the daughters of former feminist activists. These postfeminist women took for granted the gains that feminists like their mothers had secured for them, such as the right to work in formerly male-dominated occupations for good salaries, while they denounced feminism as being excessive or irrelevant. This sort of contradiction—that of accepting feminist ideals while shrinking from being *labeled* as feminist—is what Susan Douglas (1994) refers to as the "I'm not a feminist, but . . ." problem. Douglas notes that this sentiment parallels almost exactly the sort of treatment that feminism receives in the media: that media seize on the "I'm not a feminist" portion of the phrase, while they persistently refuse to examine those sentiments expressed after the "but." Those sentiments, she argues, are very often expressed as part of a "profound" connection

> between the disavowal of feminism in the first part of the phrase and its embrace at the end. The comma says that the speaker is ambivalent, that she is torn between a philosophy that seeks to improve her lot in life and a desire not to pay too dearly for endorsing that philosophy. (270)

The "I'm not a feminist, but . . ." problem illustrates part of the effectivity of media ideology in subtly privileging this postfeminist notion.

An increase in conservatism and material inequity and a decrease in media accolades for feminism serve as the context for political women in the 1990s, and although the Hill–Thomas hearings and Year of the Woman emerged during a historical moment marked for its extreme and far-reaching conservatism, they were constructed in part from discourses that explicitly challenged some conservative rhetoric, especially on those issues that have been of concern to women historically, such as reproductive rights and abortion. In this way, they distinguished themselves as radical departures from both standard political campaigns and from the dominant ideology of the time. The challenges that these candidates posed to electoral politics and media coverage of them were considerable, particularly and explicitly with respect to gender and socioeconomic power. To challenge the political status quo, the Hill–Thomas hearings and Year of the Woman campaigns, for example, included feminist arguments about the power abuse at the root of any sexual harassment situation, and about how this is most often perpetrated by men against women. Foregrounding this argument in the media (and, further, that such persistent abuse could constitute a hostile environment for the female victim) required an implied critique of the imbalance of gender and socioeconomic power that emerged as being prevalent in political institutions during the months the media featured these events. In featuring this woman-identified struggle as counterpoised against the male ruling powers of Congress and various federal bureaus and departments, media accounts exemplified an integral aspect of the hegemonic process—that popular resistance to prevailing power can result in social ruptures that may, in turn, shift the overall balance of power in a society at a given moment in history.

POSTFEMINISM AND HEGEMONY

A postfeminist logic undergirds public discourse about the political women and "women's issues" foregrounded during the 1990s and 2000. Although Fredric Jameson (1991) has explicated the broad cultural logic that he argues is coincident with late capitalism, he does not broach gender and how it figures into the historical and economic conditions that he outlines. Yet despite Jameson's omission, gendered references pervade public discourse—particularly around political campaigns—and often are derived from postfeminism. Postfeminism is not antithetical to feminism; rather, it denotes an ideology constructed, in part, from various aspects of both first- and second-wave feminism.[6] However, at the same time, it rejects these feminisms' more provocative challenges, such as those grounded in critiques of capitalism and class privilege. Judith Stacey's (1993) definition has been crucial to my understanding of postfeminism, as has Rayna Rapp's discussion of it. Stacey defines postfeminism as the "simultaneous incorporation, revision, and depoliticization of many of the central goals of second-wave feminism" (323). Further, such "depoliticization often takes the form of the reduction of feminist *social* goals to individual 'life style'" (Rapp 1987, 32, emphasis in original). Rapp notes that postfeminism dispenses with feminist collective politics as unnecessary: postfeminists claim that women have made gains because of feminism, but these gains have been exhausted for all intents and purposes; they take for granted rights that first- and second-wave feminists fought for, such as access to higher education, but simultaneously argue that feminism actually harms women, overall, because it gives women unrealistic expectations—that we can "have it all." However, Rapp argues that women who embrace postfeminism typically constitute a small and class-specific group: women who have succeeded in their professions, in part because of feminist work from past decades. Women who have not experienced such privilege seldom demonstrate adherence to postfeminism. Rapp's comments are reminders that postfeminism should not be generalized to describe the political commitment of most women, yet despite its narrow appeal, a postfeminist logic informs media discussions of public, political women.

While postfeminism comprises a number of ideological fragments, one primary claim undergirds it: that a politics of feminism is outdated, because the "playing field" for women and men is now level, thus "women have only themselves to blame if equality is not achieved" (Coppock, Haydon, and Richter 1995, 5). The other fragments are derived from this claim and extend it in important ways. First, and what Rapp touches on above, is the shift from a vision of collective politics for social change to an individualistic focus; successes *and* failures are attributed to individual women rather than to a complex formula of individual work, group efforts, and structural influences. Second, and in a similar vein (also mentioned by Rapp) is postfeminism's "lifestyle" character. In accounts in which it is invoked by name, feminism is not linked to a political agenda or history but is cast instead as an avenue to a higher-status lifestyle, with consumption of high-status commodities (Goldman, Heath, and Smith 1991). Such a commodification of feminism is readily evidenced in the many advertisements targeted at professional women—mothers, often—for products marketed to ease the burden of their second shift at home—once their paying work is over for the day. These professional women embody one of the assumptions of second-wave feminism—that women can, and should, be financially independent and able to develop in their chosen professions even if they choose to have a family as well. The value of education and financial independence though is not touted in postfeminism for its intrinsic benefit; rather, it is an inroad to a better place, a place with meals prepared by someone else, with reliable (if not luxurious) transportation, with a beautiful home, and with clean toilets and white laundry. This connection between feminism and consumerism assumes that women have significant disposable incomes, and it precludes consideration of the women who do not. This then is the third fragment in postfeminist ideology: that white, heterosexual, and middle-class women's issues can be generalized to all women, including those whose identities include none of these traits.

This postfeminist logic is elitist in its appeal and outlook, and in many ways it parallels the class interests of the political elite and media corporations of the United States. Postfeminism's relationship to these exclusive interests suggests that it might do some of the ideological work of legitimating these interests to media audiences—its ascendancy an illustration of hegemony in mainstream media during the late twentieth century. The hegemonic process, originally conceptualized by Italian Marxist Antonio Gramsci (see, for instance, Gramsci 1971) in the early twentieth century, is a struggle for the ideological dominance of the interests of the ruling classes of a society through the institutions of civil society—popular media, for example. Hegemony stands in contradistinction to a process in which class dominance is achieved through coercion and the exercise of force and absolute power (Gitlin 1987), those actions typically associated with the state and not with civil society. Hegemony exists when a population responds to ruling class ideology by "voluntarily" consenting to be ruled, and ruled in a fashion determined by the classes above them in the social hierarchy. Eventually this sort of power relationship comes to seem like the natural order of things rather than a construction that benefits a minority, often at the expense of the majority. The concept of hegemony is useful for conceptualizing the give-and-take relationship between the power blocs that struggle for control in any society and their relations with less powerful (what Gramsci refers to as "subaltern") populations.

Hegemony requires continual ideological work and gradual adaptation. When it is achieved, it is not through a process of inculcating false consciousness but through a process in which less powerful groups—more or less actively—capitulate to ideological positions advocated by power blocs (this process has been referred to by Herman and Chomsky [1988], as "manufacturing consent" for the prevailing order). Hegemonic struggles are successful only when the ideologies of which they are composed resonate and mesh with those of the subjects from whom cooperation must be forthcoming. In theory, political subjects will not consent to be ruled if their needs and desires go utterly unsatisfied. To achieve hegemonic power, the goal is not to exercise absolute power gained through coercion and violence but to gain that power that is secured through a process of usually nonviolent assent (Gitlin 1987).

One of the most significant contributions that Gramsci made to political analysis was theorizing the varied and complex relations between culture and politics, and how these relations could maintain and challenge hegemonic power. Indeed, "to think in Gramscian terms requires . . . an attentiveness to existing social and economic structure precisely to consider, rather than to occlude, the multiple factors involved in understanding the relationship between culture and politics" (Landy 1994, 75). A Gramscian analysis, therefore, is one predicated on a historically specific examination of relations between significant cultural and political institutions, such as those between media (including their texts) and their relations with electoral politics.

For Gramsci, the relations between the state and civil society were those that determined much of the fate of the subaltern, but rather than relying upon this broad but limiting dichotomy to theorize hegemonic struggles, contemporary theorists have modified it to reflect contemporary conditions and to depart from a polarized view of culture. Grossberg, for example, argues that today hegemony is fought for by a process in which blocs with "significant economic power" struggle to lead through "a continuous 'war of position' dispersed across the entire terrain of social and cultural life" (1992, 245). Further, to be successful, a hegemonic struggle must "ground itself in or . . . pass through 'the popular'" (Grossberg 1992, 247). Appealing to common culture is crucial to fight and to win any hegemonic struggle.

The institutions of civil society, such as schools, family, and the mass media (in the United States today), are those most active in the production of hegemonic ideologies and in the manufacture of consent to them; today, mainstream media, as institutions of civil society, are crucial as channels of discourse and as power blocs with a major stake in particular outcomes of the hegemonic process (Bagdikian 2000; Gitlin 1987; Hallin 1994; Kellner 1992, 1995; McChesney 1997, 1999). Because the maintenance of hegemony depends on forging effective connections with political subjects, mainstream media institutions (and the content they create) contribute largely to securing consent to the ruling order by being the primary producers of the discursive terrain upon which cultural meanings that prescribe and proscribe practice emerge, get struggled over, and change. Mainstream media continually work at the level of common sense; that is, in order to be assimilated, mediated ideology has to appear commonsensical: "naturally" obvious and immediately verifiable. Gramsci used this conception of common sense to understand forms of capitulation to power.

Common sense is constituted from the fragments of unquestioned, and typically unexamined, thought that guide practice almost unconsciously; beliefs that are historically determined yet so seemingly fundamental that they come to seem almost instinctive. Specific commonsense beliefs vary from group to group and bloc to bloc, although society-wide commonsense beliefs also exist. In addition, Gramsci (1971) points out that

> [c]ommon sense is not something rigid and immobile, but is continually transforming itself, enriching itself with scientific ideas and with philosophical opinions which have entered ordinary life. "Common sense" is the folklore of philosophy and is always half-way between folklore properly speaking and the philosophy, science, and economics of the specialists. Common sense creates the folklore of the future, that is as a relatively rigid phase of popular knowledge at a given place and time. (326, FN 5)

The mainstream media of the United States figure largely in circulating this historically specific common sense, therefore playing a role in the shaping of popular knowledge.

In representing some ideas prominently and with a positive valence, the media legitimate them; over time, they become virtually immune to question.

In omitting consideration of other subjects, or subjecting them to dispropor-
tionate amounts of criticism, media texts encourage incremental movement
toward making certain beliefs operate as common sense in a particular historical moment. In this view, the media do not foist false consciousness upon vulnerable media users. Instead, media institutions engage in continuous struggles
for power (often ideological) with their publics and with political institutions,
such as legislative bodies, through the attempt to assimilate commonsense
beliefs that benefit them as profit-making institutions and as organizations that
wield a good deal of political clout in their own right (e.g., see Bagdikian 2000
and McChesney 1997, 1999, for accounts of media organizations lobbying to
influence the terms of the Federal Telecommunications Act of 1996—a law that
afforded enormous economic benefits to media corporations). This struggle to
naturalize ideologies as common sense is elemental to the representational politics that constitute media texts.

Gaining, maintaining, and strengthening hegemony all depend upon
articulations: connections from hegemonic ideologies to personal and political
practices (Hall 1986; Grossberg 1992; Laclau and Mouffe 1985). Articulations
often are rhetorical links created to achieve specific political purposes, such as
influencing groups of people to accept a candidate's message. Stuart Hall argues
that as an analytic device, the examination of articulations "is both a way of
understanding how ideological elements come, under certain conditions, to
cohere together within a discourse, and a way of asking how they do or do not
become articulated, at specific conjunctures, to certain political subjects" (Hall
1986, 53). Hall's words point to the importance of context in understanding
both successful and failed articulations; historical conditions must be right for
any articulation to take hold in the imaginations and actions of those for whom
it is intended.

A crucial part of the second-wave women's movement in this country,
for example, involved a two-step process of articulation: that of articulating
women—as a class—to an ideology of independence and equality; concurrent
with this move was an attempt to *dis*articulate *from* women (as a class) popular
discourses of hearth and home. In other words, the ideological work of the second-wave women's movement consisted of disarticulating and rearticulating in
an effort to create "liberated" women—what Hall refers to above as "a new set
of social and political subjects." The articulation between femininity and
domesticity had been, to a large extent, naturalized: that is, it kept some women
out of the workforce,[7] doing unpaid household labor and caring for children
in the bosom of the patriarchal nuclear family, because these activities were
popularly represented as "natural" for women. (Articulations like this that rely

upon biology for their epistemological grounding seem to be unusually intractable; because biological explanations rely upon "natural" elements and processes, they are more easily accepted as "the way things are.") Such is the case with postfeminism in the 1990s: I contend that it has been naturalized, assimilated and reproduced by news workers: the journalists, editors, and, most importantly, corporate managers, all of whom make conscious and subconscious decisions about how to tell stories about women in/and politics.

An articulation, once made, is neither permanent nor unbreakable, although some articulations are steeped in such powerful imagery, symbolism, or materiality that they are practically impossible to break. In other words, to break these links—to disarticulate ideologies from political subjects and rearticulate them to others—is far from simple (Slack 1989; Stabile 1992). The more naturalized and hegemonic ideologies are, the more difficult their articulations are to challenge, indeed, even to perceive, yet these challenges do occur, and some, like the second-wave women's movement, can be considered successful, thus becoming counterhegemonic.

The way in which articulations have been conceptualized marks them as contingent and even mobile, although it is not the case that these attributes make them easy to disconnect and reconnect for use in other political projects. For applications within feminism, however, these features are crucial in understanding and theorizing the ways in which women are invoked variously for use in different political work, sometimes to oppressive ends. Chantal Mouffe (1992) thus theorizes the category of "woman" as "a multiplicity of social relations in which sexual difference is always constructed in very diverse ways and where the struggle against subordination has to be visualized in specific and differential forms" (373). Ultimately, Mouffe challenges feminist scholars to examine how different discourses construct women, and in ways that are never reducible to one single subject position, such as gender, race, or class. Such a project, she adds, helps "grasp the diversity of ways in which relations of power are constructed" (382). For a feminist media project, this approach necessitates an analysis of mediated discourses and how they work together to universalize their definition of women; in postfeminism, it is a definition with little regard for the particularities of a majority of women's lives and needs.

Gramsci's theory is useful for analyses of the relations between gender and mass culture because, as Landy notes, he insists upon a synthesis of the "discourses of politics, economics, and production and reproduction." Such an emphasis reveals not only "dominant discourses" but also the "heterogeneous elements" constitutive of representations that fix women in patriarchy (1994, 100). Hegemony presupposes struggle and conflict in the constitution of meaning in dominant cultural texts (from media such as television, film, music, etc.). In feminist media studies, the analysis of discourse for the hegemonic ideologies it privileges and the articulations it creates and maintains has been limited mostly to entertainment texts. One exception is Steeves' (1997) use of hegemony theory in her study of newspaper accounts of a rape and murder rampage that occurred in Kenya in 1991 at St. Kizito Secondary School; she found that patriarchal beliefs saturated these news stories, coalescing around several organizing themes, or frames. Steeves, using Mouffe's notion of expansive hegemony, "a more pervasive and subtle type of hegemony, [which] is exercised by intellectual and moral leaders to create active consensus" (5), identified nine frames that reinforced what she refers to as "patriarchal hegemony" (40). These frames delineated the ways in which Kenyan leaders and news workers secured consent for their positions on the crime itself and on the trials of the male perpetrators afterward. Although some feminist interpretation emerged in the coverage of the events around St. Kizito, the hegemonic process ultimately worked against a feminist interpretation and instead privileged a patriarchal perspective on the female victims and survivors of the crime, on rape in general, and on heterosexual relations broadly.

In a similar vein, popular news accounts of political women in the 1990s serve to reinforce some and subvert other patriarchal beliefs about women's relationships to power. Ultimately, however, the expansive hegemony of mainstream media—in the context that I have delineated—is one that is not strictly patriarchal (i.e., beneficial mostly to men) but postfeminist; as such, it secures the ascendance of an exclusionary logic suitable to only a minority of privileged women in the United States at the end of the twentieth century. The postfeminism prevalent in news narratives is not only a phenomenon unto itself but serves as commentary on the status of feminism in the mediated public sphere as well. Just as postmodernity works as modernity's Other, and alter ego in some ways, postfeminism emerges from feminism and its vision of an activist sisterhood only to dispense with the notion of collective action altogether. The incarnation of postfeminism that I detail in this book is in part based upon an essentialist, cultural feminism (such as that which Alice Echols [1989], documents from the second wave) and in part dependent upon a neoliberal discourse of choice and individual merit.[8] That is, news accounts of political women during the 1990s seem insistent upon tethering women to their biological sex, claiming that they bring unique attributes to politics as a result of it. At the same time, these accounts valorize the individual gains and talents of female politicians and exhibit a conspicuous absence of an articulation to a politics of feminism (despite the importance of feminist agitation in forcing changes in laws and attitudes that enabled much of the success these women can claim).

Postfeminism is intriguing for what it suggests about hegemony: many women appear to accept a postfeminist set of beliefs, and they even embrace it, yet it offers no vision of transforming oppressive conditions and seems to contribute more to their continuation.[9] This postfeminist logic is predicated on an assumption that social and economic problems based on sex have miraculously vanished because of laws against sex discrimination and harassment. One effect of this, pointed out by Tania Modleski (1991), is that of "negating the critiques and undermining the goals of feminism—in effect, delivering us back into a prefeminist world" (3). "Prefeminist" is too harsh a condemnation perhaps, for one of the most appealing things about postfeminism is not that it advocates patriarchy (which I associate with prefeminism) but that it appropriates some aspects of feminism while rejecting other, more radical, aspects. What it rejects is twofold: a critique of patriarchy as a structure of oppression, and the use of collective action directed toward changing exploitative conditions for many different women, conditions that have an unfortunate tendency to persist when they go unchallenged.

Who then might be a member of postfeminism's club? Membership is exclusive: "at best 'post feminism' is a concept appropriate to professional women" (Coppock, Haydon, and Richter 1995, 182–83). Professional women are those who have benefited tremendously from feminism, yet the only aspects of feminism many of them seem willing to retain publicly are notions of free choice—especially around reproductive rights and parenting. The women who are not hailed by this class-specific discourse continue to suffer economically, physically, psychologically, and socially from a range of power abuses. The fact that their public voices are inaudible does not render their experiences with oppression nonexistent; it just moves them to the margins of—or outside—public consciousness.

An integral component of postfeminism is an emphasis on consumerism (Coppock, Haydon, and Richter 1995; Dow 1996). The manner in which feminism has been eclipsed by postfeminism in certain contexts suggests that postfeminism works better as a promotional discourse for luring new consumers to a proliferating set of products for today's new women. Studies of postfeminism's cultural functions point to its wide circulation in cultural texts. Modleski (1991) and Dow (1996), for example, have investigated postfeminist ideology in literary and film criticism and in television situation comedies and dramas, respectively. Dow notes that postfeminism's depoliticized character—rooted in class privilege and financial security—is perfect for mass mediated texts where

it works to sell products via television advertising to women: the largest segment of television audiences that makes decisions about which household
items to purchase. When considering postfeminism's varied appearances in
media texts, this class-specific aspect of it cannot be overstated for its potential
to draw viewers and readers into the discourse of consumption.

Stacey (1993) notes that postfeminism is coextensive with what she calls
"postindustrial conditions." For the participants in her study, these conditions
were based on a massive economic shift, post–World War II, from an

> industrial to a service-dominated occupational structure [in which]
> unprecedented percentages of women entered the labor force and the halls
> of academe and unprecedented percentages of marriages entered the
> divorce courts. Unstable and, often, incompatible work and family condi-
> tions have become the postindustrial norm as working-class occupations
> become increasingly "feminized." (324)

Coincident with this shift is another, noted by political economists, the emergence of the "information society or information economy," characterized by a

> shift [in] the balance in the cultural sector between the market and public
> service decisively in favor of the market and [a] shift [in] the dominant
> definition of public information from that of a public good to that of a
> privately appropriable commodity. (Garnham 1993, 363)

Garnham's point is crucial in understanding the importance and utility of postfeminism and its deployment in media texts. Postfeminist ideology, as Dow
(1996) argues, works to construct media audiences not as critically informed
publics prepared to organize against oppressive conditions but as individual
consumers for whom freedom to choose is of paramount importance as an
abstract principle, yet typically limited to exercising commercial choice.

POSTFEMINISM AND THE MEDIA-INDUSTRIAL COMPLEX

Postfeminism is pervasive in media entertainment texts, as Dow and Modleski
demonstrate, but it is prevalent in news stories as well, if for no other reason
than its appeal to the "quality" demographic so desperately sought by media
management (Bagdikian 2000, 115). As research into the news, particularly
television news, has documented (Bagdikian 2000; Hallin 1994; McManus
1995), the line between news and entertainment has become blurred for a

number of reasons, not the least of which is the competition for ratings between departments in any media organization. News programs have adopted many of the techniques of entertainment-oriented programming, such as a tabloid format and sensationalistic tone. News departments are no longer vastly distinct from entertainment departments, formerly separated to prevent the temptations of news departments slanting their stories to suit advertisers and other powerful entities (McManus 1995; Underwood 1995). This move toward a more entertaining variety of news is one that has been occurring for years, and it has been traced, in part, to greater corporate control of news production (Bagdikian 2000; Herman and Chomsky 1988; McChesney 1999).

Ben Bagdikian has explored the structure and consequences of oligopolistic media concentration[10] for over a decade and a half now, and he notes that it results in a "total news picture of society [that] is skewed in favor of corporate interests" (2000, 16). His contention is extended by Goldman and Rajagopal (1991), who show that the news, through the promotion of its worldview as neutral, "replicates the logic of the market within which it is produced" (22). News providers, in increasingly fierce competition with one another, present the news in a fashion that will hook consumers; they thus compete in a "public attention market" (McManus 1995, 315). This public attention market comprises commercial appeals grounded in constructed commonsense views of corporate owners, who promote their news coverage as being credible and accurate—the truth about important events, public figures, and issues. With television news in particular, news is a model of "fairness and neutrality; its idiom and manner have become universally recognized signs of dispassionate inquiry" (Goldman and Rajagopal 1991, 1). News coverage thus may be perceived as a reflection of reality, when it should more accurately be considered a partial, selective, and ideological narrative.[11] The free-market ideological orientation of news coverage, both television and print, has long been an established fact in critical media scholarship (e.g., Herman and Chomsky 1988; McChesney 1997, 1999), which rejects the notion that news is reported objectively. Particularly in today's media environment, news stories cannot produce significant challenges to the economic and political systems that have made them the extremely profitable organizations the media are today, resulting in a conspicuous silence on the social consequences of industry consolidation.

Bagdikian's latest figures show that the number of media parent corporations was six, as of early 2000 (2000, x),[12] a trend of increasing oligopolistic corporate control over the vast majority of information produced by media outlets.[13] In 2001, only four corporations controlled half of all on-line, Internet time, down from eleven in 1999 ("Four sites account" 2001; Roberts 2001). The word coined for these coporations is "cyberhogs" (Roberts 2001), for obvious reasons. One of the problems that Bagdikian elaborates on as a result of intensified concentration is that the corporate bottom line becomes the ultimate factor in decisions about what to print or broadcast. The information and formats that promise to be most profitable are favored over those that may not produce a big, and fast, profit. Fast profit is of particular concern to many parent corporations, whose mergers and takeovers often are financed by junk bond deals—deals that result in interest rates so high that they are nothing short of usurious. This has encouraged greater involvement by the owners of media corporations in the news production process, and, "when a large corporate owner intervenes [into news reporting], alterations in coverage and analysis affect reports reaching millions in one silent stroke" (Bagdikian 1992, xvii). In such a context, the most powerful influences on what and how news appears are exerted by the owners of media corporations (McManus 1995, 311).

Newsrooms have become microcosms of the corporate shift in media ownership and news content. Within the last decade or so, a proliferation of news editors with MBAs has emerged, resulting in a restricted range of ideas presented in the news as well as in the type of ideas found there—less controversial, more upbeat, and more like *USA Today*, whether print or broadcast media (Underwood 1995). Of the 400–plus journalists surveyed in a study conducted by Douglas Underwood (1995), most reported great dissatisfaction with this trend, noting that their autonomy and judgment were consistently diminished in newsrooms where decisions were made with a corporate mindset—a mind-set that has come to dominate newsrooms in the United States.

This corporate shift is particularly evident in television coverage of political events, where the foremost relationship determining content is that of vendor and consumer (Hallin 1994, 35). Hallin's longitudinal study of TV news election coverage documents the effects of the corporatizing of the news media: between 1968 and 1988, the sound bites of candidates used in election coverage decreased from an average of about forty-three seconds to about nine seconds per sound bite. During this same span of time, the use of "experts" to comment on campaigns almost totally edged out the use of actual statements by candidates (137). Hallin attributes these trends, among others, to the use of outside consultants who advise media executives to shorten the length of their stories and to make their presentation of the news fast paced. This is part of an effort to compete in a deregulated market structured by cable and independent stations vying for the audiences that network news had always counted on; news programs, too, must now compete for ratings. For news departments to make themselves more competitive, they select "both sources and quotes or 'sound bites' more for their audience-building qualities than their informative aspects" (McManus 1995, 324).

Recent structural changes in and among media institutions have affected news content adversely. To wit, increased concentration among media corporations has led to newsroom environments dominated by MBA-influenced managers whose primary responsibility lies in seeing that their news programming gains and maintains good audience ratings. As former correspondent Marvin Kalb (2000) laments, "budgetary constraints, imposed by corporate management . . . have reduced the standards of journalistic performance. . . . News, like Mickey Mouse or lightbulbs, is treated as disposable tissue if it doesn't turn a profit" (A39). Recently, ABC news anchor Peter Jennings echoed a criticism of television today, made by former FCC chair Newton Minow, that it has gone from being a "'vast wasteland'" in the early 1960s to a "'toxic waste dump'" today. Jennings decried the bottom-line influence on reporting: "I cannot remember a time when we have been under such pressure to get an audience . . . because that's what the advertiser wants" (in Black 2001). To make the necessary profit, news stories must have advertiser appeal. Because news coverage of political women in the 1990s and 2000 was produced by these institutional structures with commercial constraints, I consider it an artifact of the media–industrial complex.

Bagdikian (1992) claims that "the power to create ideas and movements" (42) is one of the most profound that media organizations possess, and Hallin (1994) points out that television news is a particularly strong carrier of social meaning (2). Postfeminism in news accounts of political women serves the overall interests of corporate media by diluting or jettisoning aspects of feminism that are incompatible with corporate goals while retaining others, often for the purpose of commodifying them. I am not suggesting, however, that political women are constructed in a seamless or monolithic fashion in media texts; rather, they are constructed from struggles to fix meaning, and these result in the circumscription or negation of some meanings alongside the creation, extension, and rearticulation of others.

The Hill–Thomas hearings, for example, expanded meanings associated with sexual harassment and African-American history (see Hill and Jordan 1995; Morrison 1992). These were managed in such a way that they evoked intensely emotional rhetoric from a number of different power blocs, including white male senators, white feminists, African-American leaders, and media commentators. Anita Hill's introduction to media audiences was in the context of a crisis of meaning around the limits of white, patriarchal authority. As Stuart Hall

(1982, 69) has argued, such crises—"when events in the world are problematic (that is, where they are unexpected), where they break the frame of our previous expectations about the world, where powerful social interests are involved, or where there are starkly opposing or conflicting interests at play"—are ideal sites to examine for their role in the hegemonic process. Such events demonstrate the non-necessary, constructed nature of meaning and reveal "ideological power and the power to signify events in a particular way" (ibid.). Hill's account of sexual harassment perpetrated by her boss, Clarence Thomas, threatened not only to obstruct Thomas's path to the U.S. Supreme Court but, on a grander scale, to threaten the organization of corporate and political hierarchies with negligent attitudes toward sexual harassment and sex discrimination. While Clarence Thomas is black, as a judge and a bureaucrat he represented the interests of a predominantly white, male power bloc. His mentors and political patrons were powerful white men, and he argued stridently against judicial or legislative remedies for racial minority groups experiencing anything other than the most extreme forms of racial discrimination. In other words, while his skin color was black, the laws and policies he supported were overwhelmingly those traditionally upheld by conservative white males (e.g., see essays in Morrison 1992; Phelps and Winternitz 1992).

The crisis character of the Anita Hill–Clarence Thomas hearings is vitally important in understanding the cultural function of the hearings as the originary narrative of the Year of the Woman. I argue that the discourses of the Year of the Woman, particularly its postfeminist character, functioned to quell some of the more volatile and irresolvable conflicts while doggedly evading others, functioning, in essence, to write them off of the political agenda. Following the Year of the Woman, in the 1996 and 2000 presidential campaigns, these issues were virtually absent from coverage of political women vis-à-vis electoral politics.

Chapters 2 through the afterword analyze a variety of print media and television programs. Most of these are news texts, although some—such as *Ally McBeal*—fall under the category of entertainment. I regard mediated feminism both as a social movement that has been partially assimilated and as a site of cultural tension and controversy. It is, in other words, a conflicted site. Because the media are vital for teaching audiences about events and people outside the realm of that which is directly accessible, media texts warrant close attention for the stories they tell us—particularly those stories that concern historically and politically significant social movements, such as feminism. As Fiske and Hartley have noted, the media have become the bards of contemporary life (in van Zoonen 1994, 38).

To discern the stories told through media texts and the range of meanings in these stories, I gathered texts that invoked the subjects that are the topics of each of the following chapters: the Anita Hill–Clarence Thomas hearings; the Year of the Woman of 1991–1992; the "soccer moms" of the 1996 campaign season; Hillary Rodham Clinton's U.S. Senate campaign in 2000; and, in the afterword, feminism and media commentary on women's lives.[14] I cast my research "net" as widely as I could to obtain texts produced by both television and print media, and to obtain the majority of these. Because homogeneity of news coverage has been increasing over the last two decades (Bagdikian 2000; Underwood 1995), and because stock footage of public figures is used widely and shared by news workers on the television networks (Parry-Giles 2000), the texts I examined are reliably representative of coverage of these events. In addition, competition among media corporations has decreased, which contributes to homogeneity across parent corporations' subsidiaries, such as NBC and CBS. McChesney (1999) asserts that today's media parent companies act more like an information cartel than a group of competitors; that is, they increasingly cooperate to share their resources (which, importantly, include information), so that each parent corporation maximizes its own profits while contributing to other parent corporations' profits.[15]

This book addresses the emergent, constructed relationship between women and socioeconomic power found in widely circulated media texts. Because these texts appeared in mainstream media outlets, their patterns of inclusions and omissions—when considered together—can reveal much about a prevailing view of women and feminism during the 1990s into 2000; they betray commonsense beliefs that inform media culture. I am not suggesting that this process of privileging postfeminism is conscious or intentional for media workers and institutions. Representations need not be intentionally produced to be ideological; common sense is neither conscious nor intentional but can be powerful nevertheless. Part of the ideological effect of media lies in producing accounts that appear to be simple reflections of the world, although they are selective and jibe with the needs of the power elite. In obscuring their constructedness, media texts help manufacture consent to their "reality" using "the most skillful and elaborate procedures of coding: mounting, linking and stitching elements together, working them into a system of narration or exposition which 'makes sense'" (Hall 1982, 76). By masking their investments in particular representations, media institutions do their most important work: the ideological work of naturalization and garnering consent to a particular order of things.

The way in which women appear in news and entertainment texts shows them to be evocative of a number of unresolved cultural tensions. Those that emerged most consistently in the print and television narratives used in this book were around race and class, neoliberalism, and paid and unpaid domestic labor (including child care). The representational politics that govern the production of these discourses are thus reflective of the historical cultural contexts in which they emerged, but they are also constitutive in that their interpretations reconstruct these cultural tensions in the stories they tell about them. The stories they tell and re-tell, the metaphors they use consistently, and the persistence of particular omissions they make create a map of the media's hegemonic process as it relates to feminism in the United States during the 1990s and 2000.

Ultimately this book illuminates specific processes by which issues associated with women become ascendant in the mediated public sphere while working to reveal the status of feminism at a culturally significant historical juncture: the end of the twentieth century. This project traces the intersection of gender, race, and class and how these are mobilized in news coverage of political women during the 1990s and into 2000, in both television and print news. To do this, the following chapters produce a "thick" description of this symbolic terrain to map the hegemony of mainstream news. The result of this study is an illumination both of individual media texts and how these work together ideologically to produce hegemonic, commonsense beliefs about the status of women, those politically powerful and not; about the status of feminism; and, importantly, about the ways in which feminist ideology—postfeminism, specifically—can be deployed to target audiences for specific purposes.

CHAPTER TWO

ANITA HILL, CLARENCE THOMAS, AND THE CRISIS OF WHITE PATRIARCHAL AUTHORITY

Personally I have to say that I believe that in some ways [the hearings] may have hurt, but in many ways the airing of this issue, I think has been healthy for the nation. I think it's brought a greater degree of sensitivity to all of us because I think a lot of men just—you know, we don't always think—in fact I don't think we think very much like women think, and they happen to be pretty serious people, very sensitive people—and rightly so. And I think there's a lot of sexual harassment going on out there that a lot of men just don't consider to be sexual harassment and I think this has raised the awareness and, as I mentioned, the sensitivity of men and women all over this country and I hope it helps to stamp it out.

—Orrin Hatch, *Larry King Live*

Despite Orrin Hatch's (CNN 1991e) prophesy about the disappearance of sexual harassment, it has remained a problem, even since the Anita Hill–Clarence Thomas U.S. Senate hearings. The hearings were important in a number of respects, one being the way they brought clearly gendered struggles for meaning into homes across the United States. Anita Hill and Clarence Thomas came into our living rooms and our cultural parlance in early October 1991. As a first-year doctoral student, I was preparing answers for a take-home exam about the Chicago School and the Birmingham Center when I heard, via radio, the first suggestion that a woman (at that time unnamed) had accused President George Bush Sr.'s U.S. Supreme Court nominee, Judge Clarence Thomas, of sexual harassment. Thomas's Supreme Court nomination hearings had just begun, and, while they had been mildly controversial because of Thomas's mediocre judicial record and his extreme conservatism, the questions the senators of the Judiciary Committee had posed to Thomas at that point indicated that he was practically a shoo-in. Given what I figured would be his inevitable ascendance to the Supreme Court, I tuned out the hearings to make mental space for the more challenging task of being a doctoral student.

But on October 6, *Morning Edition*'s Nina Totenberg reported more detail, and the story became irresistible to me: University of Oklahoma law professor Anita Hill had accused Thomas, her former employer at the Department of Education and at the Equal Employment Opportunity Commission (EEOC), of sexual harassment, and she wanted to testify to her story before the all-white, all-male Senate Judiciary Committee. That stopped me in my tracks, as I considered the significance of Hill's request and the fact that the Judiciary Committee might actually hear her. (The Judiciary Committee did not agree to hear Hill's testimony immediately after receiving her accusation, and Hill herself was a reluctant witness.)

After this originary moment, the mini-dramas started to unfold—at all hours of those early days in October. Would Anita Hill testify? Would Clarence Thomas respond to her testimony? How would the White House respond to all of this? How would sexual harassment be "spun"? I moved from listening exclusively to radio to watching television news shows too. These were plentiful, and I devoured them eagerly: from the moment Anita Hill, flanked by her legal team and large family, entered the Senate hearing room until the vote on Thomas's nomination in the full Senate, I was hooked, and I was as hooked by television's depiction of the hearings as a tawdry soap opera subplot as I was by the commentary on feminism, gender, and race relations that was woven through television's accounts of the hearings.

During Hill's testimony, the senators of the Judiciary Committee subjected her to questions that impugned her story, her reactions to Thomas after allegedly being sexually harassed, her credibility, and her character. As the senators took turns interrogating Hill and making charges that time and again betrayed their ignorance of sexual harassment's effects, she remained calm. When Senator Howell Heflin, a member of the Judiciary Committee, asked Hill if she were a "fallen woman," Hill never even raised her voice when she answered this—or any other question. Yet she was clearly uncomfortable at having to recount the incidents of which she was accusing Clarence Thomas during the time he had been her employer: he had joked openly about his sexual prowess, he had compared the length of his penis to that of porn star "Long Dong Silver," and once, as he picked up a soda can, he had asked Hill, "who has put this pubic hair on my Coke can?"

After Hill's testimony and her exit from the Senate chamber came Thomas's responses to Hill's charges—the most famous of these was his anguished plea that Hill and the Judiciary Committee not subject him to racialized sexual stereotypes that men like him had suffered for centuries, incurring violence and even lynching as a result. Witnesses who testified for Thomas and Hill produced wildly disparate stories, each an attempt to fix the meaning of who Thomas and Hill *really* were. Witnesses for Thomas claimed that Hill was mentally unstable, obsessive about pursuing men, and seemingly devoted enough to Clarence Thomas that she accepted employment from him at the EEOC, even after the events she alleged had occurred. Witnesses for Hill testified to her quiet intelligence, good teaching, and politically unbiased legal work.

Clearly there was much conflicting and salacious material here for television news stories to take up. As a number of media critics have pointed out, the hearings made great TV: they included sex, struggles for power, passion, and treachery. The networks were anxious to broadcast them; they were perfectly situated between news and melodrama, and they worked well to satisfy the dictates of each. But the hearings were not strictly about sexual harassment; rather, they represented a constellation of issues concerning gender, race, and the fitness of the U.S. political system to represent the needs of all of its citizens. They also demonstrated the ways in which race, gender, and class can be mobilized in the media's representational process to produce a perceived or felt crisis.

In this chapter, I explore television news stories about the Hill–Thomas hearings, and their construction of what I argue was a crisis of white patriarchal authority. That is, four different constructed panics—around political ideology, race, gender, and institutional integrity—together constituted a perceived or felt crisis of white patriarchal authority; of these, discourses of gender instability and institutional breakdown were given the most attention. The first day that Anita Hill's name was used in conjunction with allegations of sexual harassment by Clarence Thomas was October 6, 1991; up until that time, the sexual harassment charges were made as rumors with no mention of Hill's name. October 16 was the day following the Senate vote that confirmed Thomas as a Supreme Court justice. The divisions between panics were less rigid than my taxonomy might suggest, for these were not utterly discrete entities but often overlapping and sometimes simultaneously occurring—on the same day (on different networks), or even during the same program. There was, however, enough sustained emphasis on these four panics' main ideas that they held up as particular and distinct entities. These panics worked together to form a felt crisis, one that was managed subsequently by the discursive construction of Year of the Woman political campaigns (see chapter 3). The discursive construction of both panics and crisis made almost inevitable a feminist intervention of one sort or another. That the Year of the Woman functioned as such an intervention reveals much about the sociopolitical climate at this historical juncture—and about the possibilities for feminist politics in the mediated public sphere.

This is a historical case study of crisis coverage, one that also exemplifies how easily television news coverage slips into a representational mode that relies on the language, tone, and imagery of crisis. This is not altogether surprising, given the ways in which media industries' economic exigencies have influenced all departments within television; television news is thus no exception to growing demands from media executives for good ratings, often based on quasi-tabloid sensationalism. This example also provides a perspective on representational processes in TV news and how these constitute meaning around important axes of identity: race, gender, and class all figure simultaneously into television's representation of this crisis, and in ways that are more readily apparent than usual. We can expect more coverage of this kind in TV news, I suspect, given the rapid consolidation of media corporations and the coinciding dissolution of the "wall" that separates editorial departments from those with clearer ties to commerce.

CONSTITUTING A SEXUAL HARASSMENT CRISIS

Probably the most discussed dimension of the Hill–Thomas hearings was how they foregrounded sexual harassment as a grave problem that threatened the well-being of professional women. The Senate Judiciary Committee's reaction to Anita Hill's testimony caused strong and angry reactions among many women; in the two months after the hearings, 13,000 new members joined the National Organization for Women (NOW), 9,000 more than its average 4,000 for a two-month period (Women's Action Coalition 1993, 23). The situation was not so clear-cut for African Americans, many of whom used the hearings as further evidence of institutionalized racism, signified in part by the sexualization of Anita Hill and Clarence Thomas.

The Supreme Court nomination hearings of Clarence Thomas (and Anita Hill's place in them) have been examined from a number of perspectives, including what they portended for the confirmation process (Burnham 1992; Higginbotham 1992; Resnick 1995); what they indicated about the ideological makeup of the participants in the process (Phelps and Winternitz 1992; West 1992); what they said to women of all races about their place in structures of powerful political institutions (Eisenstein 1994; Fiske 1994; Higginbotham 1995; Hill 1995; Lawrence 1995; Norton 1995; Ross 1992; Stansell 1992); what they said to African Americans about the importance of race in political decision making (Alexander 1995; Crenshaw 1992; Lacour 1992; Marable 1992; Painter 1992); and what they said about the political beliefs and practices of African Americans (Patterson 1995; Thelwell 1992). However, the hearings were important in another way as well: they served as the originary narrative of the Year of the Woman, the thirteen-month year in which a record number of women ran for office at local, state, and national levels—and won in unprecedentedly large numbers. The way in which residual anger and resentment about the hearings was channeled into successful political campaigns for women was nothing short of remarkable. This feature of the hearings makes them crucially important in understanding how gender, race, and electoral politics can mix.

Both in the hearings themselves and in media commentary about them, Anita Hill's story, and its timing with respect to Thomas's nomination, was viewed with suspicion. Her account of what had transpired between Clarence Thomas and herself when she worked for him as a staff attorney at the Department of Education and the EEOC was cast variously as lacking veracity, as the product of the psychotic mind of a temptress, "erotomania," as a vindictive act of a former admirer, as plagiarism from the pages of schlocky satanic thrillers (*The Exorcist*), as evidence of race traitorism, and, by outraged groups of feminists, as a tale of resonant authenticity.

The language of media accounts was divisive, implying the formation of a war between the sexes. Interestingly, however, the line in the sand was not always drawn between sides based on the biological sex of the troops; rather, gender-based ideological *systems* seemed to be at the root of whether or not individuals felt Anita Hill could be believed. Women, often as not, disparaged Anita Hill in "person-on-the-street" polls and interviews, while a number of men in the same polls expressed their belief in the truth of Anita Hill's testimonial. This is not unusual, albeit relatively unexplored, but as Robin Clair (1994) points out, "both men and women participate in the social construction of gender, and both may discursively frame sexual harassment in a way that perpetuates the current situation" (60). In the hearings, race, class, and political ideology were as important as gender in affecting alliances around Hill and Thomas.

My reading of television news coverage of the Hill–Thomas hearings suggests that one discursive formation was particularly influential in structuring the narratives surrounding the hearings and their participants: a crisis of white patriarchal authority. That is, the language and narratives of the news coverage both foregrounded the presence of white patriarchal authority *and* created a sense that it was breaking down. Breakdown was conveyed through images of and messages about the unsuitable way in which the white male senators of the Judiciary Committee—as well as their general Senate counterparts—framed the problem and ineptly tried to make their way toward a solution. This was very much related to the Year of the Woman phenomenon that followed the hearings. The cultural tropes and themes that formed this crisis illuminate the Year of the Woman's emergence and trajectory, as well as the ideology in news coverage of feminist issues and political women. The tropes and themes found in television news and news-talk programs (e.g., *Larry King Live*) about the hearings were partially responsible for a context in which issues of gender, race, and democratic processes were interrogated intensively in the context of panics. Such panics did not work independently of one another but were meshing, overlapping, and contradictory elements of the hearings and of the shifting meanings associated with the figures of Anita Hill and Clarence Thomas.

A crisis of white patriarchal authority was created in part by issue-specific panics, with one—gender panic—exhibiting particular dominance (ultimately articulated to the Year of the Woman). This was a narrowly focused, intensive (albeit far from exhaustive) examination of gender relations in American workplaces and, to a lesser extent, in other spaces as well. The gender panic comprised discussions of male behavior patterns (deemed unacceptable in much of the coverage) and dire predictions about untenable rifts between women and men. Constructed by volatile language predicting the end of traditional gender hierarchies and the stability associated with them, this discourse emerged the moment Anita Hill came on the scene (first as a rumored victim of Thomas's harassment), intensified throughout the week of the hearings, and then became an integral part of postmortem commentary.

The term *crisis* in this context refers to cultural crises that are symbolically constructed and managed. In this context, crisis refers to a drastic shift in representations and public perceptions of the relations of power that structure social and political institutions. Such a shift occurs through a process of ideological work and struggle to contest meanings around key social norms, such as "law and order," or cultural and ethnic identities (such as gender), with far-reaching ramifications. Crises are constructed by conveying a sense that traditionally secure structures or social systems (such as "the family") are breaking down, usually as a result of external influences. The idea of externality is key; groups or concepts targeted as disruptive, destructive, and bringing conflict and strife to previously stable and functional realms are located outside the mainstream—and made to remain there, functioning, in essence, as outside agitators.

The established use of crisis is in the analysis of the hegemonic process as it occurs around public discussions of crime and deviance, and narratives about law and order. Stuart Hall's, Chas Critcher's, Tony Jefferson's, John Clarke's, and Brian Robert's (1978) pathbreaking study, *Policing the Crisis*, examined a crisis of "mugging" and the way in which crime and criminals were constructed in public discourse so as to necessitate a rigid system of social controls in England in the 1970s. They argue that "mugging" was discursively constructed and articulated to particular subjects in post–World War II Britain to gain public consent for reactionary responses to class struggles around the allocation of national resources and wealth.

Crises may be composed of panics, distinct in this way: a panic is a relatively short-lived burst of attention given to a particular issue. Typically, it works along with other panics, that, together, are symptomatic of a larger, perhaps structural, crisis. That is, a crisis functions as an intensely affective discursive formation, the constitutive events of which are managed in such a way as to mobilize public support for its proposed resolution. Ideologically, a crisis can help win public support for "increasingly coercive measures on the part of the state, and lends its legitimacy to a 'more than usual' exercise of control" (Hall et al. 1978, 221). Media narratives typically play a large part in ascribing meaning to and perpetuating the feel of crises. Charles Acland (1995) demonstrates this in his analysis of news and popular culture treatments of youth crime in the United States as a constructed youth crisis during the 1980s. He argues that these discussions created what he calls a "felt crisis" (8): they evoked affective responses to a diffuse set of crimes (such as the high-profile "Preppy Murder" of Jennifer Levin by Robert Chambers in 1986) committed by young people during the 1980s. An analysis of panics and crises necessarily includes an examination of the groups that create and contest the terms of particular crises. Such groups stand to gain authority and credibility—and even affirmation for their existence—based on the way they manage crises. This suggests a need to understand the discursive dimension of crises in order to track the terms with which they are created, framed, and made socially meaningful.

Tracking crises in this way may reveal aspects of the hegemonic process as well; Gramsci (1971) asserts that examining a crisis is a means of demonstrating how hegemonic power may be asserted and reasserted or how counterhegemonic blocs may seize power. To Gramsci, crises of authority signified a weakening grasp on power, that the power dominant classes had over their minions was not secure. He also noted that such crises were not observed passively by those in power; rather they were used to mobilize against those elements deemed most threatening and to reestablish social control (210). In contemporary times, crises work effectively as sites for public relations work, for urgency is part of their tone; they seem to demand fast solutions and a restabilization of social institutions and relations. They also can be constructed and managed to justify strong and aggressive control measures. Thus the construction of crisis—and the resolution that it demands—occurs as part of what Acland (1995) calls "the logic of a form of hegemony" (41).

> [C]risis as discourse, which is experienced and determined historically, is omnipresent in the formation of hegemonic alliances. Crisis operates as a *mobile signifier* that migrates from debate to debate and carries with it a field of connotations and referential indices. (40–41, emphasis in original)

In the Hill–Thomas hearings, media discourse constructed Anita Hill as an outsider to the world of formal political institutions because of her gender, her race, and the nature of the complaints she made against Clarence Thomas. As Wahneema Lubiano (1992) points out, cultural stereotypes of African-American women, the "loose cannon, out to subvert . . . the 'American' family," embodied by Hill made her the perfect "outlaw" to enable Clarence Thomas's emergence as a "hero" (337).[1] One of Hill's cultural functions thus became barometric, signifying the status of societal and institutional relations. In particular, she showed the instability of gender relations among women and men, both African American and white in the United States, and particularly within workplaces. Over time, she became a tacit—and then an outspoken—critic of the masculine codes of formal political institutions.[2]

The Senate Judiciary Committee's acts toward Anita Hill and Clarence Thomas underscored the presence of deeply ingrained patriarchal authority in democratic institutions. Many of these acts were challenged publicly by feminists and civil rights activists as being deeply flawed for the outmoded attitudes that informed them. By 1991, the racism and sexism that manifested themselves behaviorally and institutionally on the Judiciary Committee had been contested in the United States by the civil rights and women's movements for at least three decades, so the senators who confronted Anita Hill should not have been wholly unprepared for the anger that would be directed at them when they lambasted Hill from race- and sex-biased positions. Their visible abuse of power and its contestation by political groups constituted the driving force behind this crisis and helped shape and channel it into its subsequent form: the Year of the Woman.

The Year of the Woman was spawned by the felt crisis of the Hill–Thomas hearings, a crisis that served both Hill and Thomas at different times, but at all times was a part of a struggle for hegemony around gender, race, and political power in the United States. Its composition was the result of historically specific debates that had been occurring during the 1980s, including those about the dismantling of affirmative action programs, appropriate remedies for poverty, the representation of women and minorities in democratic bodies, and so on. Thus it highlighted the interests of and the power blocs struggling for ideological dominance around all of these related issues (e.g., the National Association for the Advancement of Colored People (NAACP), the National Organization for Women (NOW), the Republican National Committee, and evangelical Christian political action committees).

During the Hill–Thomas hearings, televised news accounts proliferated and provided prodigious amounts of commentary. Like the Persian Gulf crisis earlier that same year, the Hill–Thomas crisis was constructed from "special reports" that broke into regularly scheduled programming, from constant coverage of the hearings each day they occurred, and from domination of the networks' news holes. Commentators for the hearings interpreted the events and ascribed to them a sense of urgency and import. Hall and others (1978, 220) contend that, in this regard, the media perform a crucial role: in the creation and dissipation of crises, they are "among the most powerful forces in the shaping of public consciousness about topical and controversial issues. The signification of events in the media thus provides one key terrain where 'consent' is won or lost." To understand the construction of social crises today, it is crucial to understand how they are mass mediated; it is on the mediated management of crisis that public consent depends.

Television news represented this crisis primarily as a contest between the white patriarchs of electoral politics and the outside agitators of feminism. This perceived threat to white patriarchal authority comprised a number of issues and questions, particularly those concerning employment, and, specifically, the ways in which women and men might share power at work. For example, feminist organizations asked that, if men were able to harass women at work (and get a subtle nod from the EEOC), was this not a clear subversion of women's progress in workplaces in the last few decades? If so, and if the former director of the EEOC had indeed engaged in sexual harassment, then where could working women turn? Was the deck not stacked against them? These sorts of questions were taken up in the hearings and conveyed a need to restructure relations of power around gender, race, and class. The conflicted character of the hearings is quite evident in televised news accounts, and the narratives that constitute these texts are rich with tropes and direct invocations of schism, instability, chaos, and outrage. Together these contributed to a perceived or felt crisis, one that served to illuminate the constructed and sometimes provisional character of social identities and political institutions.

FEAR AND LOATHING ON THE SENATE JUDICIARY COMMITTEE, 1991

> . . . a superheated Washington controversy.
> —Tom Brokaw, *NBC Nightly News*

> Pick any of the old clichés—bunker mentality, hunkered down, under siege—they all seem like understatements here today.
> —Susan Spencer, *CBS Evening News*

> George Bush ought to go directly to the American people who voted for him and tell the American people exactly what is going on in this God-forsaken city.
>
> —Brent Bozell, Conservative Victory Center,
> *CBS Evening News*

As these quotations demonstrate, network news coverage of the Hill– Thomas hearings exhibited no shortage of hyperbolic prose. Along with potent cultural metaphors, such prose helped frame the hearings as a site of irresolvable conflict. The discursive practices of mainstream news programs constructed panics based on extreme positions from which negotiation or compromise seemed all but impossible. These dichotomous spaces were issue- or identity-specific, and together they conveyed a sense that the hearings represented the disintegration of control and dominance by predominantly white, male ruling bodies in the United States.

IDEOLOGICAL PANIC

Television news constructed an ideological panic chiefly by representing Anita Hill and Clarence Thomas as ideological extremes and then reducing their conflict to an interpersonal one, based on dichotomous, partisan loyalties. The effect was polarization: personalizing their disagreement obviated any structural or critical analysis of Hill's or Thomas's accounts, while it begged the question of inevitability. That is, are not these sorts of personal disagreements exactly what we would expect from two diametrically opposed ideologues?

This coverage coalesced in the creation of Hill and Thomas as representatives of extreme points on a sociopolitical continuum.[3] Emphasis on interpersonal conflict was directed toward the breakdown of relations between Hill and Thomas as a result of their respective belief systems and was at times broadened to include witnesses and other figures, categorized by dint of their loyalties to either Hill or Thomas. For example, NBC's October 10 news program discussed the prospect of Hill testifying[4] against Thomas in terms that emphasized the personal background of each, where their personal politics diverged, and the conflict to come. Tom Brokaw's dramatic opening statement set up their relationship this way:

> They share a common heritage. Born poor and black, bright and hard-working. They earned law degrees at Yale and went to Washington to start their careers. Now, in the nation's capitol, they're at opposite ends of a personal, legal, political, and emotional dispute of historic proportions. Clarence Thomas and Anita Hill. (NBC 1991b)

News accounts shuttled back and forth between her account and his, juxtaposing them in a he-said, she-said argument. CBS's October 11 story exemplified this as a male voice-over pitting Thomas's account of what he was enduring against Hill's: "He called it Kafkaesque, unlike anything he'd ever experienced." This was followed by a shot of Thomas stating angrily, "I will not provide the rope for my own lynching, or for further humiliation." The next shot was of Anita Hill, accompanied by this voice-over: "She began by talking about working with him at the Department of Education," followed by the most lurid excerpts from her testimony. Hill's testimony was broken up by voice-overs that set the stage for the content to come. This montage concluded with correspondent Bob Schieffer's comments:

> And it went, Dan, like that, back and forth, most of the day in some of the strongest language anyone had ever heard here. But at the end of the day the same question was to be asked that was to be asked at the beginning: Who's telling the truth? (CBS 1991d)

In focusing on the interpersonal elements of the conflict, these accounts and others like them individualized and personalized the story of Hill's complaints against Thomas, a trend also noted by Lubiano (1992, 326). Such a focus could not only depoliticize sexual harassment—an issue feminists had long

struggled to politicize—it could obscure the larger and perhaps more threatening dimensions of the phenomenon, such as the persistence of sexual harassment across different social and political institutions and the structural components that underpin it. Personalizing the events suggested that Hill's charges
were inappropriate for adjudication; after all, "who's telling the truth?" is a
question that reduces the conflict to a personal one, more simply resolved in
this realm than in judicial proceedings. Such allegations, it seemed, were better settled privately. Nancy Fraser (1992) claims that White House press han-
dlers were responsible for attempting to contain the events in the private
sphere; that it occurred as intended without critical comment in network
news demonstrated a susceptibility to White House "spin" and perhaps an
absence of a more critical framework within news organizations for evaluat-
ing sexual harassment allegations.

Fraser argues as well that the hearings were very much a matter of dis-
tinguishing, strategically and overtly, private actions from public ones: "the way
the struggle unfolded . . . depended at every point on who had the power to
successfully and authoritatively define where the line between the public and
private would be drawn. It depended as well on who had the power to police
and defend that boundary" (1992, 596). She notes that Anita Hill was never
permitted to declare any part of her life private, and therefore off-limits to
questioning, whereas Thomas was permitted to assert that most aspects of his
life were private and unavailable for scrutiny or discussion. Yet much of the
anger that politicians and politicos directed at Hill seemed to come from their
own dismay and confusion about the way Hill's charges breached the line of
demarcation between public and private worlds. Take, for example, this ram-
bling diatribe by Senator Alan Simpson made the day after Anita Hill's name
was first publicized. Simpson was reacting to *Nightline* reporter Jeff Greenfield's
suggestion that many women were angered when they perceived that the Senate Judiciary Committee had not considered Anita Hill's allegations serious
enough to warrant the prevention of his nomination.

> Let me tell you, we did look at [the FBI report] and we knew [Anita Hill's]
> name. This woman's name was presented. That's how we got the FBI
> report, and the FBI put together a folio and we read it, and when we
> found the name of the person that she said said what, it was all hearsay. I
> can tell you it is. Some day it will all come to pass, and in the report was
> a [sic] actual name of the man, of a Democrat senator staff, that contacted
> this woman to say, "You know, come forward." She said, "I don't want to
> come forward," and then go look at the convoluted process she went
> through trying to protect herself, all of it blown, and one of the serious

rights of any person in society—and journalists are to recognize it—is to recognize the dignity and privacy of people and not crow about blowing the cover of this woman who will never recover from it. (ABC 1991a)

Simpson framed his pleas for Hill's privacy to be respected in terms of blowing her cover, a phrase that suggested her privacy was as necessary as though she were a federally protected witness or an undercover detective. Simpson's implication—that Hill's move from private to public would be fraught with difficulty—was proved by subsequent events to be correct, in part because of Simpson's *own* accusation that Hill was lying to the committee. His defense of Hill's privacy did not mask his anger at Hill's coming forward with sexual harassment charges against Thomas.[5] Rather than inviting Hill's charges as an opportunity to consider what was potentially another facet of Thomas's record, Simpson instead retreated to a defense of a seemingly undemocratic practice: withholding information crucial to the decision making of an ostensibly democratic body.

In this context, private and public were inverted from their officially stated relationship to the political process: privacy, and not publicity, was espoused as being crucial to democracy (as Simpson explained, "dignity and privacy of people" together constitute "one of the serious rights of any person in society"). At this point, very early on during the week of the hearings and before Hill had actually testified, the line between private and public was drawn in such a way that preservation of privacy was identified as democratic, while public debate and wrangling were threats to democracy—the introduction of "politics" into a process that none would admit had *always* been partisan. Reporter Tim O'Brien of ABC News expressed this sentiment when he noted that,

[n]o one disputes if Clarence Thomas winds up defeated the process will have been messy, angry and riddled with politics. History shows, however, that when a Supreme Court nomination goes down in flames, rarely has it been anything other than politics. (ABC 1991c)

The choice of the phrase "riddled with politics" suggests that Anita Hill and her charges poked holes in an otherwise whole and intact confirmation process. O'Brien's comment gives the impression that she had subverted the system of Supreme Court nominations and confirmations by introducing a corrosive influence: politics.

Both the introduction of "politics" and the emergence of Hill's charges from their private shadows were expressed in grave terms in a number of newscasts. Blowing Hill's cover was, as Alan Simpson's statement showed, construed as a profoundly anti-democratic act, yet later in the hearings, Simpson himself exploited Hill's private life (and, according to his standards, her rights) by using allegations from unnamed sources of scandalous behavior by Hill in an attempt to sully her character. Ironically, this ultimately seemed to legitimate sexual harassment as a charge that could potentially bring down a Supreme Court nominee or others nominated for powerful positions. It also highlighted a shift, one that articulated Hill to publicity and "politics" and Thomas to privacy and democracy. Such a shift inverted the terms of liberalism, foregrounding a situation in which political debate was assiduously avoided, as were topics and identities that had been suppressed in the process of nominating Thomas. It was one incident that could thus demonstrate a weakness of white patriarchal authority in electoral politics in the United States.

Television commentators used metaphors of war, violence, injury, and destruction to characterize ideological conflicts, making common ground difficult to envision. The Senate's division into pro- and anti-Thomas camps was depicted as a partisan schism, a "showdown" (CBS 1991b, 1991d), and a rift that was "ripping the Senate apart" (NBC 1991a). As Dan Rather put it, "all sides are gearing up for a bruising battle in the United States Senate" (CBS 1991c). Negotiation appeared to be virtually out of the question in such an environment. If metaphors work to advance particular worldviews, as Lakoff and Johnson (1980), among others, suggest, then these metaphors surely point to the potential for destruction by offering that political wrangling results in bloodshed and apocalypse; these limit the possibilities for envisioning a liberatory perspective on political debate, thus contradicting one foundational tenet of U.S.-style liberalism: that a noisy republic is a healthy one, when its noise can be attributed to unfettered, robust political debate.

Instead, partisan division was emphasized in the coverage of the senators' arguments about Thomas's fitness for duty. Shots of senators arguing for or against Thomas on the Senate floor were spliced together to highlight the passion and strength of their convictions, but these scenes were assembled in such a way as to pit Democrats against Republicans, with each side taking turns scolding the other. An NBC segment, "Judge Thomas: The Final Vote," depicted ideological differences that looked so intractable that they defied even the redemption that a religious intervention could offer. Tom Brokaw introduced the coverage that was to follow as a part of "the end of one of the most wrenching political battles this country has ever endured." The next image was of a minister solemnly delivering an invocation before the Senate and asking God to give the senators His "righteous wisdom." Then a voice-over: "The Senate has not had much righteous wisdom lately. Today was no different. The bitterness of the hearings spilled over onto the Senate floor." This was followed by shots of various senators vigorously staking out their positions on the floor of the Senate and tangling with their ideological opponents. Ted Kennedy was pictured calling the Senate Judiciary Committee's (of which he himself was a member) treatment of Anita Hill "shameful," while Arlen Specter subsequently rebuked him with, "We do not need characterizations like shame in this chamber from the Senator from Massachusetts" (this and a later statement by Orrin Hatch about a "bridge in Massachusetts" were barbs presumably aimed at Kennedy's involvement in the now-infamous Chappaquidik incident). Correspondent Andrea Mitchell concluded the segment with a prediction of the return of the senatorial repressed: "This chapter may not be over. The Senate still has to confront its own problems, and there is a lot of blood on the Senate floor" (NBC 1991e).

This representation of the events contributed to the ideological panic by constructing a discursive chasm (Republicans on one side and Democrats on the other) and then indicating the impossibility of bridging it. This was a standoff whose hope for resolution seemed to lie only with the shedding of blood in battle. When cast in this light, politics seemed less a process of mutual and active persuasion and more an act of predestination: progressive change was difficult to envision, and the application of pressure to effect legislative change seemed futile. The combination of political party conflict and privacy conflict worked as parts of an ideological panic by emphasizing (and, arguably, reproducing) fissures in democratic politics. Any doubts that TV viewers harbored about politicians' willingness to find common ground in political struggles before the hearings were starkly and dramatically confirmed in these news accounts.

RACE PANIC

Coverage of the hearings constructed racial difference as well as ideological difference between Hill and Thomas. During the hearings, Anita Hill and Clarence Thomas each functioned by turns as white *and* African American, a process that demonstrated the instability of race as a cultural signifier. Ultimately, it was Thomas who could fix meaning to his tactical advantage by articulating his rendering of African-American history to his own and his supporters' ideological position. A panic around race[6] emerged in the tumult caused by these contradictory positions. On the one hand, the hearings offered evidence of great variation among African Americans on the basis of political ideology, socioeconomic class, and gender politics. On the other hand, African Americans also were depicted as homogeneous—a monolithic community that acted and thought in unison. The numerous African Americans who appeared in news accounts to either comment on the hearings or participate in them made clear the gradations and complexities of support for either Hill or Thomas, but media accounts mapped over these images an interpretation that contradicted such heterogeneity, both in their repeated references to "the Black community" and with implications that its members would respond to the hearings in a unified fashion, based on their race. Authoritative, usually male, voice-overs commented this way about "the Black community" and black professionals, as though they were an undifferentiated mass whose actions could be reliably predicted.

The discursive construction of racial difference emerged for the most part from the much-discussed way in which Clarence Thomas had used race to turn the tide of public opinion in his favor (something noted by a number of critical theorists who studied the hearings as well; see, for example, essays by Toni Morrison, Andrew Ross, and Wahneema Lubiano in Morrison 1992). Even before Anita Hill's name was uttered in the context of these hearings, Thomas had made numerous references to his transcendence of the racism that he and earlier generations of his family had experienced. Probably the most infamous of these statements, made after Hill had testified, was his characterization of the charges as a "high-tech lynching," and his adamant protest that, "I will not provide the rope for my own lynching" (CBS 1991d). With this phrase, Thomas accused the Senate Judiciary Committee, Anita Hill, and the press of attempting to destroy him through their investigation of sexual harassment. This gesture of foreclosure had the power to render both whites and African Americans helpless to fight against Thomas, lest they appear callous toward him and the history of racism that his allusions invoked.

Thomas' strategy was such that no one—African American, white, Democrat, or Republican—appeared able to challenge him for using this trope inappropriately or to suggest that it might be a diversionary tactic. Although politicians and journalists reported afterward that they thought it was a transparently manipulative move (Senator Robert Byrd, for example [NBC 1991e], expressed resentment quite forcefully on the floor of the Senate), they seemed paralyzed to contest it when it occurred, or even immediately afterward. Because the brutal history of whites lynching African Americans in the United States still evokes intense emotions, even an inaccurate[7] invocation of it could effectively silence characteristically vocal groups such as the Senate.

Whether appropriate to his own circumstances or not, Thomas' words served as a reminder that racism could be present even in those institutions as

lofty as the Senate. The image of the all-white Senate Judiciary Committee acting as a tribunal for two respected African-American professionals and a host
of their supporters was powerful for what it suggested about the location of
race and power in politics. Network news programs, while not delving deeply
into the subject, attempted to explore how race and racism affected perceptions
of the hearings. At times they entertained the suggestion that Clarence
Thomas's nomination had been more for the advancement of George Bush Sr.'s
political agenda than for the advancement of the Supreme Court.[8] One
exchange based on this challenge occurred on *Larry King Live*, between Phyllis Berry Myers, a former Thomas aide, and Emma Coleman Jordan, the chief
counsel for Anita Hill:

> JORDAN: Don't forget that when [Thomas's] appointment was made in Kenne-
> bunkport this past summer President Bush said that he hadn't chosen Clarence
> Thomas because of his race. He said he was the best-qualified person for the posi-
> tion and the fact that he was black was so much the better. And now we're find-
> ing that Judge Thomas is using every vile racial tactic that would be reminiscent
> of a southern campaign prior to 1960. He's saying that black-skinned women are
> jealous of light-skinned women. He compares lynching to what's happening to
> him. So he's now suddenly throwing out a lot of racial bile and we're finding our-
> selves put on the defensive.
>
> He's trying to put the committee on defensive [*sic*] because they're all
> white males, and they don't know how to sort it out. The reality is that black peo-
> ple in this country do know how to sort it out and they understand—
>
> MYERS: And according to women supporters—
>
> JORDAN: Just a minute. They understand that a black woman is entitled to be pro-
> tected from a sexual harasser.
>
> MYERS: Oh, and it's so convenient. What did they do? Is Anita a secretary? No.
> She's a Yale law school graduate who's articulate and speaks the queen's English
> and so, therefore, we're supposed to, because they found this supposedly credible
> person to take on who's supposedly a credible man—and who is creditable—that
> we're supposed to somehow not be—we're supposed to be impressed by that.
> Well, I'm not impressed.
>
> And Clarence Thomas is not the one that's throwing out the bile. This bile—
> this garbage that she said in the committee—was dumped on him. (CNN 1991d)

This exchange between Jordan and Myers illustrates the impact of political and class differences[9] on interpretations of the hearings. Not only did each
of these women represent a vastly different perspective on Thomas and the
charges against him, but each occupied a different position with respect to the

role of race in the hearings and in Thomas's testimony. Phyllis Myers' derisive comment about Anita Hill's education and diction, for example, clearly showed her contempt for any trappings of elitism; her suggestion was that these had made Hill less believable as a victim of sexual harassment (apparently, in her estimation, elite women cannot be victimized by sexual harassment). Class conflict thus intersected with race to complicate perspectives on the hearings and the various figures involved. This exchange distinguished gender from race, so that racial identity became the allegiance that Anita Hill was said to betray. Christine Stansell (1992) argues that this particular outcome of the hearings revealed

> a dismaying revelation of the calamitous uses to which the right can turn the opposition between "blacks" and "women." How does a black woman who speaks of sexual oppression by a black man come to be seen as a white man's pawn? How does the black man whom she implicates come to represent oppressed African American men? How did Thomas's autobiographical penumbra protect him from the suspicions that would easily light on a similarly bluffing, swaggering, belligerent man in any traffic court? (266)

Such a context, in which Hill could be viewed as a race traitor, worked against a feminist critique of Thomas and of sexual harassment. To cast Hill as a woman who had betrayed her race and her former friend/boss *and* was a pawn of feminists could be more useful for its scandalous and diversionary purposes than an accusation of sexual harassment ever could. Demonizing Hill in this way helped "whiten" her and articulate Thomas more securely to a liberal racial politics— a politics which, ironically, he disavowed implicitly through his EEOC and judicial work and explicitly in the various diatribes against affirmative action and other civil rights policy he had made during his career up until that point (Higginbotham 1992, 1995).

These depictions pointed to the way in which racial identities could shift in different contexts, but television news stories also made moves that contradicted a notion that race is a "floating signifier" (Stuart Hall in Jhally 1996). These stories discussed African Americans as a monolithic group of citizens, united on the basis of their skin color. African Americans were featured repeatedly voicing opinions that varied distinctly from one another—sometimes quite significantly; voice-overs and other accompanying commentary, however, attempted to homogenize these sentiments by depicting the speakers as representative members of their race. This was especially pronounced in special segments strictly dedicated to discussing how *the* African-American community was responding to the hearings. One omniscient narrator, from CBS, a voice-over, illustrated this tactic well: "Across the country, Black Americans gave a collective cringe, a shared fear that the reputations of *all* Black professionals may have been damaged along with those of Professor Hill and Judge Thomas" (CBS 1991g, emphasis in original). Such depictions were markers of difference, for they occurred most often in the context of discussions suggesting polarity between African Americans and whites. That is, an impression of African-American unity disarticulated African Americans *from* whites (and any sense of interracial harmony) and underscored the differences between these two groups. This essentialist focus on race obviated a discussion of race as anything but a biologically determined category of identity, even though a number of circumstances, such as the array of African Americans displaying varied politics, would have suggested that the time was ripe for just such a discussion.

As Michael Eric Dyson (1993) points out, "[g]iven the variety of elements and the complexity of means by which racial identity is constructed, there can be no essential black identity, because racial identity is relentlessly reshaped" (xx–xxi). Stuart Hall also notes that race can be considered a "floating signifier" that, historically, assumes different meanings and serves different interests (in Jhally 1996). Mass mediated depictions and discussions of race are undoubtedly a part of the ways in which race is "relentlessly reshaped," so in addition to denying their complicity in this process, mediated representations that lump all African Americans together to represent *the* black community are not only inaccurate but they sidestep a more critical analysis of race as a culturally constructed category of identity: a position that critical race scholars support as being potentially liberatory.

That African Americans could be divided as factiously as whites indicated that a shift had occurred in the civil rights movement's ability to unify African Americans and impel activism as a coalition based on racial oppression. The inability of civil rights activists to block Thomas's nomination, or to mobilize effectively against him, permitted conservative politicians, such as George Bush Sr., to create an illusion of benevolence toward minorities and to articulate a progressive politics of race to their ideological position—despite such politicians' active attempts to dismantle civil rights legislation and affirmative action policies. Clarence Thomas was an ideal candidate for these purposes: his skin color marked him as black, while his political ideology had made him a darling of the Right. He was an anomaly for that time, in that he was a *very* conservative African-American public figure. Not only had he demonstrated his opposition to civil rights policies, he distanced himself from liberal African-American politicos and movements and thus showed great promise as an ideological fit with Antonin Scalia—the most right-wing justice on the Supreme Court. It was with Thomas, William Rehnquist, and Scalia that George Bush Sr. had hoped to form a judicial coalition (Burnham 1992, 291).

Contradictions between racial heterogeneity and an imposed (illusory) homogeneity formed a race panic. Representing homogeneity indicated a need for control over the multiplicity of ideological positions that African Americans could be seen embodying and voicing. In this context, then, essentialism could work to manage and secure race under the sign of a biological attribute—skin color. In direct opposition to this essentialist position was the tacit but nevertheless clear presentation of heterogeneity among African Americans. Both Thomas and Hill occupied this camp at different times. Thomas and his supporters actively disarticulated themselves from a civil rights agenda and sought instead an extreme right-wing politics. On the other hand, Hill, while not a radical leftist, was more liberal than Thomas and allied herself with very liberal advisors and supporters (many of whom had been active in civil rights politics) to assist her in Washington. Hill, Thomas, and their respective cadres pointed to the varied views and politics that African Americans could hold and were willing to fight for with passion. In this context, Hill functioned synecdochically as the victim of the breakdown of a traditional articulation—that between liberals and civil rights politics. Conversely, Thomas functioned as the fortunate recipient of a newer articulation—between conservatives and the rhetoric of empowerment, and he demonstrated the ease with which civil rights rhetoric could be voided and rearticulated to a conservative political agenda. This race panic thus indicated a significant breakdown in the power that civil rights coalitions had wielded since the 1960s, and it suggested that conservative politics held more promise for African Americans in the long run.

GENDER PANIC

Like race, gender panic was constructed from a narrow range of terms that pointed to the failures of a formerly stable system. For the most part, these occurred by representing Anita Hill as socially deviant or through the use of war metaphors, such as this male voice-over's lament that, "the recent hearings have triggered yet another round in the war between the sexes" (CBS 1991e). Using the definite article, this reporter and others like him suggested that a war between the sexes was inevitable and ongoing, its tensions simmering until *provocateurs* such as Anita Hill emerged to initiate a skirmish. Hill's deviance was in part constructed around accusations of prevarication. Conservative politi-

cians such as Senators Orrin Hatch and Alan Simpson went on record a number of times to claim that Hill had been either manipulated by Democratic
politicians into making false statements to bring down Clarence Thomas
(Hatch) or had been lying of her own accord (Simpson). Politicians and commentators featured in these newscasts repeatedly expressed great alarm that
Hill's charges were being taken seriously enough to delay Thomas' confirmation hearings. If the charges, suspect as they seemed to many, could present a
major obstacle to Thomas's progress, would this not be a signal to all women
that they too could make spurious charges and have them considered seriously?
If so, would that not allow every woman with a petty grudge to make sexual
harassment charges if she wanted to oust a man from her workplace? And
would this not instill suspicion in both women and men and thus irreparably
damage the tenor of relations between them?

Early on, news accounts established a pattern of constructing Hill's charges
against Thomas as the start of a ripple effect that would irreparably harm all
men. In part, this was accomplished by equating Anita Hill with Everywoman,
and then repeating this equivalence *ad infinitum*. Senator Orrin Hatch, on *Larry
King Live,* for instance, noted defensively that there was "a very strong feeling
that when you say anything to Professor Hill you're sort of challenging all the
women and that if you are for Judge Thomas then you're discouraging women
from coming forward, and it becomes personalized" (CNN 1991d).

Special reports on sexual harassment (five aired between October 7 and
October 15) that occurred as parts of these news programs were particularly
prone to divisive strategies; these reports on sexual harassment used essentialist
notions of gender and failed to take up the issue of power disparity and its
function in sexual harassment. This is a conspicuous absence. If nothing else, the
most elementary lessons about sexual harassment address the way in which
harassers exploit power differences, both in choosing their victims and in hid-
ing their activities. Second-wave feminists had tried to politicize this important
aspect of sexual harassment by understanding it as a tool that workplace supe-
riors (typically male) wield over their subordinates (typically female) to keep
them in line. As in rape, sex becomes a means to an end—an end that typically
leaves women disadvantaged. News segments did not explore this dimension at
length, if they explored it at all. What they did do was predict that the hearings'
social effects would make relations between women and men uncomfortable
and difficult, if not impossible, to negotiate. Men would be forced to reevalu-
ate their actions toward women to ensure that they were not acting in a way
that could be construed as harassment. Such self reflection was presented as odi-
ous and even unjust. A man polled in one of these segments commented that

men would no longer be able to compliment women on their appearances for
fear of being accused of harassment. These alarmist predictions were typical and
also contributed to the intense urgency associated with hearing coverage: gender relations were going to hell—and fast.

Suzanne Fields, columnist for the *Washington Times* newspaper, argued
along these lines on a *Larry King Live* broadcast.

> KING: Suzanne, is the workplace of America—and that's what we're talking about
> when we talk about sexual harassment; this is job-related, the workplace, or with
> your employer—is it safe?
>
> FIELDS: Well, I don't think it's safer. In fact, I've never seen men and women so
> angry at each other—at every dinner party, in every office. In fact, you have
> executives and editors saying they're not going to talk—if they're males they're
> not going to talk to a woman unless they have a witness, such as a gynecolo-
> gist would have another person in the room to make sure there's not going to
> be anything . . .
>
> KING: Well, that would make it safer from that aspect, but . . .
>
> FIELDS: But there's another problem here, Larry. A woman called me from
> Nashville, Tennessee, and she said she was in an all-male world. She was a sales
> rep., and she said she travels with these men alone, she goes on airplanes with
> them, she goes in cars. And she said they're not going to want to travel with her
> now. They're not going to want to bring women into these male-dominated
> workforces because the men are going to be afraid about, "What will she say
> tomorrow or in 10 years?" (CNN 1991f)

Fields' statement demonstrated that women *and* men were concerned about
how men's actions toward women in their workplaces would be perceived, perhaps to the detriment of women's overall professional advancement, but men
expressed fear about *their* careers in light of publicized sexual harassment. An
Atlanta man polled on *This Week with David Brinkley* complained that, "It's
almost at a point where the situation can develop where you're almost afraid to
speak to a woman." Another Atlanta man on the same program went even further: "They wear seductive clothing, and when you compliment them, they get
mad. So it's—that's how some women are" (ABC 1991e). These men implied
that women were the problem: workplace sirens who dressed seductively and
lured their unsuspecting colleagues to their professional deaths.

This sort of war between the sexes scenario often appeared in conjunction with a larger sense of doom—as a sign that the old boy political network
was falling apart. Jack Smith, a reporter for ABC News, joked informally that,
"As Americans this week put down their work and watched, women every-

where said that guys just didn't get it" (ABC 1991c). This was illustrated dramatically on October 8, the day before the Senate voted on whether or not they would hear Anita Hill's allegations against Thomas. On this day, news stories were replete with coverage of the oscillations between female and male politicos and politicians, as each group tried to dominate public opinion and prevail in the Senate. After showing a shot (now well circulated) of Democratic female House members storming the Senate Office Building, CBS aired a sound bite from one of these women: Congress member Patricia Schroeder opined that, "I think America's women really want to see this body doing something *for* them than *to* them" (CBS 1991a). This male voice-over on NBC, also from October 8 asserted that, "Today there were questions about a boy's club mentality in the Senate, and Hill seemed to speak for millions of women." This broadcast was concluded with a prescient comment by correspondent Bob Kuv: "And so, in this capitol city, where men have always made the rules, a political firestorm over sexual harassment just might help to even the score" (NBC 1991b).

These commentators set the stage for the discussion of gender issues that would follow and impugned the male senators' misunderstandings and the short shrift they gave to women's issues. The comments of CBS correspondent Bruce Morton, in a concluding commentary segment, argued that the hearings cast the Senate in a very bad light—as a men's club that was not only ignorant about the rudimentary aspects of sexual harassment but calculated in its ignorance. After Hill had concluded her testimony, Morton argued that the result was disastrous, "and the Senate looks like a collection of a hundred losers" (CBS 1991e). Morton's description was especially apt when a number of male politicians were shown expressing sentiments that demonstrated that they had virtually no knowledge of how sexual harassment affected its victims yet were perfectly willing to dictate the terms of redress by which victims should comply. This quote by Senator Dennis De Concini was particularly illustrative:

> And if you're sexually harassed, you ought to get mad about it, and you ought to do something about it and you ought to complain, instead of hanging around a long time and then all of a sudden calling up anonymously and saying, "Oh, I want to complain." I mean, where is the gumption? (ABC 1991a)

Statements by Senators Orrin Hatch and Alan Simpson, both on the Senate Judiciary Committee, also exemplified a general "not getting it" style of paternalism. These senators, when asked about their stance on the issue of sexual harassment, expressed protective sentiments and a desire to protect "their" women from harassers. Simpson, responding to a charge that the Senate had been irresponsible in investigating Hill's charges because they were men and did not understand sexual harassment, stated angrily: "No, that's a crude statement. That's a sexist, guilt-ridden statement. We are people that have spouses and daughters and mothers. You know, I think that's a really—a really cheap shot" (ABC 1991a). Hatch's statement, made on *Larry King Live*, was in response to Larry King's suggestion that Anita Hill's following Clarence Thomas as a staff attorney from the Department of Education to the EEOC Office was not necessarily a sign that Thomas had not harassed Hill. Hatch, disputing this, yet at the same time attempting to mark himself as being sensitive to the issue of sexual harassment, commented defensively:

> I think sexual harassment is a terrible thing, and it does exist and it should be stamped out. I've got three daughters. I've got nine granddaughters. If anybody harassed my daughter I'd be so doggone mad I couldn't see straight, and so I'm not debating that. I think that goes without saying, and I don't want to find fault with [Anita Hill]. (CNN 1991c)

Armstrong Williams, a former aide to Clarence Thomas and featured on a different *Larry King Live* broadcast, also strenuously defended his respect for women via his familial relations. When discussing whether Anita Hill's charges were credible, he asserted,

> [l]et me tell you, I think sometimes we're very insensitive to how women are harassed and how they're disrespected. And there's no one who has more respect for women than I do, because my mother's a woman and my sister's a woman, so therefore I have the utmost respect. (CNN 1991d)

Hatch's and Williams's similarly protective sentiments suggested concern for women's welfare on the basis of family bonds alone: Simpson, Hatch, and Williams insisted that they recognized abuses of women but wanted to invoke paternal privileges to protect them from it (rather than wanting to invoke their own institutional power to codify protective measures). What they seemed to not realize was that familial relationships with women were not unique to men who do not harass women; even convicted harassers have female blood relatives, and family bonds alone are not proof for claims of sensitivity.

An ominous tone accompanied many of these reports; not "getting it" was depicted as an intolerable situation in desperate need of change—and perhaps retribution. Even before the first Senate vote (on whether to delay the confirmation vote to include Hill's testimony [October 8]), Tom Brokaw observed that senators were under "heavy pressure" from "angry women" to postpone the confirmation vote. Brokaw's statement was made in conjunction with a shot of Arlen Specter, being mobbed by women chanting "vote no, no, no!"[10] (NBC 1991a). On the October 8 broadcast of *Crossfire*, journalist Juan Williams asked Senator Arlen Specter if the Senate Judiciary Committee was investigating Anita Hill's charges because they were fearful of the reaction from women if they did not: "Is the point then, is the Senate being steamrolled at this point because the Senate is afraid of public opinion, of women saying you're not being sensitive to women's issues? Is this what this is all about, Senator?" (CNN 1991a). Specter denied the accusation, although he conceded that the investigation of Hill's charges had not been handled as well as they should have been. Both Specter and House member Maxine Waters, on the same program, asserted that Anita Hill's charges needed to be heard and considered, but neither Williams nor his rabidly right-wing co-host, Patrick Buchanan, agreed with them. The two co-hosts seemed livid that the charges were being investigated, not only because the two of them clearly sympathized with Clarence Thomas, but because they were fearful about what this could mean about unleashing anger in women, *en masse*. What follows is the revealing exchange between Williams and Buchanan that concluded the program.

> BUCHANAN: Juan, I agree with Professor Woodson [another guest on the program], this is a horrendous charge at the final minute and—against Judge Thomas—it's already been aired apparently in that committee and I saw that woman Anita Hill up there today. She didn't look very self-confident to me. I think there's a real potential for a horrendous backlash against the Judiciary Committee and against the Senate.
>
> WILLIAMS: Well, Pat, you know, I think that there's a potential for this backlash you speak of but there's a potential for something worse here which is I think that this guy, Clarence Thomas, can get steamrolled. I think a lot of those senators now feel a great deal of pressure from women in this country who have legitimate grievance in terms of the number of women in the Senate, only two, and . . .
>
> BUCHANAN: Knowing what you know, Juan . . .
>
> WILLIAMS: . . . they feel their issues have been ignored.
>
> BUCHANAN: Knowing what you know, though, if he loses the Supreme Court seat based on this allegation from a woman who came back to town and calls him up ten times and leaves nice little messages on the pad, is that not an outrage?
>
> WILLIAMS: It's an outrage and it's an injustice, and I tell you injustice like this makes me want to scream, Pat. It's just wrong. (CNN 1991a)

The next day (October 9, 1991) *Good Morning America* explored a similar theme, albeit in a somewhat more complex fashion. Co-host Charles Gibson queried both former Senate Majority Leader Howard Baker and former
congressperson and vice-presidential candidate Geraldine Ferraro about the
Senate Judiciary Committee's behavior, specifically the handling of the charges
and the FBI leak. Gibson was particularly probing about the issue of what all
of this indicated about sexism in the Senate. Ferraro charged that the Senate
showed that "they still don't get it," while Baker blustered that, "I served in the
Senate for 18 years, and I must say, I do not think it's a sexist group" (ABC
1991b). This conflict between Baker and Ferraro was fairly typical of the news
programs broadcast during this time: liberal feminist spokesperson (usually
female) pitted against conservative establishment spokesperson (usually male),
expressing untenably disparate perspectives on the same situation. Construing
the problem in these narrow, dichotomous terms constricted the boundaries of
exploration around this issue so that possible solutions were seldom, if ever, discussed. When this rigid dichotomy was paired as it was with an almost dogged
focus on the alleged leak of the FBI's report,[11] journalists and political commentators were then free to discuss the legalities and ethics of that, rather than
to engage in sustained explorations of the ramifications of Anita Hill's charges
for women and for power relations between women and men.

As the week of the hearings wore on, the suggestion that women were
not going to stand idle and watch the goings-on without a significant intervention became louder and clearer. Tom Brokaw's opening statement on October 14 forecast some of what was to come:

> [W]ith 24 hours until the vote, nothing is certain. And when the vote is
> counted, this ordeal will not be over, for there are too many unresolved
> issues beyond the charges of sexual harassment, too much anger, too much
> anguish. (NBC 1991d)

Later in the same broadcast, an anonymous voice-over noted that "women's
groups threatened retaliation at the polls," followed by a shot of National
Abortion Rights Action League (NARAL) director Kate Michelman saying,
"women will remember this vote" (NBC 1991d). Framing implications of the
vote in terms of backlash and female wrath suggested a direction for crisis
management upon closure of the hearings and after Thomas's confirmation
vote—management that was, I argue, delivered in the specific construction of
the Year of the Woman.

Constructing a panic around gender was a matter of exploiting and exac-
erbating historical tensions around women and work and women and politics,

but with a twist: the suggestion that doing something about sexual harassment—voicing sexual harassment complaints—would cause irreparable damage to relations between women and men. Thus even though some analysis of sexual harassment had circulated through the channels of mainstream news, an implied warning of widespread social damage accompanied it so that all possible remedies looked problematic. The consequences of women speaking out about their sexual harassment were clarified both in the way Anita Hill was treated and in the predictions of social dysfunction if many women were to make these accusations. However, one solution was presented as palatable: the electoral one. The ballot was promoted as the best remedy for male domination, just as it had been among women and feminists of decades earlier (Evans 1989). As a familiar and relatively tame solution, it could diminish any possibility of a feminist revolution, suggesting instead that a dose of electoral power was the best medicine for female outrage.

A PANIC OF INSTITUTIONAL INTEGRITY

The challenge to male politicians voiced by Kate Michelman and Congress member Pat Schroeder dovetailed with two other phenomena: concern that the political system had become corrupted through its exposure to Anita Hill's allegations, and repeated suggestions that, in its treatment of Anita Hill, the Senate (as representative of the U.S. political system) had failed its citizens. The latter sentiment often was expressed in terms of an abstract community whose norms had been violated; such a violation was offered as evidence that the government was not a servant of its people. The first phenomenon revolved around the depiction of Anita Hill as hypersexualized, a figure who, in some contexts, represented sexual excess, something most often associated with images of African-American women (Fiske 1994).

When Anita Hill emerged in public, her private life opened to public scrutiny, some media accounts chose to focus on her sexuality. Journalists not only raised the issue of her sexual orientation (Phelps and Winternitz 1992), but they pathologized her sexuality. Hill was diagnosed as erotomaniacal, a disorder characterized by the presence of sexual desire so strong that it overwhelms sufferers, with a psychiatrist's testimony before the Senate Judiciary Committee. Ultimately, erotomaniacs cannot distinguish between their fantasies and the "real world."[12] (This psychiatrist had never before met Hill, let alone examined her.) About Anita Hill's treatment in this regard, Nellie McKay (1992) writes:

[I]n the deadly game of make-believe [the Senate Judiciary Committee] played, the intelligent, articulate, conservative, ambitious young black woman who faced the extraordinarily trying circumstances of the Senate hearing with dignity and calm became the delusionary opportunist who bided her time while she planned the destruction of Thomas for imaginary wrongs he did to her, the calculating, frustrated spinster whose amatory intentions toward her ambitious, aspiring superior had been rebuffed, and the woman rejected because of her insane sexual drive. Once vested with these images, [the senators] could recognize her and find a place to fit her into their concepts of black women. Then they treated her as such. (285–86)

Television news programs foregrounded sexuality further in the selections of Anita Hill's testimony about the graphic language that Clarence Thomas had used to harass her. This was seized upon by the members of the Senate Judiciary Committee, who claimed that the use of such language was indicative of Hill's psychosis. John Fiske (1994, 110) notes that, following a long line of African-American women in popular culture, Anita Hill represented hypersexuality and the image of the African-American woman with an insatiable sexual appetite. Although sexuality functioned in this panic mostly around the figure of Anita Hill, Clarence Thomas also drew implications of hypersexuality; Thomas, however, worked this to his advantage by expressing his outrage at the sexual stereotypes used in conjunction with African-American masculinity, present in Hill's testimony. Thomas accused Hill of having conjured up injurious, racially stereotyped charges as part of a campaign to disparage him.

The specific way in which Anita Hill (and Clarence Thomas at times) was articulated to sex and sexual images was in terms of what Mary Russo (1994) calls the "female grotesque." She defines the grotesque body as "open, protruding, irregular, secreting, multiple, and changing; it is identified with non-official 'low' culture or the carnivalesque, and with social transformation" (8). The grotesque image threatens the established order, for it calls attention not only to its own abjection, but to that which is collectively repressed. That images of and public discussions about women—most often women of color and poor women—often occur in terms of their bodies, bodily functions, and sexualities places them in the realm of the grotesque. Television news situated Anita Hill in this space during the hearings and afterward.

News coverage of the hearings suggested that the male world of formal politics had become polluted in its association with Anita Hill: she had stained the white sheets of democracy. The space of political deliberation was represented as an Eden against which no transgressions could be permitted. Clarence Thomas was cast as the moral and ethically pure Adam, worthy of admittance to the pristine landscape, while Anita Hill's Eve introduced taint, shame, and trouble to paradise. Her behavior and the behavior of other harassed women, in one *Larry King Live* segment (October 8), was even discussed in terms of whether or not the professional ambition that fueled them was "a sin" (CNN 1991b). On that same day, on *Crossfire*, Arlen Specter referred to Anita Hill's charges as "the fruit of a poisonous tree,"[13] a suggestion that had the charges been brought up in a less politically significant context, they might have been dismissed out of hand. But, he said, "this is a situation where we have to be sure [to investigate charges]. We're dealing with the integrity of the Supreme Court" (CNN 1991a). The nomination process, the Supreme Court, and the world of electoral politics generally were discussed in terms of a need to maintain their integrity and credibility, attributes seemingly threatened by Anita Hill.

At times, news accounts directly invoked the term *grotesque* to describe the hearings, such as Ted Koppel's, "It is difficult to remember a more grotesquely riveting day before a U. S. Senate committee" (ABC 1991d). Orrin Hatch described the hearings as one example of several "tremendously grotesque battles" in the Senate (CNN 1991e). The Oxford American Dictionary defines grotesque as "very odd or unnatural, fantastically ugly or absurd," thus to categorize sexual harassment—a familiar and widespread problem for women—as grotesque was especially inappropriate and further underscored the male senators' distance from the indignities of a typical workday for many women.

Constructing Anita Hill as a grotesque occurred through the repeated use of metaphors that articulated Hill and her allegations against Thomas to abjection. News stories represented Hill's role in the hearings using the terms Russo describes when she discusses constructions of the female grotesque: abject metaphors of blood, dirt, ugliness, insanity, and sexuality. The most obvious of these metaphors was one that reports invoked frequently: the metaphor of dirt and mud.[14] For example, Senator John Danforth, Clarence Thomas's Senate sponsor, argued against the Senate Judiciary Committee bringing in Anita Hill to testify, saying, "It cannot be true that we are going to tolerate a situation where anybody who wants to throw the mud gets to throw the mud, and if it sticks, that's just wonderful" (ABC 1991a). Along with this was the use of the term *smear* to describe the process by which Thomas was allegedly attacked (e.g., "an eleventh hour smear," "a savage political smear" [CNN 1991a]). On a *Larry King Live* episode from October 15, Orrin Hatch described the influence of special interest groups whom he accused of having set up Anita Hill: "I have to tell you, it's vicious out there. I have seen them scour the earth for dirt— they're not interested in truth; they want dirt—and then smear the guy when they can't find it" (CNN 1991e).

Metaphors that referenced mental illness, physical injury, and savage battles also were used to describe the hearings. Jeff Greenfield of *Nightline* suggested to Senator Paul Simon, a member of the Senate Judiciary Committee,
that Hill's charges represented the "scent of blood in the water" of Thomas's
nomination hearings (ABC 1991a). Orrin Hatch, on ABC's *World News Tonight*,
predicted ominously that neither Hill nor Thomas was "going to walk out of
here a whole person. They're both going to be badly damaged" (ABC 1991c).
Additional aspersions were cast on both Hill's and Thomas's (but mostly Hill's)
psychological well-being. In the midst of the week of the hearings (October
11), Ted Koppel observed that "one of these two people, Judge Thomas or Professor Hill is—if not by clinical definition, then by almost any other measure—
a liar of near-psychotic proportions" (ABC 1991d). On *Larry King Live* (October 14), J. C. Alvarez, a former employee of Thomas's, commented:

> I don't know how else to say it, but I have to tell you that it just blew my
> mind to see Anita Hill testifying on Friday. Honest to goodness, it was like
> schizophrenia. That was not the Anita Hill that I knew and worked with
> at EEOC. (CNN 1991c)

These comments construed Hill's charges as significant threats to an otherwise intact, clean, and healthy democratic system. Equating the charges with
injury or evidence of mental illness made them seem less worthy of adjudication and more appropriately the subject of *medical* intervention, and because
sexual harassment has been coded as a woman's problem, the pathology, by
extension, became sexed. The thrust of this was to suggest that Hill, and perhaps women in general, threatened the harmony and consensual nature of formal politics. Importantly, these interpretations of Hill's charges were composed
primarily of metaphors associated with abjection, thus suggesting that women's
complaints should perhaps not appear in association with politics: pathologies
have no place in the senatorial Garden of Eden. Not only could this move
diminish the institutional legitimacy of women's accounts of sexual harassment,
it could serve a larger purpose as well. That is, it seemed to discredit one of the
most significant critiques of the second-wave women's movement: that what
goes on in private is both affected by and generative of sociopolitical effects; in
other words, that the personal is political (Davis 1991).

The hearings were viewed as a threat not only to democratic institutions
but to community norms as well. This impression was created using several tactics. First, the use of polls—both on the street and with reported data—provided a sense that newscasters were reporting information that had come
directly from ordinary citizens. Whether they were used to gauge reactions to

gender-related issues, such as how the hearings would affect gender relations in workplaces, or more juridical issues, such as whether or not Thomas should be confirmed, these polls constructed a community of citizens and responses that appeared as though they were the norm.[15] Regarding the use of polls in the Hill– Thomas hearings, Andrew Ross (1992) writes that polls operate, "[a]s a medium"; in other words, "polls rarely carry a message; they *are* the message, to cite McLuhan's consistently misunderstood dictum" (44–45). In news coverage of the hearings, polls constructed and fortified the mainstream so that it was resistant to outside threats such as those Anita Hill introduced.[16]

The hearings and their attendant events were depicted as otherworldly, weird, and a blight on the U.S. political and social landscape. They were thus Other to the norms of the community implicitly referenced here. In describing Anita Hill's allegations, for example, Senator John Danforth said that Hill's charges were a last-minute, sleazy attack on Clarence Thomas and were "contrary to the values of most of our people" (CBS 1991a). Dan Rather introduced a postmortem of the hearings by noting that they were "extraordinary, unprecedented, and sometimes . . . they were downright weird." Following Rather's comments, Rita Braver described the hearings as having "drifted into the twilight zone where one bizarre event followed another." "Things were so topsy turvy," she observed, that Hill's supporters and friends, "mostly liberals," who opposed the use of lie detector tests, were bragging about Hill's having passed one. Braver concluded her comments by stating that the hearings constituted "one of the weirdest episodes in Congressional history" (CBS 1991e).

"Bizarre" and "weird" mutated into even graver and more significant descriptors; in this vein, the typically florid Garrick Utley of NBC began the October 12 newscast with this comment on the hearings: "It has been another day of pain and politics, of human emotion and, yes, partisan bickering, of what one senator called today 'a God-awful experience.'" Later in the newscast, Utley introduced an interview with Arlen Specter and Patrick Leahy by arguing that, "we have to remember . . . the credibility of the institution known as the United States Senate" was under fierce attack. Prior to questioning either Specter or Leahy, Utley offered them these soothing words: "We know what you have been going through, as has the witness [Thomas], as has the nation today." Interestingly, Anita Hill's name does not appear on the list of those to whom Utley extended his sympathy, again a subtle indication that Hill was Other to this community. Utley concluded the program with a commentary piece in which he argued that the hearings were not about justice but about spectacle. Would this "further weaken public confidence in government, the process? Yes" (NBC 1991c).[17]

Newscasts using the words of politicians, politicos, and journalists repeatedly echoed the fear that citizens would have no faith in their government or legislators after the hearings. The system was in disarray, they claimed; power had run amok. Both Anita Hill and Clarence Thomas were painted as victims, although by the end of the week's coverage (October 15), both ABC's and CBS's coverage seemed tilted in Anita Hill's favor. The big picture though was of electoral political institutions in crisis, run by anachronistic white males who were generally clueless about gender and, to some extent, race relations.

Interestingly, a number of different newscasts mentioned public relations strategies used by the White House as being at least partially responsible for the direction the hearings had taken. Newscasters noted specifically that White House public relations workers had orchestrated the events of the hearings by influencing Clarence Thomas's testimony. The evidence cited for this claim was Thomas's revision and deployment of race history to gain a public opinion advantage over Anita Hill. Media commentators and politicians suggested that this had been a result of coaching by savvy White House aides who knew how Thomas should position himself vis-à-vis the very white Senate Judiciary Committee and, more generally, the electorate. There seemed to be a consensus that such stealthy manipulation, while impossible to prove, had indeed occurred; however, the tone of these comments was disapproving. This panic of institutional integrity suggested that electoral institutions needed to circle the wagons, rebuild their credibility, and recuperate from their association with Anita Hill.

FROM PANICS, A CRISIS

The panics I have described in the foregoing sections were not mutually exclusive; they functioned alongside and overlapped with one another. While each seemed to foreground a different weak spot or fissure in the political system, they worked together to construct a perceived or felt crisis of white patriarchal authority. This was most readily apparent in the candidacies of the numerous women who objected specifically to the hearings' events. The perceptions of this crisis concerned the inappropriateness of a group of privileged white males adjudicating and legislating for citizens whose needs they clearly did not understand and led to what Lubiano (1992) refers to as "the blurring of the lines between real and cultural politics" (350).

Nancy Fraser (1989) argues that during tumultuous times public discussions of social needs may produce incommensurate solutions. She argues that runaway needs that have broken out of domestic or official economic enclaves enter that hybrid discursive space that Arendt aptly dubbed "the social." They may then become focuses of state intervention geared to crisis management. These needs are thus markers of major sociostructural shifts in the boundaries separating what are classified as "political," "economic," and "domestic" or "personal" spheres of life. (171)

Coverage of the Hill–Thomas hearings laid bare a number of such "runaway needs" by constructing scenarios that pointed to the inadequacies of political and social systems for addressing a constellation of problems experienced by traditionally oppressed groups, such as African-American women. That these needs were featured publicly and dramatically fostered a general recognition that shifts were occurring in the boundaries between what Fraser refers to as "spheres of life." They also helped illuminate some of the dark corners where power brokering occurs, thus providing a look at the process and the players that can influence the political process (politicians' protestations to the contrary notwithstanding).

The constitution of this crisis was advantageous for different reasons to both Hill's supporters and Thomas's. Neither the panics nor this crisis though can be attributed to any one person or group; rather, these were constructed from and managed by the efforts and resources of various power blocs and oppositional groups. One of these, as I have mentioned, was the White House and its corps of public relations workers. News accounts were quick to credit the White House with backstage issue management, as were critics. The White House's desire to create a conservative majority in the Supreme Court was a strong reason for its support of Thomas. Other conservative groups, such as the Conservative Victory Center, vocally supported Thomas and denied Hill's charges. Conservative groups and the White House constituted one major power bloc, one that could influence media accounts decisively.

In opposition to this conservative bloc was one composed of established feminist groups such as NOW and the National Abortion Rights Action League (NARAL). This bloc attempted to make gender issues, particularly sexual harassment, dominate public discourse, and in some contexts it succeeded— as the Year of the Woman's candidates' slates demonstrated. Although unintended, some of this group's work was accomplished for it by the Senate Judiciary Committee's self-described blundered interrogation of Hill.

As all of this demonstrates, cultural crises are not monolithic; rather, they represent the activities and interests of different power blocs and oppositional groups. However, despite the different interests of which a crisis is composed, a dominant ideology inheres within it, and it is to this that consent must be won; this is the substantive basis in "reality" to which public opinion continually refers. In this way, by "consenting" to the view of the crisis which has won credibility in the echelons of power, popular consciousness is also won to support measures of control and containment which this version of social reality entails. (Hall et al. 1978, 220–21)

Hall and others and Acland (1995) assert that the goals of "control and containment" are crucial to the social and cultural functions of crises, and the Hill–Thomas hearings were no exception to this. They demanded an array of responses that took account of power differentials around workplace sexual harassment, race relations, and formal political institutions and practices. The Year of the Woman (discussed in chapter 3) was such a set of responses.

One of Mary Russo's contentions about the female grotesque is that along with abject imagery, the figures and practices of the grotesque have worked historically to subvert social conventions and open up new spaces for imagining identities; Russo argues that, specifically, female grotesque images have served liberatory purposes for women and for feminism, and I argue that Anita Hill's use as a grotesque was progressive in several respects. By her own admission, Hill's experiences were valuable for the space they opened around the discussion of sexual harassment.

> One of the things that has happened over the last week is that people have started to talk about [sexual harassment]. It's almost as though a silence has been broken and women are talking about experiences that they had never spoken about before and that should not die today. It should continue on. We should continue to come forward, and I hope that no one will feel they could not come forward. I hope that this does not prevent someone, or make someone afraid to come forward. This has not been a pleasant experience, but it was an experience that was worthwhile. (CNN 1991f)

Cultural critic Nellie McKay has said that Anita Hill was the best thing to happen to the feminist movement in twenty-five years, because her circumstances encouraged the meshing of African-American and white feminist activism (in Fiske 1994, 95). Such activism crystallized in the moment of the hearings and, because of the crisis felt in association with them, newly energized activists had a space in which to address the problems and issues of which the crisis was made. Because the crisis was located rather narrowly in the realm of formal politics and in workplaces, however, addressing and controlling it meant generating solutions using the terms from which it had emerged. Thus the notion that women should run for political office *en masse* emerged as one such remedy—and one that was promoted almost exclusively as the antidote. The way in which television news constructed and managed this crisis permitted particular meanings to emerge, while eclipsing others or rendering them invisible. In a very concrete sense, the numerous voice-overs in the coverage provided a commonsense map of the hearings. Disembodied and usually male, they provided a deified voice of authority that rose above the fray and gave a definitive interpretation of events. By weaving certain postfeminist ideals into the stories they told about the hearings, television news helped defuse this crisis.

For example, personalizing the issue of sexual harassment as a disagreement or misunderstanding between two people displaces an analysis of sexual harassment as a social problem that affects many women; as an individual concern, it can be remedied through individual choice rather than structural change. This is a crucial move in postfeminism and a reversal of second-wave feminist teachings; that is, it reduces the political to the personal (Rapp 1987; Stacey 1993). Moreover, one strain of postfeminism lays claim to the idea that relations between women and men were much easier before feminism came along and drew attention to sexual harassment as a *problem* (e.g., Senator Simpson's remark about "this sexual harassment crap") (Bonnie J. Dow, personal communication 1999). Thus sexual harassment could be promoted as a chimera created by feminists. After all, some of Thomas's supporters claimed that women were now liberated enough to stop harassers in their tracks without legal intervention. The subtext to this suggests that those who are not capable of this must surely be weak.

Postfeminism also was enabled by the way in which race and class were elided in favor of a focus on gender. In other words, news stories that used gender as their favored category of analysis overlooked the ways in which race and class work *along with* gender as "interlocking systems of domination" (hooks 1990, 62). This too is vintage postfeminism, in that it oversimplifies the circumstances of everyday life and, by default, constructs a subject position for women that is white, middle class to elite, and straight.

In the world of television news, Anita Hill's charges conjured up threats of social chaos and inspired concurrent moves to suppress those threats. They could thus reveal something about the representational politics of TV news. In their drive to represent complex issues such as sexual harassment as simply dichotomous (the women against the men, for example) in the face of all kinds of information that contradicted such a simplistic view, news stories both succeeded and failed. They succeeded at mapping a bipolar field of choices over the hearings' gendered, raced, and classed nuances. In this way, they simplified a complicated situation and thus contributed to a prevailing commonsensical (in the Gramscian sense) view of gender and race, but they also failed in that their maps of meaning were necessarily constructed out of the messy admixture of humanity that is the basis of social reality. Anyone who watched the hearings could see how difference—racial and gender, particularly—marked these news stories. Old stereotypes just did not hold up in many of the images that news stories included, but the speech that accompanied these counter-stereotypical images was anything but reflective of this variability—particularly the speech of network correspondents whose bookending commentary seemed designed to tame chaotic imagery and diminish any discomfort their coverage may have caused. Relying on familiar themes and a simple he-said, she-said structure, news commentary participated in the process of crisis construction and dissolution. Notwithstanding attempts at quelling crisis, however, the residual "reality effect" here was the representation of the American community in a state of chaos, a condition that made its resolution seem even more urgent. Poll results and informal interviews in news programs suggested that certain segments of the public had consented to this interpretation. Year of the Woman candidates and their supporters confirmed this as they referred to the hearings as their rationale for candidacy. The hearings thus provided a conflicted, yet vivid, point of reference for the body politic.

Voice-overs were just one tactic used in this coverage; others, including polling and informal street interviews, worked with voice-overs to perform what I consider the most signficiant ideological function in this discourse—that is, they attempted to control and contain suggestions of the all-out, system-wide shake-up that some experts and protesters were visibly demanding. Over-laying disruption and debate with vocal authority that expressed familiar inter-pretations of events was a tactic that attempted to legitimate and reassert the authority of the democratic system as it had been before Anita Hill's arrival. The seeming need to control and contain by reverting to the norms of an imagined community—what Lubiano calls the "'American' family"—revealed what this community/family was imagined to be. This imagined community was a com-monsensical one in that it appeared to represent neutral territory, devoid of gender, race, and even class until Anita Hill's charges brought all of these to bear on electoral politics. Hill's presence—and all of the attendant wrangling—made visible African-American women and men, white women, feminists, and, to some extent, class hierarchy.

A by-product of television's version of these events was the "naturalistic illusion" (Hall 1982, 76) that a ruling system run by elite white men was the norm—an unraced, ungendered, and unclassed norm that simply represented the natural order of things without ideological bias. The community norm represented in these hearings thus suggested that "race" is African American; "gender" is something only women have; and "class" is a category reserved for the rabble—all of those Others who might contradict the rule of this elite minority. That hearing coverage made visible the presence and demands of these Others—much to the apparent dismay of the Senate patriarchy—illuminated the status disparity and attributes of the outsiders and revealed the privilege of those *inside* the sanctum.

The next chapter discusses the political events that immediately followed the Hill–Thomas hearings that became known as the "Year of the Woman." While there had been other years of the woman in the United States, this one altered the complexion and tenor of the very institution that had given Anita Hill so much trouble. By using some of the discursive resources revealed in the crisis around the Hill–Thomas hearings, activists made very real material gains in national, state, and local governmental bodies. The commentary that Year of the Woman coverage provides is, like the Hill–Thomas hearings, a narrative about women, feminism, and socioeconomic power that helps construct a commonsense perspective from which to judge all of these.

CHAPTER THREE

POSTFEMINIST IDENTITIES, NEOLIBERAL IDEOLOGY, AND WOMEN OF THE YEAR

As time passes, I am convinced of the enduring impact that [Anita Hill's] testimony has had on popular and political culture. Further, I am convinced that her appearance before the Senate Judiciary Committee moved the awareness of sexual harassment issues from bumper-sticker simplicity to the level of complexity they deserve.

—Julianne Malveaux, in
Race, Gender and Power in America

The crisis of white patriarchal authority that emerged from coverage of the Hill–Thomas hearings was one that seemed ripe for a remedy. Men and women were outraged by Hill's treatment and by the way in which sexual harassment had been dismissed as a form of oppression. From this outrage a new coalition of Democrats and Republicans was formed, mostly women, who pushed female political candidates into campaigns and then office as a direct response to what they saw as misogyny in the U.S. political system. At the time (late 1991 to November 1992), the new coalition seemed unstoppable: an apparent juggernaut propelled by well-endowed coffers and optimism about the possibilities for women to drastically refashion the world of electoral politics.

In this chapter, I examine television and print news treatments of this event, the Year of the Woman, and the way in which news narratives positioned feminism as a cultural signifier. I concentrate specifically on the news frames used to structure the Year of the Woman as a discursive formation, and I examine the ideology of gender that emerged as a hegemonic discourse from this formation. As a discursive formation, the Year of the Woman was constituted out of several articulations, resulting in an interpellated postfeminist identity: part neoliberal, part cultural feminist, she was an economically privileged subject with corporate and political savvy, and she became a dominant element of Year-of-the-Woman public discourse as the thirteen-month "year" wore on.

Eleanor Holmes Norton (1995), a feminist member of Congress, has delineated three factors that linked the Hill–Thomas hearings with the Year of the Woman: (1) a general fear for the future of the Supreme Court and its rulings if Thomas's nomination were permitted to go unchallenged; (2) a desire to use the power of the gender gap to correct electoral gender imbalances; and (3) a widespread visceral resonance between Anita Hill's charges and the experiences of similarly harassed women, incensed that Hill was not being taken seriously.

This NBC *Nightly News* broadcast (NBC 1992a) is emblematic of the manner in which the Hill–Thomas hearings were articulated to the burgeoning Year of the Woman political formation using the components that Holmes Norton has delineated. Correspondent Bob Kuv, covering the National Pro-Choice March on Washington, stated:

> It's become something of a spring time ritual, a march on Washington for abortion rights. And this year with freedom to choose threatened as never before, yesterday there were more marchers than ever before, half a million. Among them, women who say they're new to political activism, and planning to get involved in this year's election for many reasons. (The camera cuts to a marcher from Chicago, Wendy Fine.)
>
> FINE: This year just took on a whole new tone with the changes in the Supreme Court, and the big elections this fall and the chances that we have to really turn the tide. (The camera cuts to Anita Hill testifying at the Senate Judiciary hearings.)
>
> KUV: Many women were enraged last fall at how Anita Hill was treated by an all male Senate Committee, then accusing Supreme Court nominee Clarence Thomas of sexual harassment. . . . The Thomas–Hill hearings and abortion rights aren't the only issues women see as advantages this year. There are more open seats, and there may be a backlash against incumbents. (The camera cuts to Carol Moseley Braun waving from a podium.)
>
> (The report concludes with a head shot and sound bite from Harriet Woods of the National Women's Political Caucus, and a wrap-up statement by Kuv.)

WOODS: Maybe this is the most important year we've had in a long time. Everything seems to be right to make women winners. Now we are going to have to wait and see if that really happens in November.

KUV: See if more candidates, more enthusiasm, and more money, turn into more power on election day.

The features of the Hill–Thomas hearings that Norton cites were not only tied to the hearings specifically but arose from the sociopolitical terrain of the early 1990s—crucial in the construction of the Year of the Woman as an emergent phenomenon.

The year 1991 ended more than a decade in which a conservative political philosophy had trickled (or, in some cases, poured) down from the Reagan and Bush regimes into social and political institutions, such as schools and legislatures, and into everyday lives. Many U. S. residents, individually and collectively, registered complaints about the obvious failures and glaring injustices of such conservative politics, yet until the Hill–Thomas hearings, these issues had seen little critical analysis in the mediated public sphere. The combination of a public space in mainstream media plus a day-to-day, living demonstration of the failure of many public policies to address the grinding difficulties of many lives morphed together into the Year of the Woman, a site on which many women and some men pinned their hopes for better lives.

For many women, and particularly women of color, this was not a boom period; they experienced drops in their annual incomes and increases in their costs of living, and while the workforce expanded to include many more women, the domestic sphere offered few improvements.[1] (This contradiction is one explored at length in Hochschild 1989.) Conflicts between the demands of work and home, in conjunction with public policy and policy makers who seemed mostly insensitive to women's and working families' realities, helped spark the fire under the Year of the Woman candidates and their platforms (which were quite similar to one another). This arrangement, as Patricia Mann (1995) points out, worked to liberate some women "from the gendered forms of oppression we now recognize as endemic within traditional kinship relationships" by expanding greatly the numbers of activities and occupations women now perform. This, however, has not been without its drawbacks; because of this,

> gendered conflicts become a part of everyday life for women and men, regardless of how they position themselves toward feminism. . . . Problems and concerns previously associated with a feminist "fringe" are now recurring patterns in the fabric of daily life in our postfeminist era. (224)

As a cultural text, the Year of the Woman addressed many of these problems and anxieties, made even more urgent by the actions of the Senate Judiciary Committee and the looming presence of Clarence Thomas as a Supreme Court justice.

W(H)ITHER FEMINISM?

In early 1996, a news item appeared in the *Washington Post Weekly* concerning a feminist and the body politic. Its gist suggested an underlying problem in the relationship between feminism, political campaigns, and public policy. This two-column blurb discussed feminist Naomi Wolf's contribution to the Clinton presidential campaign. Wolf is the author of several books, including the best-selling *The Beauty Myth*, a feminist treatise on misogyny in the beauty industry. For the presidential campaign, Wolf had been contacted by the Clinton administration to be a consultant whose expertise lay in attracting female voters to the Clinton camp for the election of November 1996. She recommended that Clinton develop an "'overarching, pre-emptive metaphor'" (Kamen 1996, 15) to appeal to female voters. Her suggestion for such a metaphor was that Clinton assume the role of the "'Good Father,' building and protecting the family home from the Republican bulldozers" (ibid.). That this paternalistic trope, recommended by a well-known feminist, was made apparently without irony is startling. The recommendation seemed even more bizarre when placed in its historical context—a mere four years after the hype of the Year of the Woman in politics.

Perhaps the message sent to politicians by angry women during the Year of the Woman was responsible for a feminist being asked for input into presidential campaign strategy in the first place, but when the substance of the message is considered, its regression to a patriarchal figure is disappointing. This suggests that perhaps one problem with the diffusion of feminist politics as it has occurred within the last decade or so in the United States is the way in which feminism—as a social movement and as public policy—becomes positioned as a cultural signifier, in part a result of its treatment in news accounts. Such accounts often are nominally positive, yet are not necessarily advantageous for feminist politics in the long run. This has important consequences for democratic processes and policies, particularly when the link between feminism and electoral politics is as direct as that shown in Naomi Wolf's example. Zillah Eisenstein (1994) has noted that these circumstances are not unusual for feminists in this decade:

Feminists have often had to define their politics within a political discourse that they have not chosen for themselves.... The 1990s started with
an already narrowed feminist agenda. Positioned defensively for over a
decade, it has become more and more limited. (130–31)

Now that the consciousness-raising groups of the second wave have
declined in popularity, feminist issues circulate culturally by other means,
among them public discourse produced by the news media. The Anita
Hill–Clarence Thomas hearings' events raised issues associated with sexual
harassment, and they provide a good example of this, as does the topic of this
chapter: the (very much related) Year of the Woman. Although many more
women than ever before ran for local, state, and national offices during this
time, the Senate campaigns of Barbara Boxer, Carol Moseley Braun, Dianne
Feinstein, Patty Murray, and Lynn Yeakel became synonymous with the Year of
the Woman as a unitary entity. In the 1992 Year of the Woman, four new female
senators (Lynn Yeakel lost her race) were elected along with one incumbent,
twenty-four women were elected to the House, and in state legislatures
women's representation increased to its highest level ever: 20 percent (Wilcox
1994, 1). Political scientist Clyde Wilcox notes that these gains for women in
Congress were "unprecedented," however, he also cautions against viewing
these results with too much euphoria: "Women would need more than 10
'Years of the Woman' to reach equality in the House of Representatives" (2),
he warns. The Senate, at that time over 90 percent male, also was far from
exhibiting gender equity.

Wilcox's point leads to an interesting question: what was it about this Year
of the Woman that resulted in such gains for female politicians? I argue that the
Year of the Woman was, in part, the public face of a set of socially acceptable
feminist beliefs that dominated the mediated public sphere during this thirteen-month "year." More specifically, the feminism that emerged in mainstream
television and print media constructions of the Year of the Woman emerged as
part of an "outsider" discourse that consistently positioned the players and
events of this phenomenon outside of the mainstream as a result of both ideological and biological traits; yet despite being characterized as outside of the status quo, this discourse—toward the end of its deployment—gained normativity and strongly influenced the campaign rhetoric from this election year.

The 1992 election year was also, and importantly, as journalists and political scientists have noted, a year in which political outsiders were spoken of rev-
erently. Wilcox points out that "[r]ecord numbers of African Americans and
Hispanics were elected, and the U.S. Senate elected its first Native American.

The Year of the Woman is therefore part of a larger phenomenon, in which the opportunities of the 1992 election allowed new groups to win access to power" (1994, 21). This feature of the 1992 political terrain also helped propel Ross Perot into an independent candidacy in which he made a reasonably good showing, particularly for a third party in a system locked by two political parties.

Generalized dissatisfaction with the attitudes and practices of long-time politicians arose in much public talk prior to the 1992 election (e.g., around the Hill–Thomas hearings), so it is not surprising that one predominant component of the Year of the Woman discursive formation would be what I label the "outsider" discourse: a set of news stories that situated the campaigns and politics of the five female Senate candidates most closely tied to the Year of the Woman. Notions associated with these outsiders emerged and circulated discursively in a seemingly contradictory fashion. That is, the outsider discourse— an assemblage of news frames that marked women as being outside of mainstream culture—eventually served a normative purpose: to define and act as a point of reference for campaign platforms and rhetoric—even among candidates who, because of their political beliefs, did not identify themselves with the Year of the Woman.

Like so many political events and spectacles, the Year of the Woman was primarily a mediated phenomenon. As such, it can be understood only through an analysis of its mediated constructions. This does not in any way suggest that a media event is somehow devoid of material effects or less "real" than unmediated phenomena. (The large numbers of women elected to office in 1992 point to the existence of the material effects of discourse.) John Fiske (1994) argues convincingly that high-profile media events (and I include the Year of the Woman in this category) exhibit "no clear and obvious distinction between electronic mediation and physical happenings, or between media figures and real people" (xiv). Mediated depictions affect cultural practices, and these in turn influence subsequent mediated phenomena; this is particularly evident in political campaigns. The way most voters come to know anything about political events and candidates is through their mediated constructions, so it is especially crucial for these constructions to be scrutinized for what they reveal about the dialectical movement between discursive framing and cultural practices, such as those from the Year of the Woman.

Fiske (1994) adds that media spectacles are appealing and invite the participation of audiences: "The figures who play the key roles in these events literally embody the politicocultural meanings and the struggles over them about which America is most uncertain, most anxious, and therefore most divided" (xv). The political subjects of the Year of the Woman became players in a media spectacle that functioned precisely as Fiske describes. The Anita Hill–Clarence Thomas hearings resulted in a crisis of white patriarchal authority in the public sphere constructed from panics around race, gender, and institutional power, thus it not surprising that the female Senate candidates in the Year of the Woman—given their relationship to the hearings—came to embody specific anxieties derived from these more general issues.

The way in which these cultural anxieties were portrayed not only circumscribed the Year of the Woman but served as commentary on the content and cultural position of feminism at a specific historical juncture. Feminism is a crucial ideological component of the Year of the Woman; to examine the specific issues present in these media texts is to illuminate the type of feminism advanced as a part of this pro-woman political climate.

FEMINISM IN THE PUBLIC SPHERE

The way in which feminism was "spun" in this campaign coverage suggests that it more closely resembled postfeminism than feminism: that is, a "white, middle-class, heterosexual bias, an assumption that a 'seize the power' mind-set and more vigorous individualism will solve all women's problems, and a conflation of feminist *identity* with feminist *politics*" (Dow 1996, 207, emphasis in original). This is a concise starting point for describing news discourse around Year of the Woman candidates as well. Postfeminism's middle-class to elite orientation does not encourage social-movement-style activism, as it lacks a collective vision for the solution of women's problems. Ideologically, it is composed of beliefs gleaned from different varieties of feminism. On the one hand, its derivation is from liberal feminism's focus on getting more women into important institutions that influence women's lives, such as Congress. In other words, increasing the numbers of women occupying positions of power is one important goal, but this goal exists in contradistinction to another postfeminist ideological position: a cultural feminist, essentialist vision of women as Other—subjects tethered to practices determined by the unique aspects of their biological sex. This aspect emerged in discussions of how gender would affect the abilities of female politicians, with the clearly and recurrently stated prediction that they would behave in a fashion morally superior to that of male politicians. Both of these elements exist and intersect at times within Year of the Woman coverage, and these construct a postfeminist identity.

It is important to emphasize that postfeminism is fashioned from certain feminist beliefs, particularly those from second-wave feminism. The central goals of second-wave feminism included major issues that emerged in Year of the Women coverage, such as equal access to political office and attention to sex bias and harassment in workplaces, but second-wave feminism also was a social movement, and thus based on collective action for the purpose of effecting structural changes to benefit women. A second-wave politics of feminism then was one that could not be subsumed by other political projects—such as anti-racism—but could work alongside these and even use similar tactics and logic.[2] Postfeminism though works against a model of collective activism and a recognized need for continued improvement in the conditions under which women of all races and socioeconomic classes live their lives.

Postfeminism emerged in the 1992 election year as a complement to other ostensibly novel, hybrid forms of politics. While postfeminism was not exactly new, its hegemonic position suggested that it had gained acceptability as *the* feminist position—a move away from the radical and more militant feminist politics of yore (see, e.g., Echols 1989). In a similar fashion, during the 1992 election year, a neoliberal agenda emerged and gained respectability. Candidates such as Paul Tsongas and Bill Clinton promoted neoliberalism as an antidote to both the reactionary agenda of the New Right, which had dominated policy making for over a decade, and the Left's emphasis on social services and federal assistance for citizens and aid organizations. Neoliberal candidates eschewed the political protest tactics traditionally associated with marginalized groups; they politely promoted their agenda, much of which appeared to have been borrowed, it seemed, from a conservative economic handbook. This may have worked in their favor inadvertently, as the Republicans looked overzealous and shrill with the far-Right messages and proposals that emanated from their 1991 convention. This was a problem that they were repeatedly forced to try to ameliorate, but with little success.

The neoliberal project was promoted by candidate Bill Clinton as a New Covenant, and the Democratic Year of the Woman candidates seemed content to be associated with it as well. The Progressive Policy Institute (PPI), the policy organization and think tank of the Democratic Leadership Council (DLC), embodied neoliberalism and was influential in helping shape a policy agenda for Clinton's Democrats. The DLC is a centrist-to-conservative faction of the Democratic Party, and it exerted itself in guiding President Clinton's domestic and foreign policy, from welfare to trade issues. The PPI's *Mandate for Change* (Marshall and Schram 1993) lays out the neoliberal stance on specific issues, such as welfare reform, explicitly intended to influence Clinton's policies on each of these issues. The editors contend that their ideas are "innovative, non-bureaucratic approaches to governing" and are keys to the "new thinking that is changing the basic contours of American politics." This is "a new politics that transcends the exhausted Left-Right debate that has immobilized our nation for too long" by calling for a "radical departure from the status quo. [These ideas] are certain to upset the comfortable arrangement of politics as usual in Washington" (xv–xvi).

These policy essays advocate several general goals: (1) increasing competition within influential organizations (especially government organizations), between corporations, and between U.S. and international companies; (2) freeing markets from unnecessary constraints (i.e., increasing deregulation); and (3) increasing the opportunities for and ranges of choice for citizens in various settings. Neoliberal policy makers favor an entrepreneurial model of government, with an emphasis on recuperating losses they claim the middle class has experienced, while increasing wages and job opportunities. The words "liberate" and "empower" are used frequently throughout the essays in *Mandate for Change* to signify the radical thinking influencing the PPI, but these policy makers also exhibit a traditionally conservative emphasis on various economic and social issues, such as encouraging heterosexual marriage and discouraging divorce for couples with children (as a way of fighting poverty); they thus unabashedly advocate a family-values agenda much like that of the New Right. They depart from that agenda, however, in their statements that women will be, and should be, earning incomes—if they choose to do so—and that neoliberal family policy should take this factor into account.

During the course of the 1992 election year, this brand of neoliberal politics was articulated to a postfeminist identity through Year of the Woman candidates and their campaigns. Like the neoliberal project espoused by the PPI, the Year of the Woman campaigns featured in mainstream news were composed of both liberal-to-centrist social policies and conservative-corporate positions on fiscal issues. This brand of feminism is thus quite different from the second-wave feminist movement of the 1970s, which drew its ideology and tactics from the New Left, civil rights, and anti-war politics. Laclau and Mouffe (1985) note that new political subjects are constructed out of resistance to different forms of capitalist influence; they add that not all such subjects are articulated to a progressive politics. Thus postfeminism can stand in nominal opposition to practices that subordinate women (such as sexual harassment); however, the forms of protest used and the rationale for opposition are different from a collective, activist feminism, such as that of the second wave.

In a political context in which neoliberal policies dominated discussions about a national agenda, it is not surprising that one of the ideologies to emerge would be composed of neoliberalism and feminism, taking the form of postfeminism. This postfeminist identity is not without its contradictions, however, as its neoliberal, pro-corporate dimension conflicts with its cultural feminist aspects: those claims about women making unique contributions to the world of politics simply because of the virtues ascribed to them on the basis of biological sex. This new postfeminist identity is conflicted, for there exists an immanent contradiction between its neoliberal roots and emphasis on professional success and its cultural feminist claims to biological uniqueness.

FRAMING THE YEAR OF THE WOMAN

When used in public discourse, frames structure the terms of and "mobilize public opinion" through the ways in which they "present events and individuals" (Kellner 1992, 62). In the context of the Year of the Woman, these frames work as what Stuart Hall (1986, 54) calls "lines of tendency": they position the Year of the Woman politicians and rhetoric in public space and encourage an orientation toward them through what they exclude as much as through what they encompass. Frames are constructed of recurrent themes and tropes, and in the case of the Year of the Woman, they are replete with gender-specific notions. When viewed together as a discursive formation, a set of specific postfeminist positions emerges and becomes hegemonic in the Year of the Woman. The three frames used for Year of the Woman candidates—sometimes individually and sometimes as a group—I label "Washington outsiders," "status quo challengers," and "women as change agents." In some instances these frames overlapped chronologically, but usually they existed independently and in the chronological order in which I have listed them. The content of these frames also supported a feminist ideology that served to glorify some aspects of feminism and to contain those aspects that demanded more than superficial gestures.

Year of the Woman coverage coalesced around a few key issues—abortion, sexual harassment, the underrepresentation of women in positions of power, and "family values"—and mostly as a result of the wrangling between two factions: one of conservative Republicans and one composed of both moderate Republicans and Democrats. The composition of the Year of the Woman discourse and its trajectory during this thirteen-month "year" revealed nuance in the construction of women candidates as political subjects but also demonstrated the pack journalism practices that abounded during this time.

The differences between local and national television and print news coverage were few and consisted specifically of patterns of gendered signifiers and discourse found within news coverage of Boxer, Braun, Feinstein, Murray, and Yeakel. This finding supports a trend reported by Beverly Kees and Bill Phillips (1994) of the Freedom Forum: that the coverage of local and state races increasingly mimics national coverage (100). At the national level, these five candidates were typically grouped together for purposes of coverage, while local papers, not surprisingly, almost always covered as individuals the candidates whose races were relevant to the geographic region for which each paper was responsible. Almost all local coverage, however, made at least some mention of each candidate's position vis-à-vis the Year of the Woman and provided accounts of specific aspects of the individual race under discussion. Local coverage drew liberally from the national media's construction of the Year of the Woman as a singular movement and provided details from local races as supporting evidence for the existence of the Year of the Woman.

The most striking stylistic difference between national and local coverage was of sexist language in local Year of the Woman news accounts. That is, stories from local papers exhibited more sexism than did stories produced for national audiences. The association and discussion of female candidates through stereotypes typically connected with women was quite pronounced in many cases. One story about Patty Murray from the *Seattle Times*, for example, began with this sentence to signify Murray's place as a Year of the Woman candidate: "U.S. Senate candidate Patty Murray is feeling like the little sister who tags along on a date and yet somehow gets a fair share of attention" (Matassa 1992a, A5). The same author used the following description in a story about Murray's reaction to her opponent, Rod Chandler, during one of their televised debates: "Murray, like a mom tired of bickering with a cranky teenager, made a face and shook her head" (Matassa 1992b, B2). Dianne Feinstein's reaction to her opponent, Gray Davis, in one of their televised debates, was described by *Los Angeles Times* reporter Bill Stall as a "lecture . . . in the fashion of a fearsome English teacher chastising a wayward eighth-grader caught cheating on an exam" (1992, A-20). Not surprisingly, the male candidates were not discussed in conjunction with pejorative figures, even when they made big (and sexist) gaffes in their own speech.[3] In other stories from local papers, female supporters as well as the candidates were discussed using stereotypic notions and language. Carol Moseley Braun's supporters, for example, "women from all walks of life," were said to have cried "tears of joy as they watched Braun give her victory speech" the night of her win in the March 1992 Democratic primary (Johnson and James 1992, A1). Women, no matter how powerful and competent, just could not escape being associated with school-marm, mom, or young-girl images, or with emotions outside of the narrow range expressed through tears.

What is more surprising about the local versus national coverage is not the differences between the two but their similarities. In the news accounts that I reviewed, three frames characterized and formed the trajectory of the Year of the Woman as an "outsider" discourse.[4] In the context of the Year of the Woman, at least, these levels of coverage functioned symbiotically as part of a discourse that privileged postfeminism and provided some information about each candidate—usually with at least some mention of the race in relation to feminist politics. These similarities might be explained by several factors, three of which have been delineated by Marian Meyers (1997, 4) in her study of Atlanta's local media coverage of violence against women. Meyers notes that local media servicing major cities such as Atlanta often are professional "stepping stones" between smaller and larger professional or national media markets. A certain amount of cross-pollination is therefore to be expected, simply because of news workers' and journalists' movement between these markets. Meyers also observes that journalists are socialized in a similar fashion, and that "news values, codes, and conventions" (ibid.) share many attributes across specific outlets. To Meyers' list I would add a fourth factor: the political economy of news media. That is, some discursive practices around news production have emerged from a trend that I discussed in chapter 1: newsrooms increasingly moving toward adopting a USA Today or tabloid model of news production and presentation (McManus 1995; Underwood 1995). Thus while the content may differ somewhat between local and national coverage of the same stories, the style of reporting will be quite similar. Also, the Year of the Woman has "(wo)man bites dog" news value as well as a feature-page feel to it: angry women acting to right a system that wronged them. This has both local and national appeal.

Of course, newsrooms are not perfectly homogeneous with the coverage that they produce, nor is the culture in one identical to that in another;[5] contentious political and social issues specific to particular newsrooms and communities can affect both journalists and their coverage. Carolyn Byerly and Catherine A. Warren (1996), for example, conducted a study of political activism among journalists at eighteen large metropolitan newspapers and USA Today; their findings reveal that activism around political and/or discrimination issues in newsrooms (while it differs according to the culture and management of each newsroom) can influence reporters and their reporting—even within the confines of restrictive management practices. Their research shows that journalists' own activism "improves their understanding of events and conditions that affect them, improves working relationships, deepens convictions to continue working for social change, and is generally gratifying and empowering" (Byerly and Warren 1996, 17). Political work done at a local level then is one way in which news workers can challenge both problematic management practices and pack journalism perspectives on some issues. (Byerly and Warren note that the Anita Hill–Clarence Thomas hearings were particularly effective in acting as a catalyst in this regard.)

However, even as journalists and news workers engage in resistant acts in their own newsrooms and communities, it is important to point out that they constitute only one group struggling for ideological hegemony. Within the context of the Hill–Thomas hearings and the subsequent Year of the Woman, a number of new and preexisting coalitions worked discursive forms and engaged in practices designed to authorize the hegemonic meanings associated with the hearings and the campaign rhetoric. The stakes were high indeed; African-American feminists, for example, saw the Hill–Thomas hearings as an opportunity to educate African-American men about the conflicted loyalties of African-American women, and of the need for a strong African-American feminism that had been absent during the hearings (hooks 1992). On the other hand, there was the radical right wing, vying to make its ideological position dominant. Marilyn Quayle, for example, was trotted out repeatedly and promoted as an example of the ideal contemporary woman: a smart, professional, conservative, stay-at-home wife and parent. Mainstream feminist organizations such as NOW and NARAL held rallies, lobbied politicians, and raised funds in an effort to foreground their concerns and, ultimately, the politicians whose campaigns they supported.

So although the crisis of white patriarchal authority that ensued from the Hill–Thomas hearings opened up a space in which new meanings and identities came into the mediated public sphere, these were the result of ideological work by a number of different groups. The news frames that emerged in mainstream news narratives then cannot be attributed to one news organization or even a public relations firm or two; rather, these frames were constructed out of representational forms created by numerous groups engaged in a complex jockeying for power.

BARBARIANS AT THE GATE

The first frame to emerge in Year of the Woman news coverage was by far the most dramatic and marked the origination point of the outsider discourse: I refer to this frame as "Barbarians at the Gate." The frame appeared just before Anita Hill testified at Clarence Thomas's confirmation hearing and was formed and characterized by vivid depictions (including a front-page photograph in the *New York Times*) of the October 9, 1991, confrontation between seven Democratic congresswomen (one of whom was Barbara Boxer) and their male Senate counterparts. The congresswomen had attempted to gain physical access to the senators to insist that the Senate Judiciary Committee include Anita Hill's testimony (which had only recently emerged in public) in their hearings for Supreme Court nominee Clarence Thomas. The photograph and the accompanying story of the congresswomen marching up the Capitol steps to the Capitol room of the Senate—where they were denied entry—became almost mythic in its importance to the formation of the Year of the Woman; it could well be viewed as the *ur*-narrative of this discourse, as it signified the physical exclusion of women from an ostensibly democratic institution and foregrounded the dismissive attitude that these men showed about a women's issue. Maureen Dowd described this incident as the beginning of a

> day of highly charged sexual politics on Capitol Hill. The battles over equality that have shaken society as women have entered the workforce in ever greater numbers were reflected today in numerous tense exchanges between men and women in Congress, ranging from bitter parliamentary disputes on the House floor to private conservations [*sic*] in Senate caucuses about how women behave when they are the victims of sexual crimes. (1991, A-1, A-19)

"Barbarians at the Gate" coverage occurred in the early months of the Year of the Woman and was marked by language that emphasized divisions between female and male politicians first, and then between women and men in general. This coverage was saturated with stories about female politicians expressing anger and resentment when their requests that Anita Hill be heard were initially denied. Comments such as these, from John Chancellor's commentary of October 8 (NBC 1991a), were representative:

> There are about 100 million grown women in the United States, and I thought I heard them all growling today. . . . These women are furious because they know what it is to be ignored. . . . There are several important lessons in this drama. One is that women vote. More women voted in 1988 than men. Another lesson is that when women think their interests are not being addressed, they will act together. And the biggest lesson of all is that these days women take it very seriously when they're not taken seriously.

To further reinforce the polarity between women and men, news stories used the language of conflict and war: women and men interacted in a bellicose fashion, battled and struggled, and were engaged in combat in a war between the sexes.

The field created by this polarization was further clarified by the characterization of Washington women having been perceived by their male colleagues as representative of a weak group of fringe interests, outside the range of those traditionally considered appropriate for debate and discussion in the inner (and male-dominated) sanctums of the House and the Senate. This notion was advanced by the publication on October 15, 1991, of a *New York Times*/CBS News poll, the results of which indicated that a majority of Americans favored the nomination of Clarence Thomas—despite the charges of sexual harassment against him—and believed that his account, and not Anita Hill's, was the more believable of the two. Buried in the last paragraph of the story describing this poll was a figure that underscored the idea that the outraged women who had "stormed" the Capitol a week earlier represented fringe interests: 73 percent of those polled believed that the Senate Judiciary Committee had treated Anita Hill fairly, while only 66 percent believed that the committee had treated Clarence Thomas fairly (Kolbert 1991, A-20). In other words, more respondents believed that Hill, and not Thomas, had been treated fairly—an opinion diametrically opposed to the ideological nucleus of the Year of the Woman.

Two days after the publication of the *New York Times*/CBS News poll, the *New York Times* published an article suggesting that women would not accept the events surrounding the Hill–Thomas hearings passively but would organize actively to challenge male politicians who had voted for Thomas. The story described several incidents in which women in the Democratic Party waged organized protests against their party's elite male members, accusing them of having betrayed women in their collusion with Republican men on the matter of supporting and then voting to nominate Clarence Thomas. Through public demonstrations and private confrontations, Democratic women emphasized the importance of their fiscal and physical presence in the party: together they had contributed millions of dollars and hundreds of work hours to aid Democratic politicians and causes over the years. That their concerns fell on deaf ears was a matter of grave concern to them. The reporter, Richard Berke, cited unnamed analysts who noted presciently that this "outcry against the Democrats was the first sign of a re-emergence of women's rights organizations" (1991a, A22).

This thread foreshadowing the events of the Year of the Woman emerged further in an article published a little over a week later and marked by the headline "Thomas Hearings May Be Over, But Senators Find a War Looming." This piece described an alliance between Democratic and Republican women forming around the issue of "how they could mobilize to elect politicians who they believe would be more sensitive to women" (Berke 1991b, A-14). The women in this article gathered under the auspices of the International Women's Forum and were depicted as being furious about the Hill–Thomas hearings and ready to act decisively in their own interests. One of the participants (a columnist for the *Nashville Banner*) observed that the "sense of outrage, of power, in this room, is palpable. Incumbents will be feeling more than heat. They'll be feeling hell" (ibid.). A remark from Senator Barbara Mikulski (one of two female senators at this time) was included as well: "An old girls network will come because we take time to listen to each other. That's my message here today: let's stick together" (ibid.). Mikulski's feminist spin on a paternalistic institution offered *New York Times'* readers a glimpse into the future.

"THE STATUS QUO MUST GO"

Four months after the International Women's Forum had thrown down the gauntlet, *New York Times* columnist Anna Quindlen sounded the clarion call for a specific antidote to the problem of not being taken seriously as political subjects: run for office and rework the system to be more accountable to the women it purports to represent. Quindlen's take was that women were morally superior to men, but she also suggested that women were better suited to political office because of their practical experiences—they typically encountered a range of activities that the average male pol does not:

> If we really believe, as I've heard over and over during the last three years, that our political leaders don't have a clue about real life, look for a woman. I've rarely met a woman who didn't know more about the supermarket, the bus stop and the prevailing winds than her male counterparts. Not to mention about child care, human rights, abortion, the minimum wage, and sexual harassment.
>
> If it's so widely understood that the wives are superior to the candidate, shouldn't that tell us something about where to find the candidates to come? (Quindlen 1992a, IV-17)

Quindlen's suggestion that women move *en masse* into the ranks of elected public officials marked the transition, during the early months of 1992, to another frame: "The Status Quo Must Go" (a phrase oft-repeated by Dianne

Feinstein during her Senate campaign in California). This frame emerged in the numerous announcements about women who were doing their part to jettison the norm by running in political races at the state, local, and national levels. Citing the masculinist politics of the Hill–Thomas hearings, these women formulated their strategy to take place in the realm of politics, the site where their collective disillusionment had occurred.

This narrative stems from the American mythos of citizens assuming the reins of governmental power, perhaps best exemplified in Frank Capra's film, *Mr. Smith Goes to Washington*.[6] Crucial to this mythology is the innocent average citizen who moves into a position of importance in order to provide a cure for what ails the corrupt democratic system. Of course, the Year of the Woman's Ms. Smiths provided a plot twist to this familiar narrative: the people best suited to provide the antidote to diseased Washington politics were *women*, not men. Using a courtship metaphor, correspondent Cokie Roberts (ABC 1991c) predicted this:

> Wooing the women's vote will be a high priority for both parties this year. And both parties believe that women candidates will help win over their sisters. So the women are out there running, and the Congress could end up looking a lot more feminine than it ever has before.

Mister morphing into Ms. Smith signified a major challenge to mainstream politics. Mostly because of their sex, women seemed novel in the context of political candidacy; their campaigns were particularly unusual, because the candidates clearly invoked sexual and gender politics routinely. Anita Hill's experience was brought up frequently to represent the way in which women were mistreated by the male establishment, as was the subsequent phenomenon referred to as not "getting it."[7] Together these were presented as the catalysts for women who decided to take on the old-boy political establishment and demonstrate its shortcomings for women. In this coverage, metaphors of the female Senate candidates as moral warriors in a battle for justice abounded. Portrayed as preternaturally pure and devoid of the political entanglements of their male opponents, the new "soldiers" coalesced around the figure of Anita Hill, their martyr; reporter R. W. Apple Jr. remarked that "Professor Anita Hill is their Joan of Arc" (1992a, IV-1).

Other depictions of the female Senate candidates suggested that their fervor and strength came from a morally courageous desire to right the system that had wronged them: radical feminist Catharine MacKinnon argued that the power that women in office could wield would have broad effects, grounded in a desire to end the violence and abuse of women and children. "We can say

one simple thing: Stop. Stop it. Don't do this anymore. No more sexual harassment. No more sexual abuse of children. No more battering in the home."
Correspondent Gary Matsumoto concluded this report with: "MacKinnon and
other activists argue these goals can be best achieved by getting more women
elected to political office" (NBC 1992b). At times this coverage even imbued
candidates with messianic qualities. Carol Moseley Braun received most of this
treatment; she was, for example, described variously as a "political dragon
slayer" (ABC 1992b), "able to rise above the fray" (Wilkerson 1992a, A-19), and
as the "level-headed alternative to two men [her opponents in the primary]
caught up in a schoolyard fistfight" (Wilkerson 1992b, A-20). The language of
another piece indicated that the reporter was observing a quasi-religious spectacle in which women pledged themselves to what Braun represented.

> These days it is not hard to know when you have arrived at a Braun
> reception. It is the one where women are waving checkbooks in the air
> and applauding devotedly like converts to the Dalai Lama. (Wilkerson
> 1992c, A-13)

The righteousness expressed in this almost evangelical, quest-for-justice
narrative was closely tied to the process of expanding democratic institutions
and the political process. As one political consultant put it when discussing this
issue, "representative democracy works best when it's truly representative"
(CNN 1992c), and U.S. democracy served the interests of male elites more than
any others. These news accounts pointed repeatedly to the exclusivity of Congress and noted happily that the female Senate candidates, if successful, would
challenge the status quo by forcing a consideration of women's concerns.
Within this narrative, one of Dianne Feinstein's phrases appeared recurrently:
"Two percent may be good for fat in milk but it's bad for women in the United
States Senate" (see, e.g., Ayres 1992, A-9). The presumption in these accounts
was that democracy in the United States lacked only gender balance. Women
were presented as the fix to the homogeneity of U.S. political institutions.

A closely related point woven through stories about challenging the status quo was that of the satisfaction of women's needs being crucial to a fully
functioning and healthy democracy. The reports included many references to
women's rights not being special rights, but those that should concern everyone—male and female: "women's issues are everybody's issues" (Hinds 1992, A-
19). Anna Quindlen also noted that the "issues once called women's issues have
become cutting edge" (1992b, IV-19). Correspondent Jim Whooten (ABC
1992a) grouped women together to form their own side of a political divide.
Commenting about problems that Arlen Specter was having in his campaign,

Whooten stated that Specter's "problem rises from the other side of the political spectrum: thousands of women offended by his vote for Clarence Thomas,
and his accusation of perjury against Anita Hill."

It also was during this time—the first half of 1992—that the phrase
"Year of the Woman" began to appear with regularity. In this context the
phrase referred to the surge in women's political visibility and was usually
explained as a unique phenomenon, occurring as a result of the peculiarities
of Hill–Thomas gender politics. Two different *New York Times* editorials relied
on this notion to suggest that women candidates had "surged out of
nowhere"("Here come" 1992a, A-22), and that women in politics were the
"no-longer-silent majority" ("A woman's place" 1992b, A-22). Although it
was true that women constituted a majority of voters (and still do), to label
women as silent and invisible before 1992's election season was to deny the
long history of women's work in formal politics. About one week before the
California primaries, when that state's voters were deciding whether to vote
for two female candidates, Cokie Roberts made a claim about Barbara Boxer
and Dianne Feinstein—two experienced politicians and politicos—that illustrated this point clearly. "If voters draw the lesson that it's time to take a
chance, the throw of the dice could land two women with Senate nominations" (ABC 1992b). Roberts' gambling metaphor invokes a sense of the
uncontrolled risks associated with games of chance, but it is inappropriate in
this context: not only had women been active in politics for at least a century prior to the Year of the Woman, there had been other election years (e.g.,
1972 and 1990) in which women ran for office in large numbers for precisely
the same reasons that these five high-profile women ran—to change public
policy and legislation and to interject women's voices into male-dominated
political conversations.

Creating the impression that women came out of nowhere to thrust
themselves into politics casts them as a flash-in-the-pan phenomenon; if they
just appeared here today, they may well be gone tomorrow, and thus are much
easier to dismiss as serious contenders. It was not until much later in the election year that the actuality was revealed: women worked to make themselves
viable candidates for many years prior to 1992, although usually in lower, less
visible offices. (Barbara Boxer, for instance, was a five-term member of the
House of Representatives; Patty Murray had been a Washington state legislator
for one term; and Carol Moseley Braun worked as an Illinois state legislator for
ten years and then as Cook County Recorder of Deeds until she was elected
senator.) This perspective on female politicians marginalized and obscured
women's political work. Not only had women been active as politicians, but

they had created political action committees and lobbied on behalf of them. EMILY's List (Early Money Is Like Yeast), a PAC for pro-choice Democrats, for instance, was instrumental in propelling a number of candidates from obscurity to notoriety. Depicting these campaigns as novel and unusual obscured the mundane realities of the work, such as fund-raising, necessary to make the candidates viable; it also created a formula for covering the inevitable Years of the Woman in the future: angry women grabbing for political power made good and dramatic news copy.

"Women: They Are the Change"

Year of the Woman news accounts also framed women as outsiders on the basis of their biological sex and often invoked essentialist notions of gender difference to discuss the ways in which sex differences manifested in the candidates' campaigns and future policy making. One of the main currents running through these accounts centered on the importance of being female on the campaign trail: by their sex alone, women were depicted as being at an advantage to male candidates who, because of their sex, symbolized the established order.[8] In these accounts, gender superseded all other factors in fixing the female Senate candidates in the imagination of journalists and media commentators.

Even in a campaign in which the candidate's racial identity was mentioned often, that of African-American Carol Moseley Braun, gender superseded race as the most important identity component. In one piece on Braun, reporter Isabel Wilkerson (1992c) described her on the campaign trail as "a defiant Everywoman" with whom thousands of female supporters identified: "for some women, it is enough just to know that she has given birth" (A-13). Wilkerson included one gushing quotation that exemplified this phenomenon well: "'She's me,' Dianne Valleta, a white woman from the Chicago suburbs said of this black woman from the South Side. 'She represents everything I feel, everything I want to be. I'm so locked into her that what she says is unimportant'" (ibid.).

Resembling feminist theory sometimes known as "difference" feminism (typically associated with Carol Gilligan's [1982] *In a Different Voice*), these news stories used language to imply that women—a class by virtue of their biological sex—did things differently: in politics, more ethically, efficiently, honestly, and with greater integrity. In a *Nightline* episode from May 29, 1992, for example, viewers witnessed a number of references to the ways in which women candidates were superior to men: more cooperative, more efficient, more resourceful, and less combative. Senator Barbara Mikulski (running for a second term during this time) noted that being a woman was a strength for her campaign that year, whereas in past years she had struggled because of her gender:

> [N]ow I find that my gender is an asset, because people see me as some-
> one who's not one of the boys, who's going to be a fighter, somebody that
> they can count on and somebody, as I said, who's going to be a change-
> maker, not a dealmaker. (ABC 1992b)

Women were portrayed as being better at working together and as being lov-ing cultivators of their social networks. A point often remarked upon was that Barbara Boxer and Dianne Feinstein ran their campaigns together—as a team—after their primary victories. In an invocation of two well-known fem-inist duos, Feinstein was quoted as saying, "Just as Cagney had Lacey and Thelma had Louise, Dianne has Barbara and Barbara has Dianne" ("Year of the Woman" 1992).

Also tied to the foregrounding of gender was the notion that women, again because of their sex, were agents of change and outsiders to the Wash-ington inner circles, depicted as repeatedly betraying their female con-stituents: "The striking success of women is a clue to the later lesson as well—that voters want change. A woman as a Senate candidate, after all, symbolizes changes *even before she announces her platform*" (Clymer 1992, IV-3, emphasis added). Even when so-called real-world events contradicted this notion, sex prevailed. Barbara Boxer, for instance, a congresswoman for five terms, was able to position herself as a Washington outsider because she emphasized her femaleness (Apple 1992b). In the case of Washington state's Patty Murray, sex appeared to be the trump card in her primary victory over a candidate whose positions on political issues were much like Murray's own. When questioned by Catherine Crier of CNN about this issue in her primary victory, Murray protested that her appeal cut across gender, age, and lifestyle lines, however, she eventually conceded that perhaps her sex had placed her at an advantage (CNN 1992a).

The issues with which the five Senate candidates were associated fell out along gendered lines as well; that is, women were predicted to focus on policies that fell within their traditional (sometimes expressed as "natural") domain—the domestic. The perception advanced was that male legislators failed to formulate effective domestic policy or, as Joan Lunden put it on *Good Morning America*, "there's this general attitude that a lot of men in office have messed up" (ABC 1992d). Women were promoted as being capable of addressing the failings of men on domestic issues and of solving some enormously complex and difficult problems, all lumped together under the rubric of a domestic agenda—what Cokie Roberts called "more tender social policies" (NBC 1992c). Susan Estrich, Michael Dukakis' presidential campaign advisor, described these issues broadly as "family and the economy, education and health care" (ABC, 1992d), and Dianne Feinstein expanded the roster to include "jobs, . . . crimes, drugs, gangs, environmental cleanup, [and] the right to choice" (Reinhold, 1992, A-17).

News accounts repeatedly invoked the end of the Cold War and highlighted a need for a focus on the home front—circumscribed by the geographic boundaries of the United States and articulated to the female candidates. George Lewis of NBC (1992c) claimed that "with the end of the Cold War pushing domestic issues to the forefront, many voters believe women are better equipped to handle problems at home." The camera then cut to a headshot of Dianne Feinstein saying," What people want a United States senator to do today, is to begin concentrating on America." Another NBC broadcast, this one from the Democratic Convention on July 14 (NBC 1992d), featured the Year of the Woman theme. "Democratic consultant" Ann Lewis echoed the same domestic theme: "The Cold War is over. We're not looking for this macho style, who is going to defend us, take on all comers. We are saying, 'wait a minute, what about those of us at home? Who cares about us? Who cares about our families, about our mortgages, about our kids' future?'" These sorts of articulations insist upon situating women within the confines of an unusual "hearth-and-home" setting—that between the walls of the nation-state rather than the more confining space of home. The duties for which they were said to be most appropriate, however, were more traditional private-sphere concerns such as child care and home life.

NORMATIVITY AND THE YEAR OF THE WOMAN

After the Year of the Woman's discursive formation positioned female Senate candidates as outsiders using the three frames that I discussed above, a move to normativity occurred. That is, despite the appearance of female Senate candidates as being outside the mainstream due to various factors, eventually other players—opponents of the candidates or simply antifeminist public figures—reacted to the Year of the Woman discourse in ways that indicated that it had become normative—and formidable.

Perhaps the most notable example of this move occurred with Arlen Specter, Lynn Yeakel's opponent in Pennsylvania. When political scientists (see, e.g., Hansen, 1994) discuss Lynn Yeakel's campaign, they often attribute her success to the way in which she parlayed women's anger around the Anita Hill–Clarence Thomas hearings into support for her candidacy. The campaign advertisement that she is probably most well known for used footage of her opponent, Senator Arlen Specter, grilling Anita Hill, followed by Yeakel's voice-over asking viewers, "Did this make you as angry as it made me?" Apparently the answer was a resounding "yes," as Yeakel's support exploded immediately after the advertisement aired. As reporter Isabel Wilkerson noted, "Senator Specter has, deservedly or not, come to be seen as the parliamentarian of the men's club" (1992d, A-1) as a result of this campaign. As such, he was forced to respond to constituents who questioned his actions during the hearings and the patriarchal attitudes that he came to represent afterward. While campaigning, Specter was forced, time and again, to defend himself and to explain his interrogation of Anita Hill; his campaign strategists referred to this problem as "the Anita Hill situation" (ibid.), and developed tactics—such as preempting these comments by invoking his pro-woman voting record—for Specter to minimize the negative impact that the "situation" would have on his campaign (CNN, 1992b). One Specter supporter quoted in the *New York Times* had observed this phenomenon and with disgust commented that Specter had "done everything but emasculate himself" (Wilkerson, 1992d, A-12) to regain the respect of women. That a male candidate might have to emasculate himself to gain female supporters is a strong statement about the sex of the reference point of Year of the Woman discourse (not to mention the castration anxiety tied to women acting to effect political change).

Some reporters noted that during the Democratic Convention and afterward, another high-profile political woman, Hillary Rodham Clinton, would be undergoing a process of domestication to resemble "someone who attends teas and discusses her chocolate chip cookie recipe, as she has at this convention, in the role of traditional political spouse" (NBC, 1992d). However, Cokie Roberts noted that Hillary Rodham Clinton was still perceived by Republicans as a threat—in part because of her feminist politics. In order to reduce the possibility that she might benefit the Democrats' chance, Roberts claimed that "Republicans plan to dust off the old liberal label, and try to attach it to Hillary Clinton, who they will claim would serve as her husband's co-president" (NBC, 1992d). A similar strategy seemingly designed to defend against the popularity of issues made visible during the Year of the Woman was a move by then-President Bush.

Feeling a significant gap in support between men and women in the latest opinion poll, President Bush took his top female aides in tow, lined his
speaker's dais end-to-end with women, and cast himself today as a feminist, free-market style. (Wines, 1992, A-7)

President Bush, feeling the effects of an enormous gender gap between his
numbers and candidate Clinton's, took to the road with a group of his female
aides to try to repair damage incurred by the strident, far-right rhetoric of the
Republican National Convention. The desperation in this eleventh-hour measure is obvious, not only in the article's content (when else did George Bush
ever wish to be associated with feminist politics—however diluted?) but in the
accompanying photo of Bush, flanked closely by his female entourage, in which
his pinched countenance and uncomfortable smile suggested that this was anything but a natural situation for him.

Despite President Bush's attempts to defuse the effects of the convention
on his party, the convention was mentioned repeatedly in much of the coverage between August and November 1992 as the chief problem in Republican
appeals to women voters; often it was portrayed as an earthquake that created
an untenable gender schism. Marilyn Quayle, one of the convention's loudest
voices, found herself repeatedly taken to task for comments that were widely
interpreted to mean that mothers should stay at home with their children and
not work outside of their homes. In a *New York Times* op-ed piece that she
wrote three weeks after the convention, Quayle defended and expanded upon
her convention remarks:

> Today women don't have to dress or act like men to advance in the pro-
> fessional world previously dominated by men. We don't have to reject the
> prospect of marriage and children to succeed. We don't have to reject our
> essential natures as women to prosper in what was once the domain of
> men. (Quayle 1992, A-35)

At one point—clearly as a gesture to feminist critics—she even mentioned the
work of feminist scholars Betty Friedan and Carol Gilligan to support her position. Quayle relied upon essentialist notions of womanhood to defend herself
and to speak about women as she campaigned for the ticket that included her
husband, but despite numerous statements that she stood by what she said at the
convention, her remarks to the press often included explicit claims about the differences between male and female "natures" and further explanations about
what she actually meant in her convention speech. This was portrayed clearly as
an issue of concern both to her and her Republican campaign coaches.

Marilyn Quayle's essentialism and Arlen Specter's emasculation were just two specific demonstrations of a perceived need for defense against the momentum of the Year of the Woman. A nondefensive note that marked the Year of the Woman's move to reference point is the language of universality used in postmortem discussions of the Year of the Woman. Immediately before and after the election, public talk shifted toward making this woman-centered discourse and its associated notions stand for a more general set of issues and values. Democratic pollster Celinda Lake's words in a *New York Times* op-ed piece a few days after the election were typical: ". . . voters overwhelmingly believed that women were in touch with [voters'] concerns. . . . Female candidates were seen as populist outsiders who could make government work for ordinary people—a powerful profile in today's political environment" (1992, A-21). The fact that women were spoken of as representatives of "ordinary people" supports the idea that their interests had come to be perceived as more than simply "women's issues" but average citizens' issues. Speaking on CNN, Harriet Woods, president of the National Women's Political Caucus, expanded on this idea when she emphasized that not only did women vote for women in record numbers, but large numbers of men voted for women candidates as well (CNN 1992c). While these commentators may have had partisan motives for their comments, this point also was emphasized by other journalists, political commentators, and political scientists.

"EVOLUTION, NOT REVOLUTION"

In her post–election euphoria, the newly elected Carol Moseley Braun predicted that her campaign would live on as a symbol not only of a progressive, coalition-built campaign but of a reconfigured U.S. society, "a multiracial, multiethnic, multicultural society." "This election points the way to the future" (CNN 1992c), she noted. Braun's words—along with those of other candidates, public figures, and reporters—suggested the necessity of a radical revisioning of the U.S. political system to accommodate members of the body politic who were neither white nor male. Prior to the election, a recurrently invoked remark concerned the lack of representativeness in U.S. politics and political institutions. Because women candidates were part of the predicted sea change in democratic processes, it is useful to consider what the public talk regarding these political women suggested about feminist politics, since this informed the ways in which change was conceptualized in this context.

As the heading of this section indicates, the dominant mode of discussion about political change via the Year of the Woman was in terms of evolution, not revolution. This phrase was, in fact, a part of a *New York Times* headline from October 1992, about two weeks before the election: "Women Advance in Politics by Evolution, Not Revolution" (Manegold 1992b). This declaration could be construed as both descriptive and placating: a move to soothe the fears of voters concerned about the prospect of women winning public offices in large numbers. Reporter Catherine Manegold argued that "actual victories at the ballot box will be not so much a result of sputtering anger as of the long, little-noticed efforts of a band of well-spoken political guerrillas" (1992b, A-1). To further alleviate any doubts about the modest nature of women's political goals, she included a quote by Harriet Woods: "It's not like we are taking over the country. But men left to themselves are like tribes on the Hill. We just want to try things our way" (Manegold 1992b, D-21).

The themes that appeared in these texts, as well as the manner in which they were discussed, showed that feminist ideas and values permeated this public discourse—a not surprising feature given the focus on women and women's concerns. The perpetual male domination of centers of power, such as Congress, was the issue that took center stage in the coverage of the Year of the Woman candidates, although abortion was mentioned almost as often. Abortion was most often discussed in the context of its importance for galvanizing women and determining their votes rather than as an issue that significantly affected women's lives outside of voting booths. Various other themes associated with feminism were scattered throughout the coverage: sexual harassment, family leave, day care, and employment issues such as pay equity, job opportunities for women, and the glass ceiling.

That these issues had some prominence in public discourse during this year is a noteworthy feature of the political landscape, yet not all journalists were swayed by the mere appearance of women's issues in political campaign rhetoric. As two *New York Times* journalists noted, after awhile the appearance of feminist issues looked more like window dressing than an attempt to engage these issues in a substantive way. For example, Barbara Presley Noble's lead paragraph, for her article "The Missing Issue in Campaign '92," expressed dissatisfaction even with the amount of air time given to women's issues, noting that these were "curiously inconspicuous during the Presidential campaign" (1992, III-23). Citing the work of a group of feminist economists headed by Heidi Hartmann, Noble observed that despite the pro-woman rhetoric of the campaign, economic policies benefiting women were almost entirely absent

from the agendas of the two presidential candidates. Yet according to Hartmann's group, economic policies that focused on the needs of women were
those that could actually help large numbers of women more than almost any
other policy. In a similar vein, Catherine Manegold (1992a) argued that the
near obsession with abortion as a campaign issue caused other issues of great
importance to women to be overlooked and underappreciated for their potentially positive impact.

Both Manegold and Noble make valuable points. The appearance of this
configuration of feminist issues conferred legitimacy upon it and demonstrated
that some degree of public support existed for these issues, but the next step—
concrete plans for ameliorating or resolving problems, such as sexual harassment—was left virtually untouched in mainstream public talk. That some feminist ideas have gained a toehold in the mainstream media and with media
consumers is supported by the findings of recent research on feminism's move
inside into influential cultural institutions. Political theorist Mary Katzenstein
(1990), for example, has noted that the 1980s saw a strong movement to "insti-
tutionalize" feminism: to get feminism and feminists inside of powerful institutions—even those as male-dominated as the Catholic Church and the military.
Katzenstein demonstrates that this has occurred in the last decade and a half
through a process of "unobtrusive mobilization" (27) in which women and
men who support feminist reforms have risen in the hierarchies of their respective organizations, attempting to implement feminist policies along the way.
The fact that many Republican women voted for Democratic candidates
(Wilcox 1994) in the Year of the Woman because of their progressive views on
women provides one suggestion that some feminist political positions have
broad appeal.

Although feminist issues associated with the Year of the Woman campaign gained public visibility, it is difficult to see the treatment of these as much
more than a public relations campaign that doggedly evaded questions about
underlying causes of gender-related problems. The feminist issues raised in the
coverage of the Year of the Woman showed that feminism can be deployed
strategically to influence campaigns and win votes; some foundational beliefs of
feminism could even be reduced to glib sound bites. The problem with this is
that the promise of a substantive feminist agenda is left unfulfilled.

In the case of the Year of the Woman, the assumption seemed to be that
the placement of more women in political office was the panacea for women's
needs. Almost no discussion occurred about how this increase in numbers
would improve the lives of *constituents* or of what reforms, specifically, the new
agendas would be composed. In other words, feminism became a virtually

empty signifier—a position used opportunistically, for the purpose of campaigning, and one that permitted structural problems and material inequities to
remain unaddressed. This is despite the fact that demographic figures showed
that women—and particularly women of color—were suffering during this
time as a result of gross disparities in income distribution in the United States
(see chapter 1).

In an exhaustive historical survey of second-wave feminist politics and
organizations in the United States, Johanna Brenner (1993) argues that second-
wave feminism, once a formidable political movement, has foundered considerably. One of the critical problems to which she attributes this loss of strength
is the dominance of a feminism in which most political efforts have been dedicated to (and exhausted by) reactions against threats to abortion rights. Yet
many women experience crises around a set of problems irreducible to abortion: "the inner cities, lack of health care and child care, [and] low wages" (130),
for instance. Brenner makes specific recommendations for a third-wave feminist politics that could surpass the popularity and strength of early second-wave
feminism if it attends to the material realities of women's lives and includes
these in programs for social transformation. She argues that feminist demands
for change and the

> ways of arguing for them have to transcend rather than capitulate to exist-
> ing political worldviews. We need to develop a politics that combines the
> liberatory moments . . . of the movements for democratic inclusion . . .
> with new struggles over material needs. (157)

The missing link in the Year of the Woman is what Brenner discusses: the connection to disenfranchised constituents adversely affected by the policies of
elite, white, male-dominated political institutions.

Although the Year of the Woman's celebratory slogans and hype may have
worked, on the one hand, to publicize a few feminists and feminist issues, they
fell short of being a campaign of far-reaching influence. The Year of the Woman
outsider discourse positioned feminism strategically and propelled more feminist women into insider status in the Senate and the House as a result, but postfeminism—with its undergirding in neoliberal politics—offers little more than
a superficial gesture to the set of structural problems that beset the U.S. electorate. For instance, one of the most important votes for the Year of the Woman
senators was that on President Clinton's welfare reform package. All but one of
the new senators, Carol Moseley Braun, voted for the package despite strident
opposition to and vigorous lobbying against it by feminist organizations, such
as NOW and the Women's Economic Agenda Project, for the negative impact

that it would have on women. When asked about their votes afterward, Barbara Boxer, Dianne Feinstein, and Patty Murray retreated to a *realpolitik* defense or reactionary excuses; Feinstein, for example, defended her vote by claiming that her constituents had a "growing resentment of people who won't work" and offered virtually no sympathy for those who would suffer as a result of the package's cuts (Kirshenbaum 1996, 17–18).

This example from the welfare reform vote suggests that the postfeminism with which the Year of the Woman was suffused remains hegemonic. It has become the commonsensical position from which legislative and policy decisions are made; it has become part of the Year-of-the-Woman senators' *realpolitik*. The common sense of postfeminism, as Feinstein's comment about welfare recipients "who won't work" suggests, is based on fairly conservative positions: welfare recipients not wanting to work, government as an entrepreneurial entity, and the valorization of the free market, for example. Yet these positions are not beneficial to a majority of women; they are arguably even detrimental to most women, as feminist economist Nancy Folbre (1994) has pointed out. Indeed, Folbre argues that collective action based on political economy is the most effective way to begin to make economic arrangements more beneficial to women, and to families overall. Both women and men could benefit from a program for social change that attempted to redress structural inequities, such as the virtual impossibility of finding jobs in the inner cities, but the Good Father of Naomi Wolf's creation does not do that; moreover, he appears to take patriarchal tough love to new extremes.

The Year of the Woman's mediated postfeminism blended neoliberalism with cultural feminism to produce a hegemonic female subject. While she seemed to represent the needs of some women, she focused attention on those women (white, middle class to elite, and straight) and away from those who did not occupy that subject position—many of whom were future constitutents of Year of the Woman candidates. Amidst the glamour and attention given to the Year of the Woman, a sharper feminist critique could be eclipsed by postfeminism, and while I am not suggesting that this was conspiratorial (in the sense that it was either surreptitious or maliciously intended), this privileging of postfeminism coincides with a neoliberal hegemony in *media* politics that McChesney (1999) discusses. That is, like neoliberal politics, postfeminist politics do not ruffle the feathers of corporations or alienate the donors to important PACs (which may help support them) by challenging the corporate domination of important institutions, such as those of electoral politics and the mass media. Media corporations and politicians are tied symbiotically, as Bagdikian (2000)

has argued. In 1998, for example, media corporations contributed $186.5 mil-
lion to federal lobbying efforts and were the second largest donors in this area
(just below the real estate and banking bloc) (Center for Responsive Politics
2000). Postfeminism emerges from this as a by-product of the media–industrial
complex. Its significance is evident, for it migrates to the 1996 presidential
campaign. There it emerges in the figure of "soccer moms," the subject of the
next chapter.

CHAPTER FOUR

From Women of the Year to "Soccer Moms"

The Case of the Incredible Shrinking Women

The 1992 Year of the Woman was a set of conflicted texts, yet it privileged a postfeminist logic. This logic was one that could be appropriate for only a minority of women and was conveyed through news stories and images of high-profile women poised to gain powerful political offices. The subjects of mainstream news accounts of the Year of the Woman came to signify maverick electoral power which, although at times couched in somewhat sexist terms, were woven through with a fairly respectful tone for the candidates and their supporters. Journalists permitted women to be speaking subjects (albeit in an always already restricted conversation), perhaps based on what appeared to have been their inevitable moves into politically significant roles.

In the 1996 election year, the discursive terrain of mainstream political reporting looked very different. Instead of glowing biographical accounts of "women of the year," there were "soccer moms." In place of women, *en masse*, demanding redress for political grievances on the steps of official buildings, there was the mini-van brigade, shuttling children from school to soccer matches to home. The power behind women's voices in the electoral arena had dwindled significantly in a scant four years, perhaps a victim of the constricting influence of postfeminism.

The following letter suggests that even as much as two years after the 1996 presidential campaign, the figure of the soccer mom was a salient one—

at least to some readers and viewers of the news. On August 23, 1998, six days after President Clinton's confession of his "inappropriate" liaison with Monica Lewinsky, this terse letter to the editor appeared in the *Minneapolis Star Tribune*:

> Memo to Bob Dole: How many ways can we apologize to you for reject-ing your honesty, your integrity, your morality, your patriotism?
> I trust you soccer moms are enjoying the opportunity to explain the various forms of sex to your children. (Manther 1998, A-28)

This particular reference to "soccer moms" also suggests a desire, on the part of some citizens, to blame a swing voting bloc for the failings of the politicians who received their votes, as if soccer moms, by virtue of their votes, must have condoned all of President Clinton's infelicitous practices. Inappropriate attri-bution is one consequence of a label used to designate or characterize the traits of a group of voters, but of course there are others. This chapter examines some of these, particularly the cultural capital and liability that a label—in this case "soccer mom"—can have for a group of voters, even well after a campaign sea-son is over.

In the 1992 election year, mainstream print and television news coverage was replete with hosannas for female politicians, praised as strong and politically powerful figures during this so-called "Year of the Woman." Just four years later, 1996 election news reports relied upon a very different image to describe women vis-à-vis electoral politics: that of "soccer moms." "Soccer mom" was used most recurrently in mainstream TV and print media to describe an aggre-gate of women, vis-à-vis electoral politics, described in media texts as being crucial to the success of either presidential candidate: President Clinton or Robert Dole. The term may have originated in politics during a 1995 Denver city council election in which one candidate campaigned as the "Soccer Mom for City Council" as a way of demonstrating her populist, "everyneighbor" leanings (MacFarquhar 1996, IV-1). By the time the campaign season of 1996 was in full swing, the term was used widely in television, newspapers, and mag-azines to denote the swing vote *du jour*.

This period of time represents a dramatic shift in news discourse: from dis-cussing women as political power wielders (Women of the Year) to discussing women as a group of swing voters defined primarily by their filial obligations. This move represents a discursive connection between women voters—reduced to a demographic category characterized by their relationships to their chil-dren—and an ideology of consumerism that reduces electoral politics to personal choices around product consumption and "lifestyle." The ideology in this cover-age is important also for the cachet that it can garner in other contexts after a campaign season is over. As I argue here, the soccer mom trope of the 1996 election season exemplifies just such a trajectory; that is, its potential to affect groups and individuals seems greater as a commercial than as a political metaphor. This likely has consequences for public perceptions of women in/and politics.

Far from simply describing the world, metaphors are prescriptive linguistic devices that guide and shape thinking as well (Lakoff and Johnson 1980; McMillan and Cheney 1996). The ramifications of a metaphor such as "soccer mom" (particularly reductive when considering its contrast to the more powerful Year of the Woman of 1992) are thus worth considering: juxtaposing Year of the Woman news texts (1992) with soccer mom news texts (1996) illuminates stark differences—differences that represent a diminution in the power of women's constructed representation in the context of electoral politics at the end of the century. McMillan and Cheney, whose work focuses on the implications of the student-as-consumer metaphor in public discourse, make important points about the socially constructive and destructive possibilities of labels and metaphors. These implications are vitally important, they argue, because

> when collectively we come to share a linguistic construction, language shapes our institutions as well—in that the very distinctions and classifications we make come to affect our future thinking and behaviors in much the same way as a rule can come to "rule" its creators. (1996, 2)

McMillan's and Cheney's study demonstrates that the incorporation of particular terms and other linguistic constructions into public discourse, such as media texts, has significant ramifications for thought and action. Thus when media texts articulate the label "soccer mom" to women's lives and activities, media consumers are encouraged to think along the lines suggested in the content of such texts: in the case of soccer moms, the most significant and frequent motivations ascribed to them are explicitly or implicitly consumerist in character. Because the soccer moms of 1996 were ostensible political agents, their discursive connection to a set of behaviors and products promoted elsewhere by consumer marketers is a matter of concern for what it suggests about the way in which women's public identities in electoral politics could be perceived.

Media institutions and texts create and perpetuate catchphrases and metaphors such as "soccer moms" constantly; in the contemporary United States, this has become one of the media's chief functions, both in advertising and programming. Our common symbolic environment is woven through with these, as critical media scholars argue; from billboards to the Internet, we are inescapably immersed in what Douglas Kellner (1995) calls "media culture," a late twentieth-century phenomenon in which images, sounds, and spectacles help produce the fabric of everyday life, dominating leisure time, shaping political views and social behavior, and providing the materials out of which people forge their very identities. Radio, television, film, and the other products of the culture industries provide the models of what it means to be male or female, successful or a failure, powerful or powerless. . . . Media stories and images provide the symbols, myths, and resources which help constitute a common culture for the majority of individuals in many parts of the world today. (1)

Political rhetoric in mainstream news texts contributes to the production of particular social identities and their motivation toward democratic practice and activism—however strong or weak. A tendency toward alienation can be directly attributed to the philosophies and practices of social institutions (e.g., mainstream media, government, schools, and churches) that encourage consumerism, privatism, and individualism over collectivism, and a desire to act in concert to improve the common good (Bellah, Madsen, Sullivan, Swidler, and Tipton 1991). As McMillan and Cheney point out, far from fostering a sense of community or common good, "consumerism is self-centered" (1996, 9). Thus the production of identity—including assigning value to different identities such as the consumer—is a highly significant function of the dynamic relationship between media institutions and audiences. This is arguably the most important function of commercial media, whose very existence depends upon delivering audiences of varying socioeconomic compositions to advertisers, who in turn rely upon social identities that shift and change fluidly according to the newest consumer trend.

While scholars such as Roland Marchand and Todd Gitlin have discussed the problems associated with equating politics to product consumption, the gendered dimension to this equation has not been taken up in such critical scholarship. That soccer moms follow immediately on the heels of the Year of the Woman suggests that gender-related ideology can be invoked in electoral politics to encourage or discourage a sense of political agency among voters. In the case of soccer moms, media texts weave together both subtle and obvious assumptions about women's appropriate roles in such a way as to subdue the clamor over the strong women of 1992 and channel it into a different space: that inhabited by the nuclear families of the suburbs and their ever-expanding inventory of consumer products. Thus rather than encouraging a further increase in women's power in electoral politics in 1996, the use of soccer moms in media texts obscures women's 1992 victories in politics by substituting its language of strong and victorious female politicians and activists with the language of privatization and domestication. Such a contrast in perspective would be notable at any time, but particularly so when it occurs after such an important election year for women politicians, feminist activists, and feminist issues. The figure of the "soccer mom" works to construct a less threatening identity, one derived in part from traditional stereotypes about women's "proper" places in combination with more contemporary assumptions about women's integral function in the labor force as workers and in the marketing and advertising worlds as a target demographic.

Reframing the Gender Gap

Soccer moms likely emerged from the wellspring of the gender gap—the predominant trope used to discuss women in U.S. electoral politics. The gender gap is a feature of news discourse that bears noting, as it signifies schism and ideological distance between female and male voters; it refers to patterns of voting characterized by a significant percentage of female voters voting for a particular candidate or issue, while a significant percentage of male voters vote the opposition. The first appearance of the so-called gender gap in voting and the appearance of a majority of women voters both occurred in 1980; four years later, in the 1984 presidential race, Geraldine Ferraro became the first woman to run for vice president when she ran as Walter Mondale's running mate (Mueller 1988, 16).

In the 1980s, when the gender gap first appeared, the changing conditions of the workforce, of nuclear family life, and of the economy all created a cultural shift[1] in which greatly increased numbers of women were, because they wanted to be or had to be, financially independent. The circumstances of financially independent women strongly influenced the reconfiguration of gender relations; in this case, the shift was exemplified when a majority of women *and* men during the early 1980s reported their acceptance of ideas and policies once considered radical: government-subsidized day care centers for children, work schedules that accommodated parental obligations, and a much wider range of the roles thought to be appropriate for women (Klein 1984). Given this sea change in attitudes and lived circumstances, it is not surprising that women whose lives had changed for the better would develop voting practices that protected what they valued and would support candidates who embraced a vision of the future that was feminist in character. Joan Tronto sounds a cautionary note, however, when she points out that the gender gap is not necessarily a reflection of *many* women's experiences brought to the voting booth. Rather, she argues that "gender gap attitudes are exhibited most by women who already have achieved autonomy" (1995, 410). The gender gap is thus only partially useful as a signifier for the wide acceptance of a feminist agenda, however, it does yield information about a group of relatively privileged middle-class to elite women, whose links to feminist politics may be quite different from those of less privileged women—in particular, those for whom autonomy is a distant or an unfixed goal.

Despite its socioeconomic class specificity, the gender gap was touted by liberal feminist groups—and especially NOW—as an important sign that women's voting patterns should be considered significant for their bloc.[2] This was accomplished in large part through the work of NOW and similar groups; reporters made the issue "fashionable" by demonstrating "how specific [electoral] races were won or lost with a margin of victory secured by a women's vote" (Bonk 1988 83). This aspect of the gender gap was a feat of media management and was linked to pro-ERA (Equal Rights Amendment) feminist groups', especially NOW's, drive to ratify the ERA. By 1981, the phrase "gender gap" was appearing with some regularity in mainstream news outlets (90). This public relations style of dealing with reporters included, in 1982, a monthly "Gender Gap Update" sent to thousands of reporters each month to ensure their awareness of gender gap issues (92).

By the time the 1984 presidential campaign was underway, news coverage persistently suggested the possibility of the gender gap's reappearance. Ronald Reagan was questioned so often about his "woman problem" (i.e., that significantly fewer women than men agreed with his policies and reported that they would vote for him in November 1984) that he launched a counterattack in the press to make his politics more palatable to women.[3] Reagan's characteristic blunders, however, continued to thwart any progress made by his public relations team. The Democrats were not particularly skillful at working their advantage with women in the polls, either, and the gender gap in the 1984 election was almost identical to that in 1980 (Bonk 1988, 100).

Even Geraldine Ferraro's presence on the Democratic ticket of 1984 could not effectively widen the gender gap to the party's advantage. This fact, Kathleen Frankovic (1988) argues, is consistent with the ways in which vice-presidential candidates typically affect campaign results. That is, they usually have little or no impact on voting preferences when it comes to voters choosing between candidates. Ferraro's loss did not portend the demise of women's influence on the political process or in presidential campaigns, however. Both Frankovic (1988) and Bonk (1988) have noted that NOW controlled the issue of a female vice-presidential candidate and her connection with the gender gap in the media, and that in making their members prominent as authorities, they were able to gain and maintain access to Democratic Party heavies who consulted them about women's issues. As a result, NOW moved from the margins of Democratic Party influence closer to the center, where they were situated along with other influential groups, such as labor unions (Frankovic 1988, 123).

NOW's brand of feminism, however public, did not necessarily represent, or even address, the concerns of a great many women—even a great many middle-class women. This became apparent when Geraldine Ferraro conducted a poll to gauge the possible success of a 1986 Senate candidacy. Ultimately, her poll and focus-group results concluded that some women "feel unsexed by powerful women" like Ferraro (Witt, Paget, and Matthews 1994, 84). About the results, Ferraro observed that the women who found her objectionable were the traditional wives and mothers who wondered, "How would their husbands view them if 'all they could do'—and that's in quotes—'was be a wife and mother'? Would it jeopardize their marriages? I mean, the way people thought about this!" (Geraldine Ferraro, quoted in Witt, Paget, and Matthews 1994, 84–85).

Year of the Woman news coverage suggests that news workers interpreted the events surrounding the drastic increase in women running for political office as a significant and concrete manifestation of the gender gap, and although this coverage of the candidates was flawed in a number of respects, one of its strengths was that it included narratives and tropes of strong, empowered women who were ready to take on the political system—as candidates and then as office holders—for having wronged them historically and systematically. Year of the Woman candidates were valorized for challenging the political system and insisting that its embedded gender inequities be rectified through that all-American practice of running for political office. Mainstream coverage likened their efforts to a Holy War, in which the forces of morality and righteousness were women.

Although the tone of this coverage was decidedly pro-woman, it was not necessarily pro-feminist but postfeminist instead. Perhaps because of its white, middle-class to elite orientation, postfeminism contributes to a climate in which drawing parallels between the electoral practices of U.S. women and their consumer habits and between the ballot box and the coupon book remains virtually unquestioned. Thus explications of soccer moms in news coverage contained no mention of a feminist challenge to the term or its cultural connotations. This may be due to the fact that the soccer mom trope in mainstream news texts did in fact foreground some women's concerns and their predicted electoral influence, thus satisfying any editorial dictate to discuss the gendered dimensions of the campaign—no need to include feminist voices in a campaign media mix that could be considered at least nominally pro-woman. It also is possible that dissenting feminist voices were not raised publicly on the issue of soccer moms because, on balance, feminist political activists considered them positive for women in politics: news accounts (even conservative ones) noted the successful way in which the soccer mom strategy attracted great numbers of women—even conservative Republican women, who had been repelled by the angry tone and masculine messages of the Republican "revolution" of 1994.

Voices of discontent about the soccer mom strategy occurred infrequently and were diffuse; mostly these were raised by Republicans and other conservatives, even while they acknowledged the success of the strategy. In other words, competing frames for the gendered dimension of this election coverage were virtually nonexistent. Instead, the news coverage from this period represents an instance of pack journalism's tendency to latch onto a catchphrase and exploit it: about two weeks before the election, 302 stories about soccer moms had appeared and were listed in Lexis-Nexis; two-thirds of these had been published in the previous two weeks (Peck 1996, F-2).

The gender gap has been somewhat useful as a force for motivating both women voters and women politicians, but overall it acts as something of a smokescreen for other electoral issues. In fact, the gender gap's *deficiency* for explaining or predicting voting behavior has been demonstrated historically since the 1980s (see, e.g., Mueller 1988; Tavris 1996), and although a gender differential existed in the pre- and post-campaign polls of 1996, we might question why *gender* has become the *ur* organizing category in campaign coverage. As social psychologist Carol Tavris (1996) points out, wealth and geography gaps also are significant when analyzing voting behavior, yet these generate nowhere near the volume of public discussion or the intensity of fascination that the gender gap does. Tavris argues that 1996's gender gap can be explained as an "experience gap." That is, typically more women than men have direct experience with sex discrimination, with economic suffering, and with nurturing—the latter because historically, they have constituted the majority of the ranks of single parents and have assumed responsibility as primary caretakers of children and aging parents. To support a Democratic candidate who purports to be sensitive to those issues is not a genetically determined (or essentialist) trait, therefore, "it stems from self-interest" (Tavris 1996, A-15).

Yet despite the dubious predictive or descriptive value of the gender gap, since 1980 it has been the metaphor most recurrently deployed by news producers to discuss women and their voting patterns. Even as recently as

1996, news workers persisted in using the gender gap to predict how women would vote in the election of the same year. Not surprisingly, the gender gap was supposed to have worked to the advantage of the Democratic candidates, Bill Clinton and Al Gore. For NBC, even the idea of a gender gap could not adequately convey the perceived distance between male and female voters; on at least two occasions, NBC correspondents referred to the gender gap as a "chasm" (NBC 1996a); for then-candidate Robert Dole, it was a "dangerous political chasm" (NBC 1996b).

The soccer mom appellation personalized the gender gap and simultaneously provided it with a memorable name. As one *San Francisco Chronicle* reporter noted, "until a creative consultant came up with the soccer mom tag, these were just middle-class female voters whom the polls showed favored Bill Clinton over Bob Dole by more than 20 percent" (Garcia 1996, A-5). Tagging this group of women with this particular label though also permitted the articulation of this aggregate of women to a host of consumer products; this was a process that seemed to solidify the terms of a valuable consumer identity: that of the domestic woman.

THEORIZING SOCCER MOMS

The power with which soccer moms were associated was of a variety much more nebulous and uncertain than that of 1992's Women of the Year. Soccer moms' ostensible power was constructed discursively from a nexus of factors, including their domestic relations, their household income levels, and their somewhat uncertain political leanings, a feature that could work for or against candidates until the very last minute of the election.

The texts that I reviewed used the term *soccer moms* for the first time on August 29, 1996, during the span of time in which both the Democratic and Republican National Conventions occurred. The originary moment occurred in a *CBS Evening News* program, in which Dan Rather described them as a voting bloc that was poised to make or break the political fortunes of the Democrats or the Republicans. Another CBS correspondent, Robert McNamara, noted playfully that "this year, politicians can't score without the soccer moms." This was only the first invocation of the game metaphor used with respect to soccer moms, but it occurred through the end of the campaign season in a number of accounts, a trope that seemed to trivialize the tone of these narratives.[4] In this same broadcast, Rather described soccer moms as "working mothers in the suburbs, stressed out and stretched thin": women so busy working both inside and outside of their homes (and especially caring for their children) that they failed to take account of the political race until late in the campaign season (CBS 1996). The slant and content of this CBS newscast set the stage for public discussions of women voters in the 1996 campaign season.

News workers, Democratic and Republican poll takers, politicians, and advertisers struggled to articulate the soccer mom figure to an ideology: that of a white, middle-class, suburban woman. The particular historical and material conditions of the 1980s and 1990s make the soccer mom trope and ideology commonsensical (in the Gramscian sense of the phrase) for this historical moment. For example, by 1996, although women had been gaining political power at the local, state, and national levels (albeit slowly) throughout the century, media texts still constructed them as Other to the world of electoral politics, an "unnatural" element in an otherwise predictable mix. Women's presence in politics is thus typically constructed from implicit assumptions about gender in ways that men's presence is not—men are the unsexed norm, while women stand on the margins, the gendered oddities in politics.[5]

Working alongside this notion of woman-as-Other in politics is the economic logic of the soccer mom ideology. The MBA-dominated newsrooms, a growing trend during the 1980s and 1990s, not only confined news workers to restrictive formulas and reduced their professional autonomy, they also functioned with a basic assumption that the bottom line should be the ultimate consideration in news judgments (Bagdikian 2000; McManus 1995; Underwood 1995). They also provided a strong guide for a journalistic ideological orientation supportive of corporate class interests. As Edward Herman and Noam Chomsky (1988) have argued, this sort of orientation results in part from "the adaptation of personnel to the constraints of ownership, organization, market, and political power" (xii). They continue with the contention that such adaptation is

> largely self-censorship, by reporters and commentators who adjust to the realities of source and media organizational requirements, and by people at higher levels within media organizations who are chosen to implement, and have usually internalized, the constraints imposed by proprietary and other market and governmental centers of power. (xii)

This variety of common sense also seems influenced by gender relations strongly rooted in a corporate class structure. It thus functions as a partial means of achieving what Herman and Chomsky refer to as an "elite consensus" (1988, 302), a view that supports corporate power but marginalizes or obscures competing perspectives on possibilities for gender relations.

Although it is outside the scope of this book to speculate on whether the commonsense beliefs that undergird soccer mom discourse have society-wide permeation, it is fair to say that these beliefs drive *news industry* interpretations of gender in electoral politics. Different, and at times conflicting, notions abounded in this logic, some relatively traditional and conservative (almost pre-feminist) and others more contemporary. The conception of common sense as a contested space between ideology and lived experience or "an intersection of various conflicting positions" (Landy 1994, 98) is useful in understanding the discursive practices formed in and around the media texts that construct the soccer mom identity. The constitutive elements that characterize this logic would include the class positions of news producers and their experiences around gender and race. Add to this another layer—the ideological environment and culture of the newsrooms and media production environment—and a complex mixture results. From the interaction of all of these constitutive elements come the commonsense beliefs of news workers, evidenced in the texts that they produce.

This type of common sense is exemplified in news accounts of soccer moms, which typically disavowed any authorial role in either the proliferation of the term or in the process of ascribing meaning to it (this despite the great volume of stories produced by news outlets). The sheer volume of coverage suggests that news organizations played some role in the wide play that the term received, but volume alone indicates nothing about nuances in the term's evolution. Use of the passive voice, for example, helped distance journalists from the process: "They have come to be known as 'soccer moms'" (Tackett 1996, 1–7); and, "suddenly, some time around the Republican convention, the Soccer Mom became mythic" (MacFarquhar 1996, IV-1). One narrative even included the phoenix-like image of soccer moms rising from the ashes of banality: "This is the year that 'soccer moms' rose from suburban cliché to political symbol" (Argetsinger 1996, B-1). Apparently these were transmogrifications that occurred without any journalistic assistance (none that was mentioned explicitly, in any case).

Some news accounts, however, approached the soccer mom phenomenon with a jaundiced eye. These accounts were critical not only of the term but of what their authors argued was a condescending attitude toward these women. "Maybe there are no soccer moms," one *Los Angeles Times* reporter suggested. "Could it be that they are a figment of the candidates' too-shallow imaginations and that suburban mothers are given to more complex thought and higher political expectations?" (Scheer 1996, B-7). Another reporter noted that the soccer mom label is the "newest and silliest spin target on the presidential map"

(Garcia 1996, A-5), while still another observed that "soccer moms are the rage, having supplanted the angry white male as the trophy voter in American politics" (King 1996, A-3).

A number of stories included statements by soccer moms who were skeptical of the term in the context of campaign discourse. "Who made up that term, soccer mom," one soccer mom asked derisively, "some man no doubt" (quoted in Peck 1996, F-2). Another soccer mom, Lauren, observed that politicians "sure sound a little desperate when [they] start talking about soccer moms" (Rubenstein 1996, A-26). Yet another soccer mom voiced a different concern: "I don't like the feeling of manipulation, like we're some kind of product" (quoted in Peck 1996, F-2).

Along these same lines, some journalists treated the soccer mom phenomenon in a satirical fashion with a tongue-in-cheek quiz (entitled "Might You Be the Coveted Soccer Mom?" [Satran 1996, 5-1]) or a "field guide" to soccer mom behavior. The latter posed soccer moms as polar opposites to 1994's swing vote bloc *du jour*, the Angry White Male.

> To the angry white male, the situation atop the ticket looks grim. The women of America have something in hand for you: five dainty fingers wrapped up in one dainty fist. In other words, a knuckle sandwich. The Soccer Moms are about to do some serious kicking, and they are not aiming at a soccer ball. (Nyhan 1996, A-27)

The tone of such accounts indicated that not everyone was overcome with positive feelings for either the soccer mom label or its creators and users. This dissatisfaction, in combination with passive-voice observations about the emergence of the term and its connotations, suggests that some journalists wanted nothing to do with the soccer mom term; nevertheless, signification practices of print and television media abounded around it in a consistent fashion.

Coverage of the soccer mom phenomenon constructed their collective identity from three discursive patterns. The first was a tendency to personalize and privatize the lives of soccer moms while situating them in a predominantly domestic context. The second was characterized by an insistence on fixing them with a racial identity and class position (white, middle class). The third was a recurrent tendency to conflate the electoral practices of soccer moms with their consumer habits, virtually equating the vote to the purchase. These patterns appeared in both newspaper and television texts, although television news programs paid considerably less attention to soccer moms than did their print-news counterparts. Television news broadcasts were content to use the time-worn gender gap trope, while print news explored soccer moms almost to the exclusion of references to the gender gap.

SIGNIFYING SOCCER MOMS

The figure of the soccer mom represents a move from one representation to another: from strong women poised to gain electoral power by wresting control of it from the governing white patriarchs (Women of the Year) to harried women defined by their domestic relationships and their commitment to their children (soccer moms). What power soccer moms were said to possess lay mostly within the realm of the domestic. Thus the discourse shuttled women from public life to private life, from the House of Representatives to the home. As one Republican pollster asserted (in what was arguably a stark, reality-determining claim), "If you are a soccer mom, the world according to you is seen through the needs of your children" (MacFarquhar 1996, 4-6).

News narratives about soccer moms insisted upon drawing and then policing the line between private and public spheres, with soccer moms set firmly in the private, domestic space of home. Even the few texts that mentioned their careers were eclipsed by all of the accounts of soccer moms' supposed preoccupation: their homes and their children. CBS correspondent Bob McNamara, for example, asserted that "between the house and her husband, the kids and the dog, she hasn't had time to decide. . . . Tonight across the country, millions of women are still looking for a political home" (CBS 1996).

McNamara describes a female subject who, though surrounded by traditional evidence of a contented domestic existence, is still too frantic to develop a well-constructed political stance. "Looking for a political home" suggests that she is a nomad, wandering without the benefit of a clear, critical analysis—and wandering not toward political territory but toward the security of a home. It also seems to suggest that because she has apparently achieved a good life already, her politics are not desperate or angry; she is just looking. Still, her children are her number one priority. In this same broadcast, one soccer mom defended her lifestyle with the following: "I mean, I can't go up to God and say, 'God, I got another raise.'" She continues, "'God, I did OK with these boys.' That's what I want to feel success about." Apparently, soccer mom success can be measured accurately only with a parental yardstick. In this same vein, one woman interviewed for a *New York Times* article claimed that her politics had changed since she had kids; she had become less "me-centered" and adopted instead "that mom focus." It was this "mom focus" that the reporter for this article claimed gave President Clinton the soccer moms' overwhelming support; Clinton's "sense of caring appear[ed] to count tremendously for women who say their political approaches have altered since they had children" (Goldberg 1996, A-24). Statements such as these reduce the complexity of maternal experience and simplify and homogenize the figures of women and their place in society—particularly in the electoral process.

In a similar fashion, news stories emphasized the emotional connections that the soccer moms reported feeling for Clinton. The stated perception was that he was not only more concerned about them than was Robert Dole, but that he was more *like* them; they felt an affinity for him. Using John Gray's popular tract about the essential natures of women and men as an authority, one journalist claimed that soccer moms liked Clinton for reasons that "all seemed to boil down to a perception that Mr. Dole is from Mars and Mr. Clinton is from Venus" (Goldberg 1996, A-24). Moreover, according to one soccer mom, "Bill Clinton is popular because all the women either have a crush on him or would like him to be your [*sic*] neighbor" (quoted in Tackett 1996, 1-7). Another noted (without apparent irony) that, "I feel [Clinton] is very compassionate. He feels our pain" (quoted in Tackett 1996, 1-7).

This sort of essentialist basis for differentiating women's and men's voting behavior is not a new feature of public discourse; news workers (among other public figures) have essentialized women's and men's electoral practices since at least the suffrage movement (see, e.g., Evans 1989; Lemons 1973; Smith-Rosenberg 1985). Discursive attempts to domesticate women are longstanding; this particular construction of the soccer mom bears a strong resemblance to the "angel in the home" reference used to discourage women from the public sphere in the 1800s.[6] In this instance, however, the tendency to domesticate these women could lead to a problematic conclusion, perhaps one whose implication is that the soccer moms, by their natures and circumstances, are essentially apolitical.[7] A typical statement, in this case made by a soccer mom, went something like, "I got to go home and thaw something. . . . I spend so much time going to soccer games, that I don't think I can really be a political force" (Rubenstein 1996, A-15). One journalist described the soccer mom life as "so hectic many barely have time to think about eating, let alone voting" (Goldberg 1996, A-24). Obviously electoral political practices are not the only variety of political activism available, however, no other form of political activism was ever mentioned with respect to the soccer moms; voting was the sole form that soccer mom politics could take in this discourse.

Even 1992's public discussions of women in politics included a more expansive vision of the political work that women were capable of doing, and although mainstream news coverage of Year of the Woman candidates distanced them from feminist politics, a distinct critique of gender-based power differentials was foregrounded in much of this coverage. It was narrowly defined and privileged the circumstances of elite white women, but at least it was there to be found. When it came to soccer moms, the critique was virtually nonexistent, this despite the fact that these women's domestic conditions seemed ripe for interventions, such as the implementation of more equitable arrangements that would allow their husbands to share some of their double-shift burdens. One exception was a post-election op-ed piece in the *Washington Post*, authored by a self-described soccer mom. From her position of authority, she argued that the soccer mom "is tired of bringing home the bacon and then frying it up in a pan. She knows that the deadbeat dad is what you find at the far end of a continuum of men who assume that all of the so-called domestic responsibilities belong to women exclusively" (Foulger 1996, A-21). Hers, however, was the lone voice to break the silence surrounding the difficulties associated with domestic life.

Along with situating them at home, news accounts of soccer moms repeatedly mentioned their racial and class identity. That these women constituted a substantial part of the white, suburban, middle-class demographic became instantly clear through the repeated inclusion of statements describing them in this way, along with charts that provided visual representation of their demographic features. The soccer moms were described as "white, suburban, married women" (Goldberg 1996, A-24), for example, or as "harried-but-concerned suburban homemakers" (Argetsinger 1996, B-1). Although many of the soccer moms were employed outside of their homes at least part time, according to one *New York Times* chart, they still were most frequently referred to as homemakers, and their home and child care activities (but not workplace) were those underscored in news accounts.

Despite the relatively small segment of the electorate that they represented (most accounts claimed that they made up about 8 percent of the electorate), soccer moms were held up as the Holy Grail of the election; the candidate who could capture their vote would win what Tom Brokaw referred to as "this year's political prize" (NBC 1996c). The extent to which they had pro-Clinton leanings seemed contingent upon Clinton's rhetorical focus on the middle class; this sentiment was summed up by an Ohio soccer mom, who said: "[Clinton] seems down to earth. He seems to think about the middle class. He seems to think about the future" (in Tackett 1996, 1-7). The prize seemed to be not only the soccer mom vote but the crucial soccer mom place in the nucleus of the middle class, with all of its associated trappings: whiteness, marriage, and suburbia.

Marital status played a large role in soccer mom narratives as well: these women were married; single soccer moms were rendered invisible in this discourse. In a few accounts, soccer mom voting tendencies were discussed in relation to their husbands—allegedly, the angry white males of the 1994 congressional elections. This tendency to discuss the voting habits of women in contrast to or simply in relation to those of their husbands is a pattern that has its roots as far back as the turn of this century as well; the first post–suffrage era election was one whose results were reported according to gender—and with the conclusion that women voted for the candidates their husbands had. This seeming need to evaluate women's electoral practices in terms of men's—without the converse being true—lingers in our public discourse. This is perhaps a subtle means of suggesting that men make voting decisions and thus occupy a rightful space in the preserve of the public sphere; women are there because of their relationships to their men and to their children.

Campaign appeals to such an exclusive group though did not go unnoticed by the entirety of the journalists and commentators on the soccer mom beat. The author of one post–election op-ed piece from the *Los Angeles Times* argued that the focus on the soccer moms' perceived concerns led to a bias against "poor and minority women." The attention given to soccer moms precluded much—if any—productive campaigning based on the needs of other women. The author also argued that rather than pandering to the soccer moms, Clinton should have instead attempted to "enfranchise all those who [felt] shut out of electoral politics" (R. Rosen 1996, B-9). Yet despite this admonition, the gleeful obsession with soccer moms persisted through the campaign season, complete with its oligarchic overtones.

As the soccer mom identity emerged, couched in essentialist assumptions about sex-appropriate behavior, media texts then articulated this construction to an ideology of consumerism, an insidious suggestion that electoral practices and consumer habits were inseparable. Such a move relies upon a reduction of the concept of citizenship to a one-act show, voting. This obscures all of the other activities possible—and often necessary—to engage as a citizen and to sustain even a modicum of democratic political action. As Stanley Deetz (1992) has argued, "with the democracy-as-election conception, democratic communication is frequently little more than the handmaid of the representation of private interests, rather than intrinsic to the development of community and collective choice" (46). Such a reduction thus further privatizes the collective, potentially community-enhancing process of political work.

Continued mention of soccer mom household income level suggested the presence of a discursive connection between soccer mom voters and soccer mom consumers. This practice could, of course, have been another that simply reinforced the middle-class credentials of soccer moms. The income level of the soccer mom household was, in fact, squarely middle class: incomes from $40,000 to $50,000 and above were mentioned as being average for these households. (Almost every story I reviewed made mention of this.)

In addition to the inclusion of her household income level, however, news narratives often included mention of the products that a typical soccer mom used: the most common reference was to that of her preferred vehicle, the mini-van. This "politically hot" cadre was constituted of "comrades in the minivan brigades" (Goldberg 1996, A-1). Other consumer products mentioned were further evidence of the housewife/consumer, whose purchasing choices were determined primarily by the needs of her family. A reporter for the *San Francisco Chronicle* attended a youth soccer match in affluent Mill Valley, California, as one of the presidential debates was being broadcast. After surveying the scene, he described it in the following fashion:

> Some soccer moms served up the team snacks—organic puffed rice cakes and other Mill Valley staples. Others walked the retrievers, using spring-driven leashes. Some soccer moms waited in their minivans and station wagons, but none had their radios tuned to the presidential debate. One soccer mom was pumping up a soccer ball and another was organizing supermarket coupons in a little folder. (Rubenstein 1996, A-26)

This tendency to situate soccer moms within the realm of their consumer practices results in a characterization of them as consumers primarily and as voters only secondarily (at best).

A representative piece from the *Christian Science Monitor*, which drew a parallel between the coverage of both the summer Olympics and the political conventions and the women in the audience, limited women's power to consumerism.

> This summer, the power of women as consumers was demonstrated on television. NBC packed its Olympics coverage with female-friendly sports, such as gymnastics, and the human-interest stories of the athletes. Human-interest sagas were also prominent during the political conventions, as were female politicians. (Feldman 1996, 3)

Political news coverage thus courted women-as-consumers as their ultimate goal, while women-as-voters or politicians became a means to an end—rather than ends in themselves. This became even more apparent when marketing specialist Gerald Celente, editor and publisher of *The Trends Journal,* was cited as being an authority on women in politics. He commented: "If the Republican Party were a business, and it sold product, this campaign would be a primary textbook example on how to alienate a whole market sector" (quoted in Feldman 1996, 3). Perhaps the Republican Party and the Democratic Party are not profit-making businesses, in a technical sense, yet they function as

profit-generating businesses when they sell political ideology and public policy to demographic groups courted as market sectors. This is true of the soccer mom identity, which was adopted by a number of advertising campaigns,
including one for a soccer superstore; for Mitsubishi and Buick cars; for a variety of mini-vans; for the Chevrolet Malibu;[8] and for Maidenform lingerie.

Although the Chevrolet Malibu is not a mini-van, it is marketed as a reliable, affordable, four-door family car, with "useful trunk and cargo areas." One
advertisement for it appeared in a Chevrolet newsletter and was targeted to an
audience of Chevrolet owners, particularly "soccer moms, dads, and kids." It featured in the foreground a photo of a black Malibu LS Sedan parked on the sideline of a soccer field bathed in golden evening light, while in the background a
group of pint-sized soccer players (all white) rushed toward an adult woman on
the field, whose arms were outstretched to hug. The other adult, a man, stood
by the sideline with his arms dangling, looking a bit like an appendage himself.
To solidify the relationship between soccer and Chevrolet, this ad boasted of
Chevrolet's "partnership with the U.S. Soccer Association and the U.S. Youth
Soccer Association," and of its traveling Great American Soccer Pavilion, where
"visitors can watch a fun presentation on Chevrolet products and soccer trivia"
and "[y]oung soccer fans can . . . test their abilities in Soccer Skill Games and
play interactive soccer video games." The soccer mom functions here as the link
between Chevrolet and youth soccer—a connection that may not have been
apparent without the beneficent activity of Chevrolet and General Motors.

Lest media audiences conclude that a soccer mom is simply a *hausfrau*
chauffeur, Maidenform rescues her image by moving her into the bedroom. In a
New York Times story about a new advertising campaign for Maidenform ("Maidenform Unhooked"), the agency executive in charge of the campaign explained
it by saying, "[W]omen now play a lot of very different roles—mother, wife, soccer mom, lover, employer—sometimes they want to take time out to be a woman
and have some fun" (in Elliott 1997, D-2). The campaign was based on two goals:
"infusing the brand identity with a persona that will be perceived as liberating
but not lubricious, and reflecting the significant changes in consumer lifestyles
without being prurient or prudish" (ibid.). Maidenform thus fills out the figure
of the soccer mom by attending to her very private activities and desires.

THE SOCCER MOM MYSTIQUE

Advertisements such as those I have described work to cross-fertilize product
and market sector, developing and encouraging particular consumer behaviors

all the while. However manipulative, this practice is standard in the world of advertising and marketing, which is encroaching upon electoral politics quickly—in large part through constructing identities for women.

Using a commercial/market model to explain and understand electoral behavior, as well as to pitch campaigns, has become so common that it barely evokes a mention in commentary about contemporary politics. This metaphor though is worth noticing; its message is that voting behavior and consumer behavior are equivalent. With the existence of the commercial imperative driving today's mainstream media, news content included, it is no wonder that this model is deployed to such an extent; that the production of an electoral aggregate would rely upon the same tactics as the production of a consumer aggregate should perhaps come as no surprise. As Daniel Hallin concluded after studying the commercialization of the news, the "major relation of political communication has indeed become a relation of seller and consumer" (1994, 35). However, while not a surprise, this should be an issue of concern, particularly to those interested in reducing the numbers of and reasons for disenfranchised citizens. One subtle but persistent message here is that the ideal voter is equivalent to the ideal media audience member: a well-paid consumer whose disposable income goes largely toward product purchases.

Commercial media industries have moved to ever-tighter symbiotic relationships between themselves and advertisers (Turow 1997; McChesney 1999). Such a dependent relationship increases the chance that editorial decisions will favor individual advertisers and corporate thinking. This, according to Douglas Underwood, results in "marketing-minded editors" who are happy to play a role in "the corporate reshaping of the news" (1995, 147).

Bagdikian warns that this increased collaboration between advertisers and political journalists has become "instrumental in degrading the basic unit of American government"—that is, the democratic electoral process (1997, 188). Robert McChesney (1997) expands on this point with his observation that a dependence upon advertising dollars results in a focus upon "targeted markets" rather than citizens: thus media managers "aggressively court the affluent while the balance of the population is pushed to the side" (24). McChesney warns that media oligopoly influence, in the end,

> has negative implications for the exercise of political democracy: it encourages a weak political culture that makes depoliticization, apathy and selfishness rational choices for the citizenry, and it permits the business and commercial interests that actually rule U.S. society to have inordinate influence over media content. (1997, 7)

The soccer mom image represents an example of such a targeted market. That is, her identity as a political force is far less important than her identity as a consumer with a solid, disposable income. Her political interests are only alluded to, or are cast in the vaguest of terms. When her politics *are* mentioned, they tend to reinforce essentialist, traditional, domestic concerns—concerns well suited to product, as opposed to policy, intervention. This tendency is one that can push women out of the electoral political power centers—such as the House of Representatives or the Senate—by suggesting that they are perhaps more appropriately situated in their homes, raising their children. The spaces of the political and the domestic are constructed as mutually exclusive ones, with an emphasis on the appropriateness of the domestic.

Communications historian Lynn Spigel (1992) has noted that the process of creating a consumer identity for women—through the interplay of messages between advertisements and TV programs or magazine content—has existed since the beginning of commercial television, when network executives discovered that women (especially those between the ages of twenty-five and thirty-four) made the majority of decisions about purchasing and purchased products for their entire household. Thus the networks began a process of intensive work to deliver these women to advertisers, labeling their demographic group as the "age of acquisition" (82).[9] Acquisition of what? Consumer products. With incomes of $40,000 or more, soccer moms can afford to consume—at least modestly. Virginia Nightingale (1990) notes that in television, program content is thus driven by this relationship and

> motivated by women's role as prime domestic consumer/purchaser. Television channels desire women audiences not in their own right, but for their attraction to advertisers. And advertisers want women not as women but as consumers, and even more as purchasers for other consumers (i.e., the rest of the family). The place of shopping in women's culture is affirmed by television's definition of women. (30–31)

Although Nightingale's words address entertainment television, the need to attract advertisers and hail consumers is the same for any commercial medium or genre. The latter is particularly the case when entertainment and news departments of the same media organization are vying for audiences using similar methods (see, e.g., Hallin 1994). In an address to the Association for Women in Communication, long-time journalist Ray Suarez lamented bluntly that "the news business, as a rule, is far more interested in furthering your life as a consumer than your life as a citizen" (1998, A6). It remains to be seen whether the soccer mom identity could be a part of the trend toward creating what Suarez, elsewhere in his address, refers to as "uninformed citizenry," but it is fairly clear that this trope is a restrictive one in terms of what it allows readers and viewers to envision for women in/and politics. In this sense it also is regressive in that it seems to overlook the myriad *other* identities (outside of parenting) that women live—publicly and privately—that contribute to the richness of their lives.

This construction ties in well to the behaviors that Dow (1996) notes are prevalent in television advertising aimed at women: "caretaking . . . ranging from cooking, cleaning, and child-rearing to more general qualities of nurturance and emotional support" (xxi). Promoting the idea that women are natural caretakers and nurturers virtually ensures that they should be uniquely relegated to the realm of the private, but of course these are not the only behaviors and attributes that soccer moms exhibit; they also work outside of their homes and thus are expected to be competent, hard workers in a corporate-industrial setting as well as in the domestic sphere.[10] However, rather than addressing these strains as being indicative of larger structural problems, mainstream television and print accounts of soccer moms suggest that the solutions are individual; the road out of the morass can be constructed on personal choice—much of it commercial in nature.

The soccer mom's demographic identity is one that can be deployed without a substantive debate on the issues underlying soccer mom life. Although the substance of much of the soccer moms' words indicates that they are tired and overworked, this receives little commentary. Many seem to be in need of assistance of one kind or another, assistance that, fifteen to twenty years hence, would have been the subject of feminist commentary and political agitation. Rather than engaging a substantive critique of the domestic and professional expectations of soccer moms, however, the label and the ensuing media discussions tend to diminish them in importance, make them seem trivial or cute, and/or link them to consumer products—as if a mini-van or organic rice cakes could address the cultural and structural inequities that conspire to make even middle-class women's lives difficult. Almost nowhere is there a mention of the women who are not among the privileged soccer mom cadre: single women, women of color, and women who are not middle class. The lives of these women are far from those described in the soccer mom discourse, yet their needs could perhaps be remedied if they too had been the subject of the same intense media scrutiny directed at soccer moms. These women's needs for political empowerment are just as great, if not greater, than those of the soccer moms.

A larger but nevertheless bothersome point about the way soccer moms get deployed in the synergy between marketing political candidates and marketing, say, lingerie, is one that Susan Willis brings up in a discussion of how gender is constituted through everyday life practices: "[W]hen gender is assimilated to the commodity, it is conceived as something fixed and frozen: a number of sexually defined attributes that denote either masculinity or femininity on the supermarket shelf of gender possibilities" (1991, 23). This is ultimately what is at stake with this construction of soccer moms: the gendered conditions of their lives may become "fixed and frozen" in public discourse, naturalized and commonsensical in the collective mind of the public. The conditions of their existence appear unavailable for criticism and intervention—more like "the way things are" for contemporary women. In providing gender, personality, and drama to the political race of 1996, the soccer mom figure simultaneously elides the material conditions of many real women's existences.

Thus any contribution the soccer mom trope makes to our culture is likely to benefit a few auto manufacturers and marketing firms but sidestep the needs and good of the many women who struggle in their private lives with burdens that could perhaps be relieved with appropriate public policies and programs. McMillan and Cheney (1996) have argued that the "student-as-consumer metaphor reinforces individualism at the expense of community" (9). I want to make a similar point about the construction of the soccer mom trope: that it contributes largely to and reinforces beliefs about the appropriateness of women as being apolitical and well suited to the individual fortresses of their suburban homes. This distracts from a very different view of women: as electoral activists, capable of being both successful *and* comfortable in public endeavors. The aim of this chapter in contrasting this view of women with soccer moms has been to problematize the use of the soccer mom trope by illuminating its articulation to advertising and consumerism. This mediated articulation distances women from politics yet marks their strategic importance for marketers and advertisers. Moreover, it works to collapse the distinction between democratic politics and commercialism. Foregrounding this link reveals the insidious end to which a swing vote label may be used, particularly within the context of the gender gap. It would be disappointing indeed if women's gains in politics in the last decade were obscured by such an exploitation of the gender gap concept, for although the realm of electoral politics is a far-from-perfect space, it offers the possibility of greater and more enduring benefits than those offered by advertisers; it is a space in which to bring about positive, meaningful change for many women rather than for an elite minority of corporate executives.

The soccer mom identity contributes as well to a postfeminist logic, the "common sense" of news coverage of women in the context of electoral politics. The attempt to fix meaning to women voters follows patterns similar to those in accounts of women as politicians or, in the Hill–Thomas hearings, as *de facto* public leaders. By persistently associating women in electoral politics—in any capacity—with whiteness, suburbia, motherhood, and the middle class, the subject position available to women and men (and, importantly, young people as well) becomes increasingly restricted for its political potential but unlimited in its commercial appeal.

CHAPTER FIVE

"Pray Tell, Who Is the 'She'"?

Campaign 2000, or the Year of One Woman

When syndicated columnist Maureen Dowd posed the question, "pray tell, who is the 'she'"? early in the 2000 campaign year, she was referring specifically to one of presidential candidate George W. Bush's criticisms of his then-opponent Senator John McCain: "Oftentimes," Bush complained, "politics is nothing but this 'he said, she said' type of politics." Dowd wondered about who this "she" could be in a verbal sparring match that involved a grand total of two people, both male (2000, A-21). Dowd's arch question was intended to underscore another of Bush's numerous verbal gaffes on the campaign trail, but I use her question for another purpose: to point to the near-total absence of women—as either voters or politicians—in media accounts of the campaigns for the presidency and for Congress during the months that Campaign 2000 comprised.

News accounts gestured occasionally toward women as undecided swing voters or as moving predictably toward gender-gap voting patterns, but reporters seemed to have no success in constructing a consistent bloc identity for women—although more women than ever were running for the House of Representatives and the Senate during 2000. Instead of rallying around the largest group of women to run for national office (and then win), news accounts focused almost exclusively on only one woman's quest to win public office: Hillary Rodham Clinton's candidacy for the Senate in New York.[1] Seven women ran for the Senate, and 122 ran for House seats, resulting in a total of sixty-five women elected to the House of Representatives and the Senate.[2] In this sense, it was more a "Year of the Woman" in politics than 1992 was, but as far as mainstream media were concerned, it was a "Year of *One* Woman," and that one was Hillary Rodham Clinton. Between January 1 and November 7, 2000, news workers made a few, ultimately faltering, efforts to latch onto a gender identity that would characterize Campaign 2000, but none even approached the success of the "Year of the Woman" or "Soccer Mom." Even Cokie and Steve Roberts' "Dot-Com Mom" (2000, 7) could not capture the cultural momentum necessary for it to be used in any but their own accounts. Instead, news workers fell back on regular invocations of their old standby, the gender gap.

In this chapter, I examine television news accounts of Hillary Rodham Clinton's ultimately successful Senate campaign, broadcast between January 1 and November 7, 2000. This period represents the most important part of her campaign, including her move to New York State so that she could become a legal resident, the official announcement of her candidacy, the visits she made around the state, the debates, and her eventual triumph over her second opponent, Republican House member Rick Lazio. I restricted the analysis to television texts because of TV news's perceived credibility for news content,[3] and because of its national reach. The news stories I reviewed were available to the national television news audience, making them potentially more influential in guiding public perceptions than newspapers or newsmagazines—each of which has a much smaller reach. And newsmagazines are taking a turn toward emphasizing soft news over hard news in order to cope with increasing revenue losses, resulting in far fewer stories about politics, for example, and more about celebrities and New Age spirituality (Kuczynski 2001).

As I have in the chapters preceding this one, I examine these accounts for what they may say about feminism as it is constructed in and through the news—in this instance, feminism as it is mediated at the turn of a new century. Like the political women I reviewed in chapters 2–4, Hillary Rodham Clinton seems to inspire a mixture of respect and disdain from media personnel, and this mixture is more often than not structured by patterned references that reveal their creators' perspectives on women, power, and public life. Unlike the identities found in the preceding chapters, however, Hillary Rodham Clinton's candidacy represents one point in a schizophrenic range of treatments by media personnel who have, at times, seemed hell-bent on destroying her public image, if not destroying her altogether. Television coverage of Hillary, while explicitly acknowledging the novelty of this First Lady's candidacy, also adhered to the time-worn formulas that reporters used with political women during the

1990s: constructing them as neoliberal, postfeminist subjects, a process that results in naturalizing whiteness, middle-class to elite class privilege, and an implicit reliance on cultural or difference feminist principles to reinforce certain notions about the relationship between public and private sphere activities for women (see chapter 3).

The schizophrenia in representations of Hillary Rodham Clinton may betray a fear of feminism among the news workers on the Hillary beat (Jamieson 1995; Pollitt 1993). Their apparent trepidation at dealing with a well-spoken, intelligent woman who was unapologetic about her intellectual strengths was particularly evident during her early years on the national media scene.[4] As Kathleen Hall Jamieson (1995) concludes after scrutinizing coverage of Hillary during the 1992 presidential campaign and her early years as First Lady, this fear of feminism has spawned an inability in news workers covering Hillary to allow her relationship with both the private *and* the public spheres. In other words, the notion that women can be successful with both their public *and* private sphere responsibilities is repeatedly dismissed in news accounts of Hillary Clinton as she campaigned in 1992 and during her first couple of years as First Lady of the United States. Jamieson points out that media narratives about Hillary could not reconcile her feminist public persona with her parenthood. If she were a feminist, the logic went, she would have had to jettison her conjugal and parental duties; if she were a good wife and mother, she certainly could not be a strong feminist. The double bind that Jamieson argues Hillary was placed in is thus a classic one in its recurrent application to political women: the public/private bind, inflected with a fear of feminism. Betty Houchin Winfield (1997) makes a similar point about Hillary but calls the dilemma the "confusing paradox of independence and dependence, of attempting to have it both ways" (175).

Hillary Rodham Clinton has elicited controversy from the beginning of her appearances in the national media, in 1992, at the side of her husband, then-candidate Bill Clinton. Her conjugal tie to a presidential candidate dovetailed with her own successes in the professional and political arenas, and made her an ideal *ex officio* player among political women in the Year of the Woman narrative. A high achiever both academically and professionally, she graduated from Wellesley College and Yale Law School and then practiced law in Washington, D. C., and Little Rock, Arkansas. As a partner in the now infamous Rose Law Firm, she was rated one of the country's 100 best lawyers (Martin 1993). Hillary appears to be the quintessential liberal feminist success story: she is smart, competent, professional, and able to answer the many demands placed on her by a daughter, a power marriage with the former president of the United

States, being the chief architect of health care reform in the United States, and her duties as the junior senator from New York. As First Lady, Hillary's public role was not congressionally mandated, yet her years of political and legal experience prior to becoming First Lady, her prominent role in campaigning for Bill Clinton and other Democratic candidates, and her ability to succeed as an attorney, despite the gender bias for which her profession is notorious, suggested that she was well qualified to be a policy maker. When campaigning, Bill and Hillary Clinton also were not shy about discussing the important role that she would play in a Clinton presidency, referring to his possible win as a "two-for-one presidency" (Winfield 1997, 176).

Early in the 1992 presidential campaign, journalists reacted with predictable knee-jerk criticism of what they perceived as Hillary's power over Bill and his platform. This is standard stuff: Nancy Reagan and Rosalyn Carter also were subjected to journalists' unease with their perceived "power behind the throne." In Hillary's case, this reaction occurred surrounding two comments she made about her personal discomfort with traditional notions of womanhood. The first comment, made on *60 Minutes* and circulated widely, was apropos of a discussion of Bill's affair with a nightclub singer, Gennifer Flowers, and its effect on their marriage. In defense of her decision to stay with Bill, despite this peccadillo, she declared that she was "not some little woman standing by her man like Tammy Wynette." No public opinion polls were conducted after Hillary made this remark, yet journalists labeled it a huge public relations error with the potential to erode Bill's popular support, particularly among rural, working-class voters, the "'country music vote'" (Corcoran 1993, 28). A few months later, reporters again took Hillary to task for a remark that she made in defense of her career choice after then-candidate Jerry Brown had accused her of acting improperly as an attorney during her husband's reign as governor. This time, she said, "I suppose I could have stayed home and baked cookies and had teas. But what I decided to do was fulfill my profession."[5] The cadres of journalists accustomed to less frank language from political spouses—especially wives—behaved as though she had confessed to cannibalism. She was branded by *U.S. News & World Report* as an "overbearing yuppie wife from hell" (Jamieson 1995, 39) and, like Rosemary's baby, the Hillary Factor was born.

The Hillary Factor referred to the sway that Hillary could have had in influencing voters to vote for or against Bill Clinton. In a poll commissioned by *Time* and CNN two months before the election, 74 percent of voters said that their decision about voting for or against Bill Clinton would *not* be affected by their perception of Hillary (Carlson 1992). Despite this result, *Time* magazine's September 14, 1992, cover story (which included the results of this poll) was entitled, "The Hillary Factor: Is She Helping or Hurting Her Husband?"[6] It is worth mentioning here that poll results can vary dramatically based on the size and characteristics of the respondents sampled, and on the wording of the questions and responses. Burrell's (1997) analysis of polling around Hillary Clinton in 1993, for example, reveals large differences in the results of polls—particularly between the *Time*/CNN poll (above) and a CBS/*New York Times* poll conducted at the same time. Comparing the results of different polls is much like comparing apples and oranges and in this case resulted in different interpretations of Hillary's popularity as First Lady (Burrell 1997, 45–46).

The story that accompanied these poll results in *Time*, authored by Margaret Carlson, appeared to side with Hillary's detractors and chided Hillary for daring to challenge accepted norms of behavior: "Mrs. Clinton would have done well at the outset [of the campaign] to have conformed more to the traditional campaign rules for aspiring First Ladies: gaze like Nancy Reagan, soothe like Barbara Bush, and look like Jacqueline Kennedy. By not doing that, to some extent, Hillary played into the hands of her critics" (Carlson 1992, 30). Journalists at this stage responded to Hillary as though she were untamed, radically unpredictable, and quite problematic to her husband's campaign. By not capitulating to a stereotype of feminine submission, she was cast as being somehow deserving of the egregiously critical commentary heaped upon her.

This history of biased treatment followed Hillary Clinton into her Senate campaign, as did the fallout from two major events with significant influence both on media representation generally and on the politics of representing Hillary Rodham Clinton and feminism specifically: the Federal Telecommunications Act of 1996 (FTA) and the impeachment of President Clinton in 1999. The FTA is considered by many "one of the three or four most important federal laws of this generation" (McChesney 1997, 42). The FTA relaxed or eradicated most broadcast and telecommunication regulations that protected consumers and communities against market domination by one or a handful of powerful corporations. It spurred a flurry of mergers and acquisitions that resulted in a highly consolidated field: when 2000 began, only six corporations owned virtually all of the mainstream media outlets in the United States, including those that controlled such services as wireless, broadband, and Digital Signal Lines (DSL) (Bagdikian 2000). The structural and content effects of the FTA's passage in February 1996 were not great by the time the 1996 campaign was in full swing, but in the intervening four years they became increasingly evident and significant. Eventually they came to influence media content and circulation profoundly.

Fairness and Accuracy in Reporting (FAIR), for example, showed that the three major television networks' nightly newscasts had dedicated 503 minutes of their programs to Cuban refugee and rescued miracle child Elián Gonzalez during 2000. These same newscasts spent only 483 minutes on coverage of the New Hampshire Primary, Super Tuesday, the Republican Convention, the Democratic Convention, and all three of the presidential debates—*combined*: twenty minutes less than on one little boy whose impact on democratic practice generally could hardly compare to the events preceding the November presidential election (FAIR 2001, 2). This may appear to be an odd inclusion, given the topic of this chapter, but it richly illustrates a trend in political reporting that is relevant to the way in which candidates are covered (or not) by mainstream media outlets. In the chapters preceding this one, I argued that structural changes in and between mainstream media outlets influence news coverage. The corporate bottom line and parent corporation/owner dictates play a significant role in determining which news stories are selected for broadcast or publication and, importantly, how those stories are framed and expressed for readers and viewers. According to an executive at Rupert Murdoch's News Corporation in 1998, "We decide what the news is. The news is what we tell you it is" (in McChesney 1999, 275). (For an extensive discussion of further ramifications of the FTA, see Bagdikian 2000, preface to the 6th edition, and McChesney 1999.)

Another event, subsequent to the FTA, began to unfold in 1998 and influenced public discourse about political women and feminists in the years between the 1996 and 2000 campaigns: former President Bill Clinton's affair with Monica Lewinsky, a White House intern, and the subsequent impeachment that transpired from it. These events had an infinite number of facets, of course, and were judicially, legislatively, and discursively complicated, to say the least, but they generated repercussions well into the 2000 campaign, both for Democratic presidential candidate Al Gore and for Senate candidate Hillary Rodham Clinton. To a lesser extent, these events affected reporting on women as voters and as candidates, yet one could discern their impact, particularly in discussions of women voters' "Clinton fatigue" or in pointed questions to Hillary about the voting public's sense of satisfaction with her response to the affair, once it had been made public.

The affair between Bill Clinton and Monica Lewinsky appeared as a rumor in August 1998 and raised issues that feminists were called on to defend and interpret. Although Lewinsky's and Clinton's statements about the affair (once Clinton had owned up to it) strongly argued for its consensual nature (i.e., no sexual harassment), many pundits and politicians were not satisfied with this explanation and insisted that the power differential between a president and White House interns is such that *any* sexual contact must be considered sexual harassment; power being an undeniable aphrodisiac, they said, the White House intern had been tacitly coerced into assent. News organizations summoned feminists to comment on Clinton's alleged sexual misconduct, as though they held the franchise on public discussions of sexual harassment. If they pointed out, as Gloria Steinem did, that consensual sex really is not sexual harassment by anyone's standards, and, besides, Monica Lewinsky—and not Bill Clinton—claimed to have initiated the affair, they were discursively flogged for abandoning the sisterhood (Deem 1999). (Incidentally, this is a sisterhood that women have been vilified for supporting in other circumstances [Douglas 1994].)

Feminism did not fare well in mainstream media during this period, nor did the First Feminist, Hillary Rodham Clinton. When the affair was first alleged, in August 1998, the Clintons denied it publicly and assiduously. Hillary made a public defense of her husband after the allegations became public, and she attributed rumors of the affair to a "vast Right Wing conspiracy" that, she claimed, had been responsible for unpleasant, unfounded accusations that followed her husband from Arkansas to the campaign trail of 1992 all the way to the White House. Although it is arguable that such a conspiracy fed the venomous treatment of the Clintons in all manner of news outlets throughout the Clinton presidency, it was no longer debatable whether rumors of the affair were just that. Once an investigation into Clinton's intimate life had begun, Monica Lewinsky came forth, started to talk (albeit reluctantly), and Clinton eventually confessed to the affair. He also revealed that Hillary's earlier defense of him had, for her part, been sincere—she was unaware of his duplicity in this matter. Hillary was cleared of lying on his behalf in this instance and, for the first time, public sentiment toward her seemed to improve; as more information was revealed, she looked like a sympathetic character, one whose experience had likely been shared by many viewers and readers of the news: she had been betrayed by an unfaithful spouse. The conventional media wisdom seemed to be that her impeachment and post–impeachment image earned her improved treatment; with her marriage extremely shaky, she had indeed chosen to stand by her man to help him through the difficult months of 1998 and 1999. Apparently this was the correct choice in the eyes of feminism-averse reporters and editors.

However, Blanche McCrary Boyd, in a *Ms.* magazine essay published during Hillary's campaign, illustrates how divided even feminists were about Hillary in this context. Employees at the magazine were conflicted about what she should have been expected to do, as a feminist and a woman, regarding her husband's dalliances and what, if anything, her campaign portended for feminism. Boyd's assessment of the *Ms.* feminists' reactions to Hillary Clinton is that they sympathized with Hillary's difficulty in retaining any dignity throughout the publicity around the Lewinsky affair and subsequent impeachment.

> [W]hat an amazing response, in such circumstances, to choose to run for office. In a single stroke she affirmed her belief in herself as a woman, her independence from Bill, and her continuing faith in "the system." So whether she wins or loses, it's a win. . . . One wincing irony is that, if she ever does become president, it will be partly because of Monica; an important piece of history will play itself out as a drama between women. The subtle but indispensable dignity that Hillary developed during the Starr investigations and the impeachment trial is the result of public suffering. She has become more human, more recognizable, her rigidity transmuted into an admirable composure. All politicians have to press the flesh. Hillary seems to understand the flesh's limitations. (Boyd 2000, 52–53)

Occurring alongside the presidential affair and impeachment was public discussion of major campaign finance reform and the first stirrings of the McCain–Feingold bill (after the bill's sponsors, Senators John McCain of Arizona and Russ Feingold of Wisconsin). Although a full discussion of the contents and implications of the McCain–Feingold bill is well beyond the scope of this chapter, one aspect of it is pertinent: the media's involvement in raising the costs associated with running for public office in the United States, and how this connection was sidestepped in both the McCain–Feingold bill and in much of the mainstream media's postmortem accounts of Campaign 2000. The Alliance for Better Campaigns, a bipartisan political research group, reports that local television stations "profiteered" on campaign advertisements during the 2000 campaign and thus made a major contribution to candidates' needs for exorbitant amounts of money to finance all aspects of their campaigns. For political candidates, advertising is the most important way to publicize stances on various issues. Today, television advertising in an election campaign is like oxygen; without it, a candidacy expires.

Since 1971, the television industry has been operating under a congressional mandate to charge political candidates what is known as the "Lowest Unit Charge" or LUC, for advertising time. Congress mandated this for all commercial broadcasters in exchange for their use of the publicly held airwaves. While the LUC differs from community to community and is published on each local station's rate card, it is understood to be the least expensive rate for buying ad time. At times other than during election campaigns, the LUC is extended to those advertisers who have consistently bought advertising time from a given station. The rub with the LUC is that television stations can preempt those ads charged LUC rates, and they can do this without prior notification of the advertiser (Alliance for Better Campaigns 2001, 1). This holds true too for politicians who have been charged the LUC rate, and although a candidate whose ad has been preempted may have his or her money refunded or have the ad aired at a different time,

> this is cold comfort for the candidate. Unlike many product advertisers, whose chief objective is to build brand loyalty over the long haul and who can therefore afford to be flexible about when their ads run, candidate advertisers need assurance their ads will run exactly when and where they place them. . . . Local stations understand these dynamics and many stations exploit them. They charge a high premium for non-preemptible ad time, and as Election Day approaches and demand for such time keeps rising, the premium keeps rising with it. (Alliance for Better Campaigns 2001, 1)

Although the McCain–Feingold bill does not specifically address this relationship, a different provision—a bill that may be introduced later by Senator McCain—would mandate free airtime for candidates, thus diminishing their need to buy advertising (Broder 2001, 4). Naturally, this upset broadcasters and their lobby group, the very powerful National Association of Broadcasters (NAB): television stations raked in over $800 million in ad spending alone during the campaign ("Campaign record" 2001, 4). The NAB argues that a free airtime mandate would be an unconstitutional infringement on broadcasters' First Amendment rights, that the Alliance for Better Campaigns miscalculated the candidates' charges, and that cost is not a factor when candidates try to determine the "strategic impact" of their television ads (McConnell 2001, 11). Broadcasters claim that they charge a "fair-market price for a fair-market product" (Albiniak 2001, 16).

What comes out of this debate is some discussion of the ways in which the television industry contributes to costs associated with a campaign. The discussion questions the industry's motives for their charges and brings to light two facts that broadcasters would rather keep under wraps (McChesney 1999): (1) that they operate using a publicly held resource—the airwaves—and (2) that as beneficiaries of this privilege, they must uphold the PICON standard (Public Interest Convenience or Necessity), a standard clearly upheld in the provisions of the FTA.[7] Questioning whether broadcasters meet or attempt to meet their responsibilities to publics rarely occurs in mainstream media—news or entertainment—for one predominant reason: broadcasters do not want to draw

attention to the fact that they can be held publicly accountable for the content
that they air (Bagdikian 2000; McChesney 1999). Their reluctance to engage
the topic notwithstanding, broadcasters' business practices influence content in
a fashion that is problematic for electoral politics. In a democratic society, it is
of utmost importance that citizens be able to receive an adequate amount of
meaningful and truthful information about the candidates who will, when
elected, be making important decisions that affect the micro- and macro-issues
structuring everyday life. (If preventing that from occurring is not a violation
of the PICON standard, then I cannot imagine what would be.)

Television's role in campaign finance contributes significantly to a climate in which congressional and presidential races are attempted only by
those candidates who have raised or can afford to raise substantial amounts of
money. It also suggests that the candidates who can afford to run for office
must be treated in news reports with care, lest they take unfavorable positions
on media corporations once they are elected. Policies that benefit media corporations are not taken for granted by these corporations; they are achieved
only after intense lobbying and gracious treatment of "right-thinking" legislators and candidates. This may explain why so little substantive information
appeared about political candidates on television—in favor of endless discussions about the fate of a marooned Cuban boy, for example—and why NBC
opted not to carry the first presidential debate of the 2000 season, instead airing an American League World Series play-off game between the New York
Yankees and the Seattle Mariners.

By now, the relationship of broadcasting to electoral politics has become
one in which sensationalistic topics and coverage have substantially displaced
political topics and coverage, while political advertising—and the amounts
charged to candidates by broadcasters—has increased. This relationship is one
that clearly benefits broadcasters and their parent corporations, while it places
citizens who want to learn about candidates' positions at a rather large disadvantage. Not only is the type of political information that dominates television
found in the form of advertising, and thus inherently biased, but political advertising also can contain false or misleading information; because it is protected
by the First Amendment, it is not held even to the same standard of truth as
consumer product advertising (McChesney 1999, 262).

More often than not, news (and particularly television news) emphasizes
those themes that titillate rather than critically examine, that encourage consumerism rather than foster citizenship. These priorities were likely responsible
for relegating the campaigns of female candidates in 2000 to the bottom of the
issue heap. Although these campaigns did not have the same sort of "flash

point" event to rally their backers as women had in 1992 after the Hill–Thomas hearings, they possessed novelty value in their sheer numbers—something that suggested an overall acceptance of women being fit to hold public office. Had their only competition in the "public attention market" (McManus 1995, 315) been the lackluster presidential campaign of George W. Bush and Al Gore, surely their presence would have earned some national news attention, but the competitor these candidates faced when vying for national attention was none other than Hillary Rodham Clinton, First Lady of the United States turned New York Senate candidate. The novelty of a "lame duck" First Lady running for elected office as she left her post was extreme, to say the very least, and when that First Lady is Hillary Rodham Clinton, the stakes for coverage inch up even higher: as a news peg, she had generated reams of coverage through- out her husband's two terms as president; as an outspoken First Lady and accomplished attorney who stayed with an openly philandering husband who also had been impeached, she had elicited an extraordinary amount of media attention and controversy. Hillary was her own flash point, while the other female candidates had nothing comparable—and certainly nothing that could compete with the Hillary-hating cottage industry that had grown up around her in the national media during her eight years as First Lady.

There was probably no contest here for news workers whose choice was between Hillary Rodham Clinton—a perpetual source of easily procured material—and 129 relatively unknown women who wanted to win elective office. Even without Hillary's history of drawing extreme responses, she would have been a more likely candidate for coverage simply as a result of routine: the press had become accustomed to covering her, they were familiar with her background, and they had in place familiar and well-worn modes of coverage that they could invoke instantaneously.[8] Another possible factor to explain the onslaught of attention given to Hillary over her sister candidates is that of unre- solved conflicts about feminism simmering under the surface of (mostly male) baby boomer news workers' collective consciousness. Katha Pollitt makes the argument that Bill Clinton's administration was

> closely bound up with issues of gender: the social shift to more egalitarian marriages; the growing political power of women, who voted for Bill Clinton by an eight-point margin, two and a half times that of male vot- ers; the mainstreaming of a popular you-can-do-it feminism; and a well- spring of support, disproportionately female, for renewed government activism in the domestic sphere. . . . Attacking H.R.C. is a way of attack- ing the broad social and political transformations without actually making a case against them. (1993, 659)

Jamieson (1995, 22–52) echoes this sentiment, labeling Hillary as a social "Rorschach Test" for this reason. I would add another factor: the postfeminist common sense that I have argued informs news workers' narratives about women in electoral politics. By 2000, postfeminism was as commonsensical as the inverted pyramid structure of news writing, and surely it did not hurt that Hillary's political platform fit well with the neoliberalism espoused by and beneficial to the media oligopoly. For these reasons, Hillary Clinton's campaign eclipsed the campaigns of the other women candidates in news stories.

Mrs. Clinton Goes to Capitol Hill

It is hardly an original observation about television news today—or any other news medium—to say that it is superficial; nevertheless, the defining characteristic of television news coverage of Hillary Clinton's campaign to win a Senate seat was superficiality: a focus on the personalities and panics[9] of the campaign rather than on the substance of the candidates' issues. Although this is part of a more general trend in journalism toward "soft news" over hard news stories (Patterson 2001), such superficiality has consequences for how feminism is treated. Not only does this superficiality affect democratic practice as it is embodied in active citizenship,[10] it affects how we might imagine feminism. In an election year that could have produced stories about the unprecedentedly large numbers of women running for national office, instead there were stories about the campaign of only one woman—and even these stories were detail- and substance-deficient. Superficial narratives about one woman thus stand in for political women generally and for feminism at the turn of this century.

Television news stories were woefully short of meaningful details about Hillary Clinton's stance on the issues she named as hers (this is true of her opponents' coverage too), leaving voters who relied entirely on television for their candidate information virtually no substance with which to make their decisions. The issues Hillary named repeatedly as her own were "reasonable gun safety regulations . . . education, health care, the future of Social Security and Medicare, children and families' issues" (see, e.g., WNBC 2000) and "choice," though choice for what is not specified (ABC 2000c). In one program, Hillary's communications director, Howard Wolfson, provided information about her position with respect to some of these issues. Like most other stories, this one featured comments that promoted Hillary's issues as being of universal, or at least New York-wide, importance; this perhaps was a move designed to combat criticism of her as a carpetbagger who knew little or nothing about the politics of the state or its famous largest city. One clip of Hillary on CNN featured her recapitulation of this point: "I believe that the issues that I've worked a lifetime on, that you worked with me on here, are the issues that really matter in people's lives" (CNN 2000h). One caller to a CNN program thought that Hillary was "interested in anything and everything that concerns people" (CNN 2000g). To underscore differences between Hillary Rodham Clinton and Mayor Rudolph Giuliani (still her opponent at that point), Wolfson spelled out some details on her positions.

> The mayor has scrupulously avoided taking positions on Senate issues, but from time to time we're able to draw him out and to get a sense of how he'd vote as senator. For instance, on the issue of the budget—it was the major issue in this year's congressional debate—eight . . . almost an 800 billion dollar tax scheme that the Republicans put forth that would've jeopardized the future of Social Security and Medicare. Rudy Giuliani would've voted for it, Hillary Clinton would've voted against it. That is the most important issue for our future. How are we going to keep this economic progress going? There is a clear difference between these two candidates. On the issue of health care, Hillary Clinton, as I said, wants to pass a Patients Bill of Rights so that you can sue your HMO if your HMO mistreats you. . . . On the issue of education, Hillary Clinton has been a lifelong champion of education. She knows that we need to raise standards, but we also need to invest in our schools that are crumbling. (WNBC 2000)

Wolfson's discussion was the only one among the stories I reviewed that contained details that voters might use to discern differences between Hillary Rodham Clinton and Rudolph Giuliani or Rick Lazio. Perhaps this lack of detail came from her inexperience with holding an elected office; her opponents had held public office, and Giuliani had attracted negative attention while mayor of New York City when NYPD officers were accused of torturing and killing unarmed black men. Commentators and supporters, unable to draw on Hillary's past voting record, had to rely on what she had done as First Lady, first of Arkansas and then of the United States. So viewers learned, for example, that she had been a "highly effective advocate for early childhood education" (CNN 2000g) without further information about how, where, and when she exerted this effectiveness.

In this context, likely reasons for such superficiality would include (perhaps as its most important reason) a need to appeal to the advertisers on whose revenues television budgets are entirely dependent. Substantive descriptions of

Hillary's plans to improve upstate New York's economy, for example, never appeared in these news stories—local or national; instead, reporters used news time for things like chats about how her press conference skills had improved over the course of the campaign. Hard news that involves controversial subjects—particularly broadcast news—skirted in favor of softer, feature-type topics to avoid provoking advertisers is a trend that has had ample documentation over the last two decades (see, e.g., Bagdikian 2000; Turow 1997). Coverage of Hillary Clinton's campaign was no exception.

What does exist in the coverage, superficial as it is, is a pattern of constructing Hillary as a neoliberal, postfeminist subject, consistent with the manner in which Year of the Woman candidates were covered in 1992. News accounts of her campaign included numerous references to her as a "New Democrat," an identity most often associated with the Democratic Leadership Council that spawned the Clinton–Gore alliance and President Clinton's economic, media, and welfare reform policies (see chapter 3). Hillary Clinton's representation also could be described as postfeminist: her politics are so far beyond feminism that the word was never mentioned, nor were any feminist principles invoked in TV news reports of her campaign. The meanings that were ascribed to Hillary's postfeminist representation reveal some beliefs associated with the "difference" feminism that has emerged from the work of Carol Gilligan (1982). Television news foregrounded Hillary's web of relations from which she claimed to have gained lifelong support and insight and articulated her to an ethic of care while articulating her first opponent, New York City Mayor Rudolph Giuliani, to an ethic of justice (with a strong implication that he represented justice gone awry). Her integral web of relations, however, was utterly disconnected from feminism. That is, viewing audiences were not presented with a discussion of the influence of feminism on Hillary's politics, despite her platform's clear and obvious connections to feminism (not to mention its historical enabling of her candidacy as a woman). Like so many of the political women favored by mainstream media during the 1990s, Hillary Clinton's identity is emblematic of a postfeminism that privileges femininity insofar as it is associated with moral superiority and nurturance.

For a number of reasons, Hillary differs from the other political women I have discussed in this book, not the least of which is the public visibility she was forced to maintain as First Lady. In addition to the self-evident ways in which she stands apart from other political women, one point may distinguish her with respect to how the media have constructed her, and that is her ability to work the media system to her advantage. Scholars of Hillary's rhetoric and media treatment concur that she was mistreated by the press during her two terms as First Lady (see, e.g., Campbell 1998; Parry-Giles 2000). This would suggest that she had not quite mastered the art of media manipulation, because if she were so skilled, why would she have permitted such unflattering treatment? Colleen Kelley's (2001) investigation of Hillary Clinton's rhetoric over the course of Bill Clinton's presidency suggests that she evolved as a shrewd tactician who purposefully used strong rhetoric designed to attract negative attention so that she, rather than Bill, would catch the press's flak. Her rhetoric identified her as a presidential surrogate, a position that the press could not refashion to suit their purposes. Kelley argues that this rhetorical surrogacy in fact deflected negative attention onto Hillary as a scapegoat and thus "facilitated the discursive rescue of her husband's presidency not only from the impeachment abyss but perhaps from an historical one as well" (283). Kelley argues, in other words, that Hillary sacrificed herself to salvage and reconstruct what could be saved of her husband's reputation and legacy.

Kelley's analysis gives much credit to Hillary for having developed finely honed news manipulation skills. Although Kelley's study stops at the rhetoric that Hillary produced as First Lady, her analysis suggests that this rhetorical skill would carry over into her Senate campaign, where it would be at least as useful as it had been prior to her Senate career. I raise Kelley's argument to point out that of the political women whose media coverage I have examined in this book, Hillary Clinton surely represents the highest level of expertise of any of them when it comes to working the media to her advantage. Following this argument, it stands to reason that part of her neoliberal, postfeminist identity results from her own sense of how to frame issues and construct herself, but ultimately the question of how much of her identity is self-originated and how much of it may be media imposed is immaterial. Viewing audiences for the television newscasts I review here would not know to what or whom to attribute these characteristics, and, for that matter, neither do I. Regardless of who has created Hillary Clinton's identity in her Senate campaign, the result is the same: the information we receive about politicians, celebrities, and other public figures through the media constitutes the primary resource we have to work with in ascribing meaning to them and acting on it. Without firsthand, regular contact with Hillary Rodham Clinton, we are dependent on what we find out about her through print and broadcast media and the Internet. I cannot speculate about which one of the trends, images, or messages in her coverage is a result of her own efforts to launch herself along a particular trajectory and which one originates with news workers. In any case, the Hillary Rodham Clinton who is constructed in and through television news stories is the one to whom television news viewers were exposed; this is the representation of Hillary that I discuss here.

HILLARY AND THE NEW DEMOCRATS

Just as her husband, the president, had throughout his campaigns (and then in his policy making), Hillary Clinton was articulated to the so-called New Democrats, the neoliberals of the Democratic Leadership Council (DLC). The New Democrats represent a mix of socially liberal positions (e.g., government-subsidized health insurance and support for abortion rights) and fiscal conservatism—issues and perspectives traditionally associated with the Republican Party (e.g., welfare reform and President Clinton's oath that "the era of Big Government is over") (see chapter 3). The DLC's neoliberalism has been criticized by more Left-leaning members of the Democratic Party, such as Congress member Jesse Jackson Jr., and, during the presidential campaign of 2000, perhaps most vocally by Green Party candidate Ralph Nader; Nader, in fact, claimed that his candidacy was necessitated by this right turn within the Democratic Party that left most of the traditional liberal and progressive agenda behind.

Critics of neoliberalism generally reject its adoption of a corporate, private-sector model for handling an increasing number of services (e.g., prisons and health care), for its support of deregulation in key industries to make way for unregulated, market-based operations, and for its emphasis on the needs of the elite and middle classes at the expense of the working classes and the poor. Critics such as Bagdikian (2000), McChesney (1999), and Herman and Chomsky (1988) implicate media corporations in the process of encouraging a national adoption of neoliberalism—a political agenda that, these critics charge, privileges corporations and commercialism over citizens and democracy.

Television news provided ample and clear connections between Hillary Rodham Clinton and this aspect of Bill Clinton's regime and, importantly, his vision of what a New Democrat was. Some commentators situated Hillary as being subordinate to Bill, as in "the First Lady is very much running in the shadow of the president" (ABC 2000b), or they indicated that she was simply a cog in "the Clinton machine" (ABC 2000d). In this same vein, another suggested that her candidacy announcement speech "could have been a re-election speech for the president if he were allowed to run for a third term" (ABC 2000b). Articulating Hillary to Bill Clinton invoked the constellation of neoliberal policies and politics of "Clintonism" as cultural shorthand that needed no further elaboration.

Perhaps because this connection would not be well received by the entirety of the New York electorate, however, news stories also included claims that while connected, Hillary Rodham Clinton's politics and policies were autonomous. One claimed, for example, that "she is very much excited about the idea of stepping out of her husband's shadow"; that is, that her Senate campaign "is her way of stepping out and, in her own words, trying to establish herself" (CNN 2000d). Although she might have been moving away from Bill Clinton politically, he would not be entirely absent; rather, as a "powerful asset" (ibid.) to Hillary's campaign, he would be both a supportive spouse and a "key," but behind-the-scenes, occasional advisor (CNN 2000g). In his own words, Bill Clinton pointed out that voters were

> not going to vote for her just because she's my wife, but they might vote for her because we share some values and some approaches to the issues. And they want to make their own judgment about it. And I thought she was terrific when she announced. I was so proud of her. And I'll be happy to be a member of the Senate Spouses Club. I hope I get to be. (CNN 2000e)

Although Bill Clinton deferred to Hillary's status in the Senate if she were victorious, these other comments implied that their relationship mirrored one in which women have been placed to situate them in electoral politics for over a century now: woman as marginalized Other; man as political standard bearer.

Besides these more explicit statements that situate Hillary Rodham Clinton's politics vis-à-vis Bill's, a more subtle label accomplishes this as well: the "New Democrat." "Calling herself a New Democrat," CNN correspondent Frank Buckley noted that her agenda included "more support for public education, increased economic development, and improved health care. She also appealed to the center" (CNN 2000f). "I'm a New Democrat," Hillary exclaimed in her announcement speech, and then elaborated further:

> I don't believe government is the source of all our problems or the solution to them. But I do believe that when people live up to their responsibilities we ought to live up to ours to help them build better lives. That's the basic bargain we owe one another in America today. (ABC 2000b)

In an interview on CBS's *The Early Show*, she noted further that her policies would attempt to "make sure that everybody in this country has a chance, if they're willing to work hard and be responsible, to make their own dreams come true" (CBS 2000b). Later, from her speech to the Democratic Convention in August, CNN included this excerpt:

> What will it take to make sure no child in America is left behind in the 21st century? It takes responsible parents who put their own children first.

It takes all of us, teachers and workers and business owners and community leaders and people of faith. And you know, I still believe it takes a village. (CNN 2000i)

Media analyst Normon Solomon (1994) has pointed out that "ritual plat-
itudes" such as individual "responsibility" is one of the New Democrats' favored
catchphrases. He argued that President Clinton's repeated use of it (what he
calls "harping on it") was an effort to reshape "the Democratic Party to frame
such concepts as political goals more pressing than social justice and equal
opportunity" (152). The deployment of "responsibility" in media accounts of
Hillary's campaign suggests that it is a thinly disguised code for pulling oneself
up by one's bootstraps, preferably without any call for government assistance.
The term *New Democrat* signifies neoliberalism generally; using it allowed
Hillary Clinton to capitalize on the perceived strengths of this politics, and thus
on the strengths of the most favored New Democrat of all—President Clinton—without having to be associated with his personal problems, particularly
philandering and perjury. She thus avoided being pulled into the muck of her
husband's messy scandals while gaining cultural capital by instead claiming allegiance to a broader political agenda, neoliberalism.

Like other New Democrats, Hillary did not seem to have a problem accepting large campaign contributions. Unlike many of their more liberal counterparts
who worked for campaign finance reform and rejected large contributions with
the argument that they did not wish to be beholden to "special interests,"[11] New
Democrats such as Hillary were represented in television news stories as being
happy to solicit and accept millions of dollars. President Clinton, for example, was
so well liked and supported in Hollywood that several celebrities gave his presidential campaigns millions of dollars and helped him raise millions more for his
presidential library. These celebrities were financially supportive of Al Gore's campaign (despite vocal Hollywood critic Senator Joe Lieberman being on the ticket)
and Hillary Clinton's Senate campaign as well. Present at her fifty-third birthday
party in late October, for example, were actor Robert de Niro and the cast of *Saturday Night Live*; together these party goers helped raise $2 million in this one
night alone, a fact that all of the news outlets mentioned (see, e.g., ABC 2000d).

In this vein, the crowning achievement of celebrity fund-raising occurred
during events surrounding the Democratic Convention in Los Angeles in
August 2000. Not only did correspondents gush about how much Hollywood
supported the Democratic Party ($12 million in a year and a half, by one
account [CNBC 2000b]), but they also seemed mesmerized by the fruitful relationship that Bill Clinton had developed with Hollywood celebrities:

Not since JFK has a president so captivated Tinseltown. And in this mostly
Democratic world, not even Ronald Reagan, one of their own, attracted
Clinton's star power. They have loved him when he was a winner, and they
fought for him when he was on the ropes. (CNBC 2000b)

These news stories also were quick to mention that Hillary benefited from this
relationship as well. One fund-raising "mega-concert" during the convention's
festivities netted Hillary's campaign $4 million (CNBC 2000b). At another
celebrity fund-raiser for her campaign, film stars such as Gregory Peck, Shirley
MacLaine, David Spade, and John Travolta paid between $1,000 and $25,000
for the privilege of mingling and eating with the First Couple (CNN 2000i).

The New Democrats, of whom the Clintons were among the most
notable, do not eschew but rather invite large campaign donations. By allying
herself with the deep pockets of Hollywood, for example, Hillary Rodham
Clinton marked out a place for herself in this lucrative New Democrat terrain.
Although the Clinton–Lazio campaign ultimately was the most expensive Senate campaign ever and thus required large and numerous infusions of funds,
Hillary appeared to capitulate readily to this aspect of the neoliberal status quo.
During the first debate, in a widely circulated clip, opponent Rick Lazio strode
over to Hillary Clinton's podium, slammed a letter down on it, and demanded
that she sign it: the letter pledged that neither candidate would allow any further use of soft money in what remained of their respective campaigns. Hillary
managed to avoid signing the letter, thus permitting her to continue to receive
soft money funds while, news outlets reported, managing to gain a public-opin-
ion victory in her deflection of Lazio.

These news accounts are fuzzy on the details about what a New Democrat really is. Historically, however, Hillary Rodham Clinton *has* aligned herself
explicitly with a "politics of meaning." A politics of meaning (which she also
calls a politics of virtue) goes beyond traditional liberal political philosophy by
including Christian principles. In an interview with *New York Times* reporter
Michael Kelly, she described it this way:

> The very core of what I believe is this concept of individual worth, which
> I think flows from all of us being creatures of God and being imbued with
> a spirit. . . . If you break down the Golden Rule or if you take Christ's
> commandment—Love thy neighbor as thyself—there is an underlying
> assumption that you will value yourself, that you will be a responsible
> being who will live by certain behaviors that enable you to have self-
> respect, because, then, out of that self-respect comes the capacity for you
> to respect and care for other people. . . . And how do we just break this

whole enterprise down in small enough pieces? Well, somebody says to themselves:"You know, I'm not going to tell that racist, sexist joke. I don't want to objectify another human being." . . . Or somebody else says: "You know, I'm going to start thanking the woman who cleans the restroom in the building that I work in. You know, maybe that sounds kind of stupid, but on the other hand I want to start seeing her as a human being." . . . So I think what we're . . . really looking at is . . . millions and millions of changes in individual behavior that are motivated by the same impulses. (quoted in Kelly 1993, 63)

Far from being a clarion call for revolution, Hillary's politics of virtue relies on an atomistic notion of individual, cognition-level change—her approach suggests that a concerted effort to instill self-respect and respect for others will translate into behavior change which, she opines, will lead us to a better, more socially just place. A politics of virtue sounds eerily reminiscent of George Bush Sr.'s use of "1,000 points of light" to describe individual acts of charity toward underprivileged Others. Although a politics of virtue is not exactly on a par with George Bush Sr.'s politics, a certain elitism does creep into Hillary's discussion. For instance, who is this "we" to whom she refers? She seems not to be referring to a "we" that includes the bathroom cleaning woman or others like her. Whereas this cleaning woman is familiar with toilets, bathroom stalls, and floors, Hillary Clinton and her cohorts are more conversant in the limitations of glass ceilings. Hillary's politics of virtue seems to require a position of class privilege that most women in this country do not occupy: about 80 percent of women work in service-producing occupations (the most poorly compensated work category that seldom offers benefits to workers), and among these, 48.2 percent work in the services industry, which includes office building bathroom cleaners (Costello and Stone 2001, 241).

When public figures like Hillary, who have clearly benefited from the ideology and policy changes forced by feminist activism, do not acknowledge its contribution, feminist politics suffers—as does its purchase in the public sphere. By evading questions posed by an explicitly feminist politics, the press has constructed Hillary in ways that make her of little use to the majority of women whose struggles are in worlds far from the corporate world of glass ceilings. Glass ceilings also pose problems, but they are not women's only problems and perhaps not one of the most urgent for many women. A politics of virtue is more amenable to the class interests of the corporations that own and control most newsrooms today, so maybe it should come as no surprise that this is the "politics" to which journalists would articulate Hillary.

A politics of virtue is hardly virtuous if one considers its elision of class difference as a significant factor in oppression, such as that experienced by the cleaning woman attending to her bathroom-cleaning duties. It places a burden on individuals to change from within rather than to work collectively to effect change—transformation—from without, yet this is the platform on which Hillary has been constructed, and on which she (by default) represents feminism. A politics of virtue fits well within the neoliberal New Democrats' rhetoric; it supports the status quo by advancing "centrist ideology dressed up as anti-ideology—a commitment to adjust the status quo masquerading as a commitment to 'change'" (Solomon 1994, 171). New Democrat neoliberalism is a politics that works harmoniously with the goals of the media oligopoly, and as I have illustrated in preceding chapters, so too does postfeminism. Thus Hillary Rodham Clinton's television news image being grounded in a fusion of both of these could be predicted.

HILLARY AND POSTFEMINISM

A trend toward covering Hillary Rodham Clinton while overlooking her sister candidates' efforts is one that I categorize as postfeminist: it combined a relentless focus on Hillary as an individual disconnected from the rest of these candidates *and* from feminism as a social movement—despite her very clear articulation to a platform composed of the traditional "women's issues" that feminist politicians often run on. These news accounts also situated Hillary within the realm of female "difference" principles by relying on assumptions and stereotypes associated with women. This particular combination allows for the appearance of a pro-woman disposition toward female politicians without an acknowledgment of likely feminist critiques of their coverage or of the candidates' platforms. In this case, Hillary's platform, with its clear ties to her husband's politics, could have been subject to feminist criticism for, among other things, her support of the welfare reform policies of her husband's administration, something that a number of feminist scholars and activists have criticized for its dismissal of those issues that historically burden women (e.g., child care costs for mothers bumped out of the welfare system). Not only does the coverage focus on her at the expense of the other female candidates, but it also rarely mentions her future constituents' needs—other than to ponder the question of whether Hillary Clinton could truly understand New Yorkers' issues. News accounts implied that because Hillary had successfully executed her many duties in the private and public spheres, she had beatifically transcended oppression. When framed in this way, she embodies a meritocratic ideal as the archetypal successful woman who "proves" that the system works, and in a gender-blind fashion.

Susan Douglas (1994, 221–44) laments the loss of a concept of sisterhood in public discourse about women. She argues that a notion of women working together for a shared vision of change, rather than competing against one another (usually for available men), has practically disappeared in television fare. Because this notion conjures up images of feminist demands for policy changes governing private and public spaces, Douglas argues that it is too threatening to the television status quo. Although Douglas' study concentrates specifically on news treatments of the ERA, her analysis works with television news coverage of Hillary as well. One cannot know definitively what decisions went into producing the focus on Hillary to the exclusion of the other 129 women who ran for national office, but the fact remains that, relative to Hillary Clinton, these other women candidates were almost invisible in television news reports.[12] Feminism as a social movement *and* as a politics was similarly invisible. The significance of this disarticulation from feminist ideology is that it seems to mark both collective action and the politics associated with feminism's critique of race, gender, and class as interlocking systems of domination as being inappropriate in news coverage of Hillary. Most feminists probably would not label Hillary a radical member of the cause, but she certainly has been associated with second-wave feminism in past years. Thus an absence of any mention of feminism or of feminist influence on her platform is noteworthy. Barbara Olson, a guest on a *Larry King Live* episode, and a Hillary Clinton biographer (now deceased), was the only commentator in the news accounts that I reviewed to point to this absence as peculiar; as she put it, Hillary Clinton, "has been [*sic*] the politics of gender since the beginning" (CNN 2000e).

Perhaps this disarticulation from feminism was strategic on the part of Hillary's campaign staff or on the part of reporters and editors—or both. One Hillary biographer, *New York* magazine columnist Michael Tomasky (2001), noted a clear pattern in the way that she distanced herself from any political issues or language that could be considered remotely controversial during her campaign. At least one of her supporters noticed this: On one CNN talk show, an audience member, Vern, was bothered by her caution and advised Hillary to "step down into the streets; she needs to show a little Bella Abzug, if you will." He continued by insisting that the only way she could win in New York was to connect with voters "on a very personal human, you know, toes-to-toes, nose-to-nose level" (CNN 2000g). Perhaps this absence of explicit—and mostly implicit—feminism in news coverage is a result of her campaign's avoidance of this connection as being potentially disadvantageous.

Despite the denial of a connection to feminism, patterns of coverage remain in these news accounts that situate Hillary on terrain that has long been articulated to women—as candidates or otherwise—many of them ingrained as commonsense beliefs about gender. From the repeated litany of the issues that she has made her own for the campaign to the web of relations from which she is said to derive her politics, in these news accounts, Hillary Rodham Clinton looks like a cultural feminist, steeped in a philosophy of difference, a la Carol Gilligan (1982). As I noted in chapter 3, difference or cultural feminism posits important distinctions between a female culture and a male culture so that, among other things, the moral reasoning styles of each are significantly different. Whereas male culture is said to produce moral reasoning grounded in separation from relationships and to encourage adherence to principles abstracted from a context of important relationships, female culture produces contextual reasoning that derives from consideration and attention to important relationships in a woman's life. Male culture thus generates an ethic of justice that privileges aggression, whereas female culture generates an ethic of care that privileges nurturance. As Gilligan puts it, women experience "embeddedness in lives of relationship, . . . orientation to interdependence, . . . subordination of achievement to care, and . . . conflicts over competitive success," and even more generally, "women's sense of integrity appears to be entwined with an ethic of care, so that to see themselves as women is to see themselves in a relationship of connection" (1982, 171).

Gilligan's theory seems to provide a foundation for Hillary's construction in news accounts. First, the issues that she espouses in news stories are gun safety, education, children, health care, and choice. Although no one sex has a franchise on these issues, and many male candidates have run on platforms that include some or all of them, they have been associated with female candidates to such an extent that they are often known as "women's issues"—in large part because they have to do with nurturance of children and family and implied control over reproduction (see, e.g., Witt, Paget, and Matthews 1994).

Like that of any other political woman, coverage of Hillary Clinton contained stereotypical references to her appearance, behavior, and personality. Some of these were clearly gendered in the sense that they rely on time-worn stereotypes that have been used to diminish women for decades. Hillary Clinton was subjected to these throughout the 1992 campaign and during her time in the White House; for example, she reportedly "softened" her look to appear "kinder and gentler" at the 1992 Democratic National Convention (Corcoran

1993, 29). Since the convention in 1992, mainstream Hillary coverage has run the gamut from Angel (in a *New York Times Sunday Magazine* article, appropriately titled "Saint Hillary") to Devil (on the cover of *Spy* magazine, where she was lampooned as a dominatrix, decked out in leather and whip). Within this continuum, topics have ranged from her sexuality (frigid, lesbian, sexual temptress before whom Bill is powerless), her image (chic, sexy, practical— she does her own hair and makeup every day), her temper (slapping Bill, throwing a lamp at him), her cookie recipes (which beat Barbara Bush's in a bake-off), her policy-wonk proclivities, her similarities to Lady Macbeth, and her possible breach of ethics around Whitewater. The multiple subject positions proffered by Hillary coverage suggest complexity and at times conflict as some of these configurations seem to be at odds with one another (e.g., policy wonk and cookie baker). The trajectory this coverage has taken endows Hillary with multiple capabilities and complexities, but all within the realm of attributes usually assigned to women in order to police their behavior in the public sphere.

A voice-over on *Good Morning America*, for example, described the press conference at which Hillary Rodham Clinton announced her candidacy as a "coming out party" (ABC 2000a), implicitly invoking the cotillion scene that surrounds debutantes as their presence (and marital availability) is announced to their elite peerage. It is difficult to imagine a male senatorial candidate's announcement being described in the same way. It is similarly difficult to imagine a male being implicitly accused of inviting intrusive interrogations from reporters just by becoming a Senate candidate. But on CNN, *New York Post* columnist Robert George did just that in response to a discussion about Hillary's response to a reporter who asked her, "Have you ever been unfaithful to [President Clinton], and specifically the stories about you and Vince Foster, any truth in those?" George reacted to the question with, "I think the questions were inappropriate, but you know unfortunately, Hillary should have expected this when she got into this race because she actually brings that baggage with her because of the impeachment and the history with the president" (CNN 2000b). No suggestion here that the reporter's uncritical reliance upon Rush Limbaugh-esque character-assassinating insinuations could be to blame; instead, Hillary was asking to be inappropriately interrogated simply because she dared to run for public office. This was not the most egregious attempt to justify her mistreatment; that dubious honor belonged to conservative author (and former Black Panther sympathizer) David Horowitz, who was promoting a Web site that he had developed called "slaphillary.com," which featured a cartoon figure of Hillary and functionality that allowed visitors to operate a hand that would slap her image. Horowitz defended it against its feminist critics as being for the "terminally frustrated, the truly outraged Americans who are sick of the betrayal of women and are just plain mean spirited" (FOX 2000d). It is more than a little ironic that Horowitz promotes a symbolic physical assault against one woman as a remedy for the "betrayal of women."

Finally, the gender stereotypes in commentary about Hillary's appearance and personality abounded in television news. Although they certainly were tamer than they had been when she was campaigning for her husband in 1992 and as First Lady, they were gender-specific in content and in focus. That is, political women are routinely described according to their appearances and personality; political men seldom are discussed in this fashion. When one is, as in the scornful descriptions of Al Gore being tutored in fashion, appearance, and demeanor improvement (needs to act like an Alpha Male) by feminist Naomi Wolf, he is subject to endless ridicule (see Pozner 2001, 9). As Jennifer Pozner makes clear in a synthesis of print media stories about a number of political women involved with Campaign 2000, this coverage has significant implications for political women and for feminism: "By focusing so consistently on irrelevant personal, gender-specific details about female security advisors, attorneys general and congressmembers, media outlets imply that they are 'ladies' first, major political players second" (2001, 10).

Although there was no unanimity in television discussions of whether or not Hillary was appropriately ladylike, there was commentary on her looks and personality. NBC commentators Jodi Applegate, Asha Blake, and Florence Henderson (since when is the *Brady Bunch*'s matriarch considered a credible political commentator?) dished about how Hillary had looked during her candidacy announcement press conference.

HENDERSON: Boy, she had her hair cut, though, and really had a lot of blonde in it . . .

APPLEGATE: It looked good, though.

BLAKE: What, is that going to help? Am I—am I out of luck? I mean, does blonde help?

HENDERSON: Well of course blondes . . .

APPLEGATE: You know what?

HENDERSON: What?

APPLEGATE: If this election is decided on the basis of hair, I have bad news for Mayor Giuliani, all right? (NBC 2000b)

Discussions on the topic of Hillary's looks were edged out in favor of those on her personality. These were positively schizophrenic, perhaps an indication of the polar extremes engendered in reactions to her. One FOX network commentator's disquisition on Hillary Clinton went as follows:

> Hillary Clinton's image is one of deceit. This is the tone she set, and this is what is important. Mrs. Clinton is not anti-Semitic.[13] She's pro-Hillary. Whoever can help her, she likes. Whoever hurts her, she doesn't like. The overall picture of Hillary Clinton is clear, at least to me. She's a woman who wants power and will do almost anything to get it. She is cold. (FOX 2000a)

On the other hand, an unidentified man on a different FOX news segment speculated about her imminent appearance at the Democratic Convention: "I think there is a warm and soft side of Hillary Rodham Clinton, and I think it will be shining tonight" (FOX 2000b). But wait, former senior aide to President Clinton turned ABC political reporter George Stephanopoulos's answer to Tim Russert's questions about whether she had, in one instance, become "incensed" and "she has a—she has a strong temper?" was a "sure, sure" (CNBC 2000a). This does not quite square with *Talk* magazine's Lucinda Franks, who had interviewed Hillary and found that, "she's going to win a lot of points on personality, because when she goes one-to-one or even one-to-10 she is an extremely magnetic, charismatic personality. . . . She also has a streak of mischief about her" (CNN 2000g). Taken together, perhaps these various ruminations on Hillary's personality represent a consensus: that she is human, and thus she exhibits all of the inconsistencies any of us would when scrutinized by television. That such extensive ruminations on personality emerge in talk about women marks them as different—outsiders to the male norm.

Other aspects of this coverage mark Hillary's "difference" from male culture. Early in January 2000 she moved into the home that she and Bill Clinton had purchased in Westchester County, New York; news stories latched onto this as reporters positioned themselves outside of the house to report on the move. Of course, in this particular context, Hillary's establishing residence in New York was imperative to lay the foundation for her Senate campaign; news accounts included references to her commitment to New Yorkers being illustrated in this move. They also seemed to revel in the domesticity implied in her seeing to her various moving duties. CNN White House correspondent Kelly Wallace explained that

> the president and first lady came here to Chappaqua, last night, to spend their first night in a home they own after about 18 years in government

housing. Now, the price tag for this new home—let me get it right this time—is 1.7 million dollars. We understand that a friend of the Clintons brought over a home-cooked dinner and then Mr. and Mrs. Clinton got to the task of unpacking lots and lots of boxes. Now this is an important move for Mrs. Clinton. . . . Now she's got her residence. (CNN 2000a)

On the *Today Show*, Hillary Clinton campaign staffer (and former Deputy White House Chief of Staff) Harold Ickes elaborated on the move in an interview with Matt Lauer.

LAUER: Have you talked to Mrs. Clinton since she moved into Chappaqua?

ICKES: I have. She's delighted. It's the first time she's had her own home in, I think, 17 years. And she couldn't look more forward to moving in. Her mother, Dorothy, is up there helping get things arranged. And she's very, very pleased with it. . . . Pe-people—look, she's from outside of New York, and people wonder, you know, why she's moving here. She loves New York. She always said she was going to live in New York. She's bought a house here. She's put her roots down here. (NBC 2000a)

About a week later, the big news was that Hillary would appear on David Letterman's show on January 12. As Julie Chen of *The Early Show*—in a clear example of television "plugola" (McAllister 1999)—put it, "First lady Hillary Clinton has a TV date tonight with David Letterman." Reporter Diana Olick suggested that Hillary Clinton's decision to appear on the show was neither a result of Letterman's "charm or his daily cajoling," nor "did it boil down to cold, hard numbers" from a recent poll that showed 58 percent of New Yorkers encouraging her to be a guest on the show. Instead, it was the settledness of her domestic arrangement: "Now that she's moved into their new house, it just seems like the right time" (CBS 2000a). For a female candidate, all must be settled in her private, domestic life before she can venture into the public sphere, a suggestion that it is women who are still responsible for tending to hearth and home—even as they are preparing to tend to affairs of state.

Once Hillary Clinton was fixed, however temporarily, in domesticity, news accounts emphasized her difference by focusing on traditionally feminine behavioral traits, often contrasting them with her opponents' demeanors (particularly Giuliani's). Her opponents were cast as tough, aggressive, and macho, but she came across as a cooperative and collaborative statesperson. Whereas Giuliani was "more of a fighter . . . the First Lady would be better able to work with other senators" (CNN 2000c). Rudolph Giuliani was construed as "mean-spirited, arrogant, . . . goes after people he doesn't like ruthlessly," and as a leader "New

Yorkers have found to be a divisive personality" (WNBC 2000). Representative
Lazio, an order of magnitude more temperate than his predecessor on this campaign trail, made his masculine mark with his now-infamous move to force
Hillary to sign his anti-soft money pledge during their first debate. This seemed
to disadvantage him in the eyes of the newscasters, one of whom remarked on
this "aggressive position. . . . He was a little too close to her personal space after
a little while, and that made a lot of people feel uncomfortable perhaps in watching it" (CNN 2000j). After the debate, Cokie Roberts of ABC pointed out that,
with Lazio's performance, "women are responding to this debate somewhat neg-
atively. . . . Was Rick Lazio too hard on his opponent?" (ABC 2000d).

Not all commentary about Hillary Clinton was benevolent or temperate
of course. Various commentators made reference to problems that she had had
in personal relationships in the past, to her temper, and to her possibly uneth-
ical fund-raising arrangements. Surprisingly, given the harsh treatment that she
had received during her tenure as First Lady, most television news stories were
reasonably tame—and often positive. Reporters seemed to want to humanize
her, perhaps recognizing their industry's complicity in the production of negative sentiments about her in public discourse through most of the pre-impeach-
ment years. For example, about her performance in this same debate, and
specifically with reference to a question about her husband's affair with Monica Lewinsky, Hillary was described as "struggling for words at times, [but] she
came off as a very human person who had felt pain in her marriage, not just
the robotic, sort of policy wonk she occasionally appears to be" (CNN 2000j).
Speculation that occurred prior to her announcement speech predicted that
she was "going to speak from her heart" (CNN 2000d). A clip from the video
played at her announcement press conference featured Bill Clinton promoting
her ability, claiming it to be important in the Senate, to "bring people together
and kind of lift them up . . . she's very, very good at that" (CNN 2000f).

Despite these supportive sentiments that seemed to showcase some of her
more feminine characteristics, much was made of polls suggesting that many
women did not seem to be supporting her campaign. News workers apparently
expect women to vote for other women strictly on the basis of sex similarity
and not on the basis of political ideology—an expectation that seems likely to
have sprung from the gender gap and its use in political reporting. Tom Brokaw,
for example, asked her why she was not "doing better among the constituen-
cies that should be your natural followers? White women in New York, for
example" (NBC 2000d). Conservative FOX News commentator Tony Snow
wanted to know why "the so-called soccer moms, suburban moms, were not
flocking to her side" (FOX 2000c).

These patterns feminized Hillary, as did the emphasis on her context of family, conjugal, and maternal relationships. Carol Gilligan argues that such a context is what generates women's ethic of care; this marks their essential difference from men. Although feminists have found fault with such essentialist theorizing (see, e.g., Pollitt's [1994, 42–62] essay, "Marooned on Gilligan's Island" and Faludi [1991, 327–32]), news coverage of Hillary (and coverage of the other political women I have surveyed in this book) relies upon it. This is not surprising, given that it elevates women to a moral position superior to that of men; however, as Faludi points out, it has been appropriated to justify sex discrimination. With its historical roots in public discussions of suffrage from the nineteenth century (Dow 1996, 169), "difference" is a tenacious theory that revisits public and academic discourse repeatedly, despite its questionable value in advancing feminist politics or improving the material aspects of women's lives. (See Donovan [1992, 171–86] for a survey of the uses to which cultural/difference feminism has been put.)

News accounts invoked Hillary Clinton's web of relations as early as the announcement of her candidacy. As her husband had in his first presidential bid, Hillary's campaign produced a biographical video meant to acquaint voters with her life and with the foundation of her politics. Produced by the same friends who had produced Bill's video, the Thomassons, Hillary's video "used a dramatic story of her mother" (ABC 2000a) to locate Hillary's origins. The video clip featured on *Good Morning America*, February 7, 2000, included Hillary ruminating, "when I think of the courage and sheer resilience that was needed for my mother to become the mother she wanted to be, my heart is filled with profound gratitude." In that same segment, Diane Sawyer asked Harold Ickes about the purpose of such a get-acquainted video for a well-known public figure. Ickes replied that

> most people and most people in New York know Hillary in the context of being First Lady. What they don't know is the broader context of the fact that she was raised in a five-family, middle-class family, small businessman as a father. . . . That is really not known by many, many people in New York, and that is one of the purposes of the video that you saw and some of the things that Hillary said in her announcement speech. People just don't know the context, and they need to know that context to frame her in a broader way. (ABC 2000a)

The context that Ickes points to seems to refer to this familial one, important here to mark the web of relations that spawned young Hillary. The importance of family relationships though does not end here; news reports also speculated about the role that daughter Chelsea would play in her mother's campaign. A clip from *The Today Show*, for example, featured scenes of reporters mobbing Chelsea Clinton at a campaign stop to find out "are you—are you going to be campaigning with your—your mother more?" Chelsea declined to comment, as did her mother, but despite the silence from both Clintons, reporters pursued the question:

> ANDREA MITCHELL: Friends of the Clintons say reporters shouldn't read too much into Chelsea's campaign appearance.
>
> LISA CAPUTO (Hillary Clinton's former press secretary): She'll choose to do whatever she wants to do. If she wants to show up at an event where her mother is campaigning, she'll choose to do that just as she did back in her father's campaign days when he ran for president.
>
> ANDREA MITCHELL: But it doesn't hurt to have Chelsea in front of the cameras, especially since Mrs. Clinton's Republican opponent, Rick Lazio, likes to remind New York voters of his young and photogenic family.
>
> (Cut to historian Doris Kearns Goodwin.)
>
> GOODWIN: If they use her too much, it may appear like blatant politics rather than a mother and daughter enjoying one another's company.
>
> ANDREA MITCHELL: Politics haven't come easily to Chelsea, who is shy by nature. She struggled under the spotlight of her father's campaign in 1992, and then had to endure the embarrassment of the Lewinsky scandal. But in recent years she has warmed to a more public role and is a big crowd pleaser, campaigning first for her father, now her mother, stepping in at state functions when her mother is absent, this arrival ceremony for the king of Morocco just last week, traveling with her father to Asia earlier this year, receiving rave reviews, and holding her family together through trying times.

Mitchell concluded this segment with the following: "But no matter what else happens this year, Chelsea Clinton can only be a plus to a candidate trying to prove to skeptical New Yorkers, especially women, that she's just another suburban mom" (NBC 2000c).

It is hard to imagine any woman, let alone the First Lady of the United States, trying to sincerely convince the public that she was "just another suburban mom" after purchasing a $1.7 million home, but the placement of Hillary in relation to her family recurs throughout campaign coverage, seemingly as an attempt to mark her femininity and thus to reinvent her public image: from hellion to postfeminist suburban mom. Even when the stickiness of her particular family relations is brought into the mix, Hillary's news image maintains that these bonds—and particularly her bonds with women in her life—have been crucial to her development as a policy maker. Just as Tom Brokaw had in his interview during the Democratic Convention, Peter Jennings asked Hillary about her poll numbers with women, young women especially, and did they, he asked, "resent you because you didn't leave your husband?" Hillary responded with her version of family values—pro-choice style:

> You know, I've, for my entire adult life, argued, and fought for, and worked for the right of women to make their own decisions, make their own choices in their lives. That's what I've done, and that's what I would hope for any young woman. And someone's choice may not be mine, and mine may not be someone else's, but that's what's so great about being a woman in the 21st century in America. We have this range of choices, as long as we're thoughtful and responsible about how we compose our lives, what the choices are that we make. My family is very, very important to me. That is a, you know, primary concern of mine in my life, and I'm very grateful for, you know, the daughter that I've raised, and my mother still being with us. And I have made my choices and I feel absolutely right with them. (ABC 2000c)

Hillary's justification above also is a defense of postfeminism. Her account of why womanhood in the twenty-first century is "so great" rests on a notion of being able to choose from a range of different life options, presumably unfettered by obstacles either structural, such as poverty, or woman-specific, such as forced pregnancy from lack of access to abortion. Her rendering of women's lives seems to reveal tacit gratitude for gains achieved by feminists, yet she obscures these feminist roots by refusing to name the social movement responsible for codifying choices for women *and* by moving past this history into the twenty-first century—where the "post" prefix to feminism is well on its way to becoming permanently affixed. In racing to the twenty-first century with barely a nod to feminism's role in improving women's lives, this representation of Hillary Clinton embraces postfeminism, and in reasserting the importance of her matriarchal web of relations, it implicitly endorses the use of female difference to situate Hillary on the terrain of electoral politics in the United States.

Conclusion

The significance of a familiar public figure-turned-politician, like Hillary Rodham Clinton, being articulated to postfeminist neoliberalism is profound for feminism's place in public discourse. Television news recurrently evades feminism in its construction of Hillary Clinton as a Senate candidate but readily connects her to a "difference"-laden, postfeminist neoliberal politics. Neoliberalism and postfeminism are ideologically compatible in the way that they privilege the private over the public sphere. For solving key social problems, the New Democrats look to corporations and commerce to provide models of social responsibility—as in their embrace of what historian Thomas Frank (2000) calls "market populism." Market populism, he explains, is synonymous with the much-vaunted New Economy that neoliberals like Bill Clinton have promoted with religious fervor.

> From Deadheads to Nobel-laureate economists, from paleoconservatives to New Democrats, American leaders in the nineties came to believe that markets were a popular system, a far more democratic form of organization than democratically elected governments. . . . [I]n addition to being markets for exchange, markets were mediums of consent. Markets expressed the popular will more articulately and more meaningfully than did mere elections. Markets conferred democratic legitimacy. . . . Markets looked out for our interests. (Frank 2000, xiv)

Frank cautions, however, that although "markets may look like democracy, in that we are all involved in their making . . . they are fundamentally not democratic" (86).

The incarnation of postfeminism that I identify in Hillary Clinton coverage likewise idealizes private, domestic life and its influences as being beneficial to women everywhere. Bonnie Dow (1996) observes that a postfeminism that includes "difference" principles "reifies traditional notions that [women's] most important work is at home. . . . Although difference feminism may advocate the extension of women's qualities from the private sphere to the public sphere, it further naturalizes women's responsibilities in the private sphere" (170). Accounts of Hillary Rodham Clinton underscore her female web of relations and how it has provided her with particular insights valuable to her politics. These same accounts continually articulate her to this aspect of domestic life—nurturance—but they refuse to discuss any role that Bill Clinton may have played in, for example, parenting Chelsea. A man who felt comfortable announcing that his presidency would be a partnership of equals between himself and his spouse could reasonably be expected to extend this same egalitarian sentiment toward their parenting arrangements; but perhaps because it was too clearly tied to second-wave feminism, no such sentiment emerged in news accounts of Hillary's campaign. The web of family relations, with its filial duties, was articulated to Hillary alone. One consequence of this is that it supports a notion of women being the "primary hope for salvation in a brutal postmodern world," along with absolving

> men of responsibility for changing their ways. There is nothing wrong with women creating a vision of a humane world, but it seems to make more sense to enlist everyone in such a cause rather than to claim that only women (or mothers) can achieve it. (Dow 1996, 197)

Private-sphere idealization in neoliberalism and postfeminism is strongly related to the exclusion of class hierarchy in the ideology of both. The neoliberal New Democrats hobnob comfortably with Hollywood's celebrities in TV news, relying on their substantial wealth to finance New Democrats' campaigns. News reports focused on the great wealth and elite lifestyles of Hollywood stars who supported Hillary's campaign and gave little attention to her trips around New York State to investigate the needs of its poor residents in depressed areas of the state. More attention paid to this effort of Hillary's would have forced television news viewers to see class differences embodied in and lived out by people more similar to the "bathroom cleaning woman" Hillary discussed as the recipient of her politics of meaning's good intentions. It may be that Hillary Clinton's issues are everyone's issues, as one caller to a CNN talk show contended; however, everyone appears to be restricted to supporters who look fabulous, like the stars of Hollywood, and live in millionaire territory, as Hillary herself does now.

A discursive evasion of the importance of class oppression in affecting everyday life characterizes television discussions of Hillary Clinton's politics. Yet at a time when females of all ages and races are more likely than males to be poor—a total of 14.9 percent versus 11.6 percent, respectively (Costello and Stone 2001, 298)—class oppression and economic disparity seem quite appropriate as topics of discussion, if not legislation, and if not in the realm of electoral politics, then where? The need for a strong anti-poverty legislator like Hillary seems rather pressing, but it may be a long wait before she jumps on this old-style liberal bandwagon, destined it appears, for the symbolic dustbin of history. Frank (2000, 15) notes that U.S. political philosophy was at one time substantially based on a notion that "freedom was only meaningful once poverty and powerlessness had been overcome. Today, however, American opinion leaders seem generally convinced that democracy and the free market are simply identical." This early into her Senate career, it is impossible to know whether Senator Rodham Clinton will be an advocate for working-class and poor constituents, but in her campaign on television news she had left feminism and the hoi polloi behind her as she moved toward the November 7 finish line and then on to Capitol Hill. She thus represents neoliberal postfeminism from a high-profile position of privilege. For herself and the other political women in this book, this construction may have enabled them to receive the positive attention necessary to succeed in the mass mediated world of electoral politics in the United States.

Does Hillary's situation suggest that feminism for the twenty-first century is postfeminism? My reluctant conclusion is that it is—at least in mainstream media narratives about political women. Hillary Rodham Clinton, a privileged white woman with fairly conservative politics, thus comes to be the poster child for feminism by dint of her former explicit association with it, her success as an attorney, and her adoption of a public life to accompany parenthood. A closer examination reveals that, at least in media accounts, Hillary has jettisoned a feminist politics for a postfeminism that assumes that the death of patriarchy has occurred and reveres women's culture and choice. The responsibility is now on women to do the right thing with their lives, to choose the best career, to plan parenthood thoughtfully, and to break through any glass ceilings that they may encounter along the way. These are all noble goals, but their achievement is not equally possible for all women, a structural problem that has not been remedied with the ushering in of postfeminism.

As a system of representation, postfeminism renders invisible structural obstacles to success and stands in contrast to the material inequities that characterize the lives of many women in the United States today, such as the nearly 15 percent living in poverty, or those who must work two or more jobs to get by, a number that has increased from about 1.3 million workers in 1978 to almost 4 million in 1998 (Costello and Stone 2001, 238). Female heads of household are still much more likely to live in poverty than males who head up households; this is even worse for African-American and Hispanic women. Among families with children, Hispanic woman-headed households have a 57 percent poverty rate, African-American woman-headed households have a 53 percent poverty rate, and white woman-headed households have a 35.6 percent poverty rate (Costello, Miles, and Stone 1998, 335). Finally, across all occupations, a woman makes seventy-five cents to a man's every dollar, with even worse ratios in certain occupations like service (Costello, Miles, and Stone 1998, 306).

These figures show that many women could use some relief from material conditions that mark their disparity from the world of Hollywood benefactors, for example, or from Westchester County, New York. The media attention focused on elite lives and issues may be a boon to the careers of political women like Hillary Clinton, but it benefits them at the expense of poor and nonelite women whose life circumstances do not fit within a neoliberal postfeminist frame. Media signifying practices around electoral politics held up Hillary Rodham Clinton as being representative of women everywhere and symbolically displaced the majority of women *and* men whose lives do not resemble Hillary's in any way, yet whose needs call out for legislative intervention.

PUTTING ALLY ON TRIAL

Contesting Postfeminism in Media Culture

The preceding chapters of this book explored the political identities articulated to political women in television and print news stories. The postfeminist ideology privileged by these mediated accounts is prevalent across print and television news stories about women in politics in the years between 1991 and 2000, but what about media representations of supposedly average women, not the high-profile women who make it into the spotlight shone on electoral politics during election years? How does feminism, in any incarnation, appear in media treatments when the spotlight is shone, however briefly, on women who live their lives mostly out of the arena of electoral politics? And how does feminism fare in popular television, particularly in a program meant to appeal to young women through its odd, but allegedly typical, protagonist, Ally McBeal? To answer these questions I turned to media texts that have appeared in recent years and invoke feminism either implicitly or explicitly.

A number address women and so-called women's issues by exploring, and often implicating, the way in which feminism has played out in women's private and public lives. This afterword illuminates some of the ideological patterns that these texts share. I argue that, together, these patterns convey a culturally significant message to their audiences: that feminism is a problematic social movement that should be superseded instead by postfeminist beliefs and assumptions. Postfeminism is privileged in discursive patterns that constitute a solipsistic perspective on women: generalizing about women using a small and very particular group of women's voices and concerns to the exclusion of others. The worldview that emerges represents a minority of elite women's interests and negates the needs of other women. Postfeminist solipsism parallels a concept popularized by Adrienne Rich (1979), "white solipsism": thinking, imagining, and speaking "as if whiteness described the world" (299). Postfeminist solipsism functions similarly but is based on the positionality of elite, white, straight women. It is constructed from problematic assumptions and claims, exemplified in the mainstream media texts that I examine. I end the afterword with a discussion of possible strategies for feminists and media workers to challenge postfeminist hegemony and its attendant common sense.

WOMEN AND EVERYDAY LIFE

The everyday lives of women have become the subject of a great deal of media examination. According to a 1998 *USA Weekend* newspaper supplement, for example, women approached the twenty-first century "focused more on their families and homes, and less on meeting career goals or society's expectations, than at any other time in the past two decades. " In other words, for today's women, "now the word is balance" ("Now the word" 1998, 4). This article reports the findings of the *Update: Women* survey, conducted by two marketing researchers, which found that its women respondents were scaling back their expectations and aspirations in workplaces and replacing them with filial and domestic concerns; a typical respondent was one who was working for pay part time while attending to children and home for the remainder of her time.[1]

    This particular article, short and "factoid-y," is indicative of a trend in much popular culture (and here I include nonfictional as well as fictional media) that purports to report on women's lives: that of implicitly or explicitly blaming feminist politics and feminists for the dissatisfactions and problems faced by women today, while eschewing or negating an expansive notion of politics and community. A similar tendency exists alongside this feminist blaming: that of foregrounding a few high-profile examples of women in powerful positions—or simply public women—as representative of feminism's successes. This rests on a meritocracy argument: a few women have made it in a corporate or professional setting, therefore those who have not must be to blame for not succeeding. These representations of feminism though suggest that the solution for women who experience difficulty performing their first and second shifts—or simply do not want to do both—is to abandon or cut back on their work and public lives so that they may properly fulfill their work in the domestic realm; in other words, if they cannot stand the workplace heat, get back to the kitchen.

The word "balance" is key in the *Update: Women* survey for its perceived value in personal life, public life, and journalism. That is, balance connotes a space between extremes where one (presumably) finds harmony between competing forces, demands, and circumstances. Balance is not a bad goal for which to strive; we do not often hear of imbalance being credibly promoted as a worthwhile goal, however, it is worthwhile to consider what we mean when we talk about balance. For example, which elements are we trying to balance? To what end are we striving for balance, or is this an end in itself? Finally, is it the case that the elements we are attempting to balance are as extreme and oppositional as might be suggested in some public discourse?

Rhetorical forms used in media accounts may drive a perceived urgency to resolve "unbalanced" situations. Justin Lewis argues just that, and, further, that certain patterns in political reporting result in persistently reproducing what he calls the "hegemony of corporate center-right interests" (1999, 251). These patterns, he argues, are at least indirectly responsible for the way in which the majority of respondents to a poll that he and his colleagues conducted implicitly consented to aspects of a political ideology that work against them. One of the patterns of reporting that Lewis identifies as being both prevalent and insidious he refers to as the "Left versus Right framework of political reporting." This framework divides politicos and commentators into one of two dichotomous realms: those who represent left-wing politics and those who represent right-wing politics. One of the (many) problems with this framework is that, rather than representing liberal to actual leftist values, spokespersons identified with the Left usually are centrist in their beliefs—if not to the right of centrist. When combined with a tendency to emphasize conflict, this frame, Lewis (1999) asserts, stresses political differences "while areas of agreement are *assumed to take place somewhere in the political center*" (256, emphasis in original).

Lewis's analysis could be applied to reporting on so-called women's issues and feminism as well. In fact, the framework he describes undergirds some recent—and high-profile—mainstream media accounts of women's lives and/or feminism's role in them. As I discussed in earlier chapters, corporate interests come into play in media representation of political women, one factor in the production of a postfeminist hegemony. Just as Lewis argues that the Left is misrepresented in political reporting, so too is feminism in its construction in mainstream media. That is, feminism is vilified and depicted as an extreme politics that has benefited few and harmed many. What is constructed as middle ground, between the feminist and pre-feminist extremes, is postfeminism: an essentialist ideology that privileges individualism and the interests of elite, white, straight women at the expense of a collective politics of diverse women's needs.

News about women often is saturated with commentary about harried mothers who have discovered that parenting and working for pay are realms whose demands are mutually exclusive (though similarly draining)—an opposition that has provoked various antifeminist tracts suggesting that feminists are to blame. By suggesting that women could work for pay *and* be good parents, feminists have created unrealistic and unrealizable expectations for women, they say. In such discourse, "balance" is to be found only when women capitulate to their essential natures: procreating and then caring for their progeny as their first and most gratifying priority.

In much public discourse, feminism has become a scapegoat social movement—a straw figure easy to attack, because it has been constructed as being so extreme and counterproductive to women's lives as to be laughable. This perspective was propagated thoroughly during the 1990s by very positive media coverage given to Camille Paglia and Christina Hoff Sommers, two self-proclaimed feminists who have written antifeminist tracts (*Who Stole Feminism?* by Sommers and *Sexual Personae* and *Vamps and Tramps* by Paglia). Sommers' and Paglia's mainstream media appearances have promoted them as thoughtful academics, simply and rationally critical of the feminist movement, despite their clearly polemical tone and the factually inaccurate bases for many of their claims (Dow 1996; Flanders 1994). This version of feminism has become a social movement made accountable for any issue, problem, or concern even remotely related to women; as Melissa Deem (1999) argues about the Clinton–Lewinsky drama, feminism and women are typically conflated in media discourse, a tactic that makes feminists spokespersons for all women and feminist-sympathetic men.

The short-lived presidential campaign of Elizabeth Dole evoked similar responses in news stories, that is, commentators used Dole as a symbol of women's equality with men, and if feminists did not support her, then they were betraying their loyalties to their sex. Dole equivocated on the specifics of her political agenda, but her record suggested that she was anything but a feminist. Historically, she aligned herself with right-wing religious activists and organizations such as Pat Robertson and the Christian Coalition, stated that she would support "'the idea of'" a constitutional amendment prohibiting abortion, and fought hard against the Family and Medical Leave Act (Nichols 1999, 31–32). Yet Patricia Ireland, president of NOW, reported that she had spoken with NOW members who were torn on the issue of whether to support Dole or Al Gore—simply because they supported the presence of women in high political offices (ibid., 31). Is such support of Dole though a move that supports feminism? If women and feminism are conflated, then the answer is "yes": supporting any woman under these circumstances could be construed as feminist, but if we stop to consider the past record of Dole as a predictor of her future policies, then the answer is likely to be "no." And, although news workers seemed to enjoy covering Dole, giving her much flattering coverage, the mere fact of her persistent presence in news narratives does not translate into the concrete realities of support for policies that could help large numbers of women (see, e.g., Bayer 1999; Cocco 1999; Sobieraj 1999).

Marjorie Ferguson (1990) points out that women who rise to positions of power often are held up in public discourse as evidence of the success of feminism, and surely feminism, with its push to make powerful positions open to women, is in large part responsible for Dole's ascendance. Dole's place in power though is only part of the story. How she acts in the service of women's issues is quite another. In Dole's case, it is clear that she is far from feminist—and wants it that way. Elizabeth Dole demonstrates what Ferguson detected in Margaret Thatcher: that rather than being altruistic and encouraging women to follow her up the ladder of success, Dole instead saws "the ladder away from beneath the feet of those on the lower rungs, fearful that" if she does not do so, she will risk losing her status and power in the process of sharing it (223–24).

Ferguson refers to this expectation as the "feminist fallacy": the idea that the presence of women in media texts—including some women in positions of power—translates into "cultural visibility and institutional empowerment" (1990, 215). This fallacy was illustrated in a 1999 issue of *TV Guide*. The cover featured Katie Couric (of *The Today Show*) posing in a pink sweater, set off by a bold headline: "How Women Took Over the News." The story that followed the headline (and its suggestion of an invasion by foreign forces in the nation's newsrooms) celebrated the increased numbers of women in TV journalism and strongly suggested that women had achieved gender parity with their male counterparts. Along with that good news came Diane Sawyer's observations: that this women's coup was responsible for more "soft news" stories that women really cared about (e.g., day care) and a different slant on those about which women were less interested (e.g., "'what's happening in Sri Lanka,'" [Murphy 1999, 22]). Lesley Stahl of *60 Minutes* added that her style of reporting can now be "'more and more of me. It's a style of naturalness'" (Murphy 1999, 20).

There is no doubt that women in journalism have had to fight against sexism in their industry, but is the picture for women as rosy today as *TV Guide* suggests? Maybe not. According to FAIR, women are still nowhere near majority status in journalism: in 1998, they constituted only one-third of all correspondents, and they covered just 28 percent of news stories. None of the top twenty-five media corporations have women at their helms (FAIR 1999b). In other words, the fact that a few women have "made it" in TV journalism is no reason to think that the news industry is not still dominated by men, many of whom are far from feminist in their sympathies. Two-term FCC Commissioner Susan Ness (who recently resigned from her post) expressed great alarm about the scarcity of women in leadership or executive positions in all media industries. In her address to the annual meeting of the American Women in Radio and Television (Ness 2000), she pointed to masculinist biases within media organizations and to increased industry consolidation as two of the chief obstacles posed to women of all kinds making progress in the media business. She encouraged the audience to make the promotion of women a priority, arguing that,

> when there is a critical mass of women in key decision making positions within companies or on boards, good things happen. It attracts other talented women to join. When there is a critical mass of women, their voices are heard and not ignored. (Ness 2000, 2)

So Lesley Stahl's "style of naturalness" might work to make her more comfortable in her job, and the soft news focus touted by Diane Sawyer may be interesting to some viewers (although persistently referring to issues of interest to women as "soft news" is problematic), but what does this do for the way feminism is constructed in mainstream news? I contend that it works to privilege both meritocracy and elitism, thus constructing a postfeminism constituted of a glowing, but unrepresentative, picture of journalism for women; thus if antifeminist coverage, or coverage clearly *lacking* feminist interpretation, emerges, it must be legitimate—in other words, it is there because feminists and feminism are in legitimate need of retooling. After all, smart correspondents like Cokie Roberts and Katie Couric would not permit *unfounded* criticisms of feminism—the social movement that helped put them where they are today—would they?

Clearly this sort of cheerleading for women overlooks structural issues in media organizations, such as male dominance in the upper echelons of media management or the intense competition between network news and cable news that drives a bottom-line mentality. These structural issues make it unlikely that much feminist interpretation occurs. What else could explain the vilification of feminism woven through news reports on the Bill Clinton–Monica Lewinsky affair? During the time that Clinton's and Lewin-

sky's story was being broadcast, feminists who supported Clinton were compared to Nazis and prostitutes, were called hypocrites, and were made to seem
responsible for this consensual affair between two adults. If the feminist sea
change that *TV Guide* reported actually existed, it seems doubtful that such an
assault on feminism could have transpired.

Similarly, a *Larry King Live* exposé on Hillary Clinton's physical appearance and fashion sense would likely never have been broadcast if feminists had
clout at CNN. This broadcast of *Larry King Live* featured the commentary of
fashion and entertainment reporters on the subject of Hillary Rodham Clinton's "look" as she began to test the idea of running for the Democratic New
York State Senate seat. These reporters assessed her weight, the length and size
of her legs, her new $500 haircut, and her perceived demeanor: "hard and
bitchy and intense" (FAIR 1999a). That such commentary about male politicians is absent from media coverage suggests that this playing field is far from
level. The feminist fallacy is alive and well—and even thriving—in the news.

The feminist fallacy is just one aspect of postfeminism; another can be
found in entertainment television. Ruth Shalit argues, for example, that "postfeminist" describes many prime-time TV programs that feature women, such as
Dharma & Greg and *Ally McBeal*. These programs' female protagonists, who are
hyperfeminine even as they perform demanding jobs (such as attorney), represent "really nothing but a male producer's fantasy of feminism, which manages
simultaneously to exploit and to deplore, to arouse and to moralize" (Shalit
1998, 30). Finally, Shalit notes, these programs, particularly *Ally McBeal*, "have
made male power and female powerlessness seem harmless, cuddly, sexy, safe,
and sellable. They have merely raised conservatism's hem" (32).

My point here is to foreground some of the means by which texts and
trends promoted as feminist, or even pro-woman, do not always hold up as such
in meaningful ways. If anything, an *absence* of strong feminism is more evident
in mainstream media. *Time* magazine's treatise on the state of feminism, 1998,
titled "Is Feminism Dead?," for example, purports to comment on the state of
the feminist movement but succeeds instead in smearing it—and in predictable
ways. As both Susan Faludi (1991) and Susan Douglas (1994) remind us, this
process of trying to bury feminism in public discourse is one that recurs with
regularity in mainstream media. The *Time* editors thus once again deferred to
the time-worn formula of putting feminism to death, while simultaneously
blaming feminists for an appalling array of bad books and dubiously feminist
icons and art.

The *Time* essay was the cover story for the June 29, 1998 edition. The
cover featured the faces of four women, three of whom were stalwart feminist

activists: Susan B. Anthony, Betty Friedan, and Gloria Steinem. But the fourth—the face of Calista Flockhart representing her TV role, Ally McBeal—was the one that garnered the greatest reaction. Under Ally McBeal's face was posed the question, "Is feminism dead?" When that particular face is paired with this question, the question becomes rhetorical. If wacky, self-absorbed, apolitical Ally McBeal is considered a feminist icon, then feminism *must* surely be dead. In response to this issue, one post–*Time* episode of *Ally McBeal* even included an exchange between Ally and a typical media caricature of a feminist that made Ally's (and producer David Kelley's) stance on feminism all too clear.

As Ally exits a courtroom into a busy courthouse hallway, she is accosted by a loud woman who grabs her by the arm and then announces that she has been nominated as a 1999 professional role model by the "Women for Progress" group. The following dialogue ensues:

> FEMINIST: You're a role model.
>
> ALLY: I . . . I don't want to be a role model.

The feminist, not listening to Ally's objection, tells her that she is going to have to change how she dresses and to "fatten up" because her group does not want young girls glamorizing "that thin thing."[2]

> FEMINIST: My sources tell me that you feel an emotional void without a man. You're really going to have to lose that if women are going to look up to you.
>
> ALLY: I don't want them looking at me at all.
>
> FEMINIST: Don't be pissy. You're a role model. And you'll do what we tell you to do. And you can start by dropping that skinny, whiny, emotional slut thing, and be exactly who we want you to be. Nothing more, nothing less. Can you do *that* pinhead?

This dialogue, which turns out to be one of many of Ally's fantasy sequences, concludes with Ally turning to the feminist, biting off her nose, and spitting it out against a door. Later, as she petulantly recounts this dream to co-worker John Cage, she snarls, "I had a dream they put my face on the cover of Time magazine as the *face* of feminism!"

After viewing this episode, one need not wonder about Ally's and producer David Kelley's feelings about feminism and feminists. The fascist, abrasive feminist is a stock stereotype in mainstream media and works to discredit both feminism and its adherents (see, e.g., Kamen 1991). Ally's pure disdain for feminism—or even for being a role model for "young girls"—is obvious at a glance. A quick assessment of some of her other statements and behaviors on the program would suggest that Ally is hardly a feminist at all.[3] In one episode, for instance, Ally tells roommate Renee that yes, she does "want to change the world. But first I want to get married."

Despite such clear indications of Ally's actual politics, the *Time* author's conclusion is predictable. The article itself is standard tabloid fare: hyperbolic and replete with dubious evidence to substantiate the claim that feminism is a has-been social movement. Ginia Bellafante, the author of the *Time* story, has written a polemic which, if it had appeared in *The Star* or *The Weekly World News* would be easy to dismiss. Bellafante's piece, however, appears in a historically respectable newsmagazine and therefore benefits from the halo effect of its context. While it seems fairly obvious that she has constructed this polemic as a straw figure destined to generate increased sales by controversy, it still bears the imprimatur of the Time Warner corporation (now AOL-Time Warner)—one of the six largest media parent companies in the U.S. oligopolistic media world ("100 Leading Media Companies" 1999; Bagdikian 2000). The Time Warner corporation's importance to the media oligopoly might raise questions as to the intention of *Time's* editorial board vis-à-vis this commentary on feminism. In other words, *Time's* recycling of this topic is more of a demonstration of its commercial appeal than of its legitimacy as political commentary.

But if that is not enough to raise questions, then the spurious methods that Bellafante uses to make her argument should: she makes claims using—at most—the slimmest evidence; usually her claims are simply unsubstantiated. Her "that-was-then-this-is-now" examples signify a dead future for feminist politics—hijacked by what she refers to as the "flightiness of contemporary feminism" (Bellafante 1998, 57). Her evidence for such flightiness? Popular culture texts such as the novel *Bridget Jones's Diary* and the television program *Ally McBeal* (contrasted with their second-wave feminist counterparts *The Women's Room* and *The Mary Tyler Moore Show*, respectively). She argues that the female protagonists in these contemporary texts are further evidence of feminism gone awry:

> Much of feminism has devolved into the silly. And it has powerful support for this: a popular culture insistent on offering images of grown single women as frazzled, self-absorbed girls. . . . The problem with Bridget and Ally is that they are presented as archetypes of single womanhood even though they are little more than composites of frivolous neuroses. (Bellafante 1998, 57)

To Bellafante, Camille Paglia represents what feminism should be. She argues that Paglia's very controversial book, *Sexual Personae*, "helped catapult feminism beyond an ideology of victimhood" (1998, 58). That Bellafante accepts the notion that feminism ever relied upon an "ideology of victimhood" places her squarely in a camp with writers such as Christina Hoff Sommers and Katie Roiphe, who make the same, unsubstantiated, claim. Sommers's and Roiphe's works have been roundly criticized by feminists for their decidedly antifeminist and even at times misogynist sentiments (see Dow 1996, for an excellent summary). Moreover, Paglia's book did more to catapult her into the national media limelight to act as a vehicle for her own self-promotion than it did to raise public interest in feminist politics.

It is a damned if we do/damned if we don't equation. The media stereotype of feminism is that of a social movement confounded by seriousness and populated by grave, ball-busting women (Douglas 1994; Kamen 1991). So if feminists decide to have a little fun with a performance art fund-raiser ("The Vagina Monologues") it is evidence of the devolution of feminism. Similarly, the presence of women starring in television programs must mean that feminism is both responsible for getting them there and for the personalities that their characters possess. If there is a logic to this argument, it escapes me. Bellafante even notes that *Ally McBeal*'s producer, David Kelley, does not suggest that either he or Ally McBeal (the character) are feminist, although Kelley does claim that Ally is "all for equal rights" (Bellafante 1998, 58).

Danielle Crittenden's *What Our Mothers Didn't Tell Us* (1999) uses similarly spurious tactics to make a case against feminism. Crittenden is a spokesperson for the Independent Women's Forum (IWF) and the editor of their "Women's Quarterly" newsletter. The IWF is a conservative antifeminist group that churns out press releases blaming feminism for society's myriad ills. Like a latter-day incarnation of Phyllis Schlafly and the Eagle Forum, Crittenden aligns herself with conservative causes and politicians; unlike Schlafly, however, Crittenden never names her political ideology. *What Our Mothers Didn't Tell Us* is her book-length attempt to push women back to the days of yore by espousing a return to marrying young, having children quickly thereafter, and staying home with the children at least until they are old enough not to be traumatized by their mothers' outside-the-home job obligations (preferably when they leave home for college or other independent living arrangements).

Crittenden bases her argument on a foundation of antifeminism: for the last three decades, feminists sold women a bill of goods by telling them that they could—and should—successfully parent and work for pay, all while managing to have egalitarian romantic relationships. Crittenden especially objects to a feminism that she argues has elevated careers over family, betraying both women and children in the process. Clearly this has failed women, she argues, because evidence of an epidemic of desperately unhappy, feminist-influenced women is all around us. Her proof of this? Women's magazine headlines about the proliferation of unhappy single women and the multitude of techniques available for remedying their single status—in other words, to catch a man.

> When the magazines are not terrifying women into celibacy with articles on the dangers of "date rape"[4] and sexually transmitted diseases, they are offering desperate "tips" to catch a man's attention. . . . And once you have managed to turn a man's head, it's assumed that you will have no end of trouble keeping it pivoted in your direction. (Crittenden 1999, 15)

Because second-wave feminists had touted the benefits of single life, then surely they were responsible for such widespread dissatisfaction. When Crittenden conducted a tour of a few East Coast colleges and universities, she found that the few women who were proud to call themselves feminists were "on the fringes of student society . . . women with odd personalities and carefully cultivated grievances. . . . It is because women like these call themselves feminists that so many others have decided that feminism has gone 'too far'" (19).

What feminists failed to realize, Crittenden claims, is that women will always be unhappy when they are unfaithful to their essential natures. Their essential natures, of course, tell them to pair off into marriage early, have children when young, and nest with their babies until they are strong and confident enough to weather life's storms. Then and *only* then should women consider working for pay. Oh, and they should not consider divorce an option—the ease with which couples can become legally uncoupled is one of the main weapons in the morality-obliterating arsenal of feminist doctrine. Independent women can kiss the idea of coupling good-bye anyway: they are hopelessly self-absorbed, and all of this independence "has the perverse effect of making it even more difficult even to attract, let alone keep," a man (91).

Ultimately, the legacy of Crittenden's straw-figure feminism is that women now "think of themselves as a victimized subset of humanity and not as active participants in a free and democratic society" (189). Part of Crittenden's claim may be correct—that some women (and probably many men too) feel alienated or informally disenfranchised from politics of any kind. Crittenden's evidence though for blaming feminism for this is weak at best. In blaming feminism, she betrays her mildly obscured roots in conservative politics, but she also is a victim—of her assumptions, if nothing else. That is, she falls prey to the notion that media texts, such as women's magazines, realistically reflect lived experience—in this case, the quotidian lives of women. Using popular culture and popular media to gauge the success or failure of a social movement is at best a weak method; at worst, it is dishonest.

At a glance around the magazine stand at any grocery store one can easily see women's magazines that portray women as unhappily, dangerously single or exhausted from trying to deal with the pressures of work and family, but such magazines are, first and foremost, commercial endeavors; they are spaces in which advertisers peddle their products to a target audience of women consumers (an important market, to be sure). Editors of these magazines routinely tweak, alter, and eradicate stories that might alienate advertisers (see Gloria Steinem's "Sex, Lies, and Advertising" essay [1999] for an enlightening discussion of advertiser pressures on women's magazine editors). Advertisers dictate the placement and content of stories in women's magazines to produce a seamless flow between ads and stories; editors capitulate in order to continue to attract advertisers and thus to reproduce the commercial imperative of their industry. Crittenden overlooks the possibility that such stories may appear in these magazines, not because they are accurate reflections of the state of women's lives, circa the *fin de siecle*, but because their harried protagonists' lives could be represented in a very particular, commercially appealing fashion, as in need of the remedies offered by the consumer products and service industries that conveniently advertise in these magazines. *Cosmopolitan* and *Glamour*, to name just two magazines that Crittenden cites, regularly offer stories about the difficulties that women face in today's world, but the solutions they offer for diminishing or erasing these difficulties usually are consumerist in nature, and almost always sexist (see, e.g., Duffy and Gotcher 1996; Duke and Kreshel 1998; Garner, Sterk, and Adams 1998; Ruggiero and Weston 1985). If women's magazines are to be used as data for anything, this should be accompanied by an interrogation of commercialism, which is at the heart of their story-selection process. It is not *feminism* that is to blame for women being unhappy (if, indeed, women are) but commercialism and consumerism. It is not feminism that provides role models for anorexic and bulimic body types, or suggests that women's existential crises can be ameliorated through bath salts or cellulite cream. In other words, it is not feminism that has promoted a commercial fix for metaphysical ills. Nevertheless, feminism has been a historically easy target for public commentators of all stripes.

My point here is not to attack commercial women's magazines (that has been done well elsewhere) but to suggest that in using them to read women's lives writ large, Crittenden bases her argument on a fundamentally flawed notion: that commercial media simply hold up a mirror to the social world and publish or broadcast what they see there. What I call the reflection fallacy, and what Stuart Hall (1982) refers to as the "naturalistic illusion" (76), is one that a first-year media studies student might make—but not an experienced journalist, as Crittenden claims she is. In using this fallacious reasoning, she again betrays her purpose in writing about women's lives, and perhaps even more importantly, she has the opportunity to further publicize her book's smear campaign on her workshop tour: a traveling "seminar" for businesswomen's groups at which she inveighs against feminism.

CONTESTING THE NEW POSTFEMINIST ORDER

Postfeminist solipsism emerges from the antifeminist and feminist messages coded into mainstream media texts and is constructed using a variety of ideals and tactics: emphasizing the essentialist ideal of maternity and marriage, such as that Crittenden advances; attaching the label "feminist" to objectionable personalities, ideologies, or aesthetics (*Ally McBeal* and *Time*); reducing feminism to a push for gender parity in public and private sphere activities (*TV Guide*); publicly burying feminism (again) (*Time*); and the subtle privileging of a mostly white, middle-class to elite, straight perspective on women's lives and needs. This solipsism, of course, marginalizes or obviates the views of women who are not within this small and privileged group. These women and their lives are virtually absent from these mainstream media accounts of women's lives, thus these normative messages for women have a strong, but unspoken, class component: middle-class to elite women are those who fit the dominant definition of womanhood constructed in mainstream media accounts.

The implications of this for feminism are several. First, feminist public figures could use the media better; Gloria Steinem's and Patricia Ireland's defenses of President Clinton during his impeachment were too few and scattershot to even begin to be commensurate with the deafening roar of the opposition. A more thorough, multimedia approach to feminist issue management would be a start, as would a more broad-based cadre of spokespeople. For example, the conservative IWF makes available a group of speakers placed in different media venues, such as *Good Morning America*, to speak on a variety of topics: the Littleton massacre, gun control (or, more precisely, no gun control), the Supreme Court's decision on sexual harassment in public schools, and so on. Susan Jane Gilman's investigation of the IWF concludes by noting that its members' constant availability to journalists is probably the most important weapon in their public relations arsenal. Because they have become "mainstream media darlings,"

Gilman observes, the IWF's "influence and visibility far exceed their numbers" (2000, 64). A broad-based feminist contingent could make itself equally available, armed with issues perhaps even more resonant with women than the IWF's.[5]

From the academic side, an alliance between feminist political economists and feminist activists could be helpful. Such a collaboration could reveal and publicize institutional rationalizations for media representations of women and feminism. As Eileen Meehan (in Consalvo 1999) has pointed out, stereotypes are cheap to produce and propagate in media texts, thus media conglomerates that need to reduce their production costs are more likely to rely upon them. Hackneyed stereotypes of feminists—and women—thus represent an easy means of reducing production costs and multiplying revenues. Meehan notes that these financial "constraints do not bode well for diversity in media images" and have led to a reliance upon rape as a standard narrative component in media texts, particularly in film (in Consalvo 1999, 326). Other industry researchers, such as Martha Lauzen and David Dozier (1999a, 1999b), have uncovered what they call "dismal" trends in women's employment in the television and film industries. This research also could be useful in making a case for the necessity of *structural* changes in media industries that must precede significant discursive shifts across media texts.

Finally, a public alliance between feminism and class–race–sexual orientation politics—such as that being promoted by the National Communication Association's Women's Caucus and Feminist and Women's Studies Division—would help both to widen the lens through which feminist interpretation can occur and to increase the number of adherents to feminist principles and movements. These possibilities for intervention can help illustrate the anachronistic, inaccurate, and narrow perspective on feminism that postfeminist solipsism encourages. The return to a nuclear family ideal of domestic relations valorized in the literature I have reviewed here, for example, is inappropriate for the vast majority of the U.S. population because of economic and occupational demands. A regular critique of such nostalgia, also using mainstream media channels, could help cast it in a less positive light. A regular critique of postfeminist solipsism also could help change the question "Is feminism dead?" to one that reveals a troubling structure of oppression: "Is patriarchy alive and well?"[6] The latter question also might shift expectations so that the "style of naturalness" assumed in popular culture interrogations of feminism is revealed for what it is: a discourse that normalizes domesticity, whiteness, a middle-class to elite class position and heterosexuality as the traits that women in general should possess. Contesting this postfeminist solipsism *in toto*, including the means by which it is achieved in mainstream media, is one important way in which to effect a stronger, more inclusive, and media-savvy feminist politics.

One other professional change along these same lines is to reconceptualize journalism and news production as public journalism has. In many ways, the hegemony of postfeminism is at least partially indicative of a failure of news workers to address the needs of a large community they purport to serve: all of those women outside of the narrow band of postfeminism's appeal. In saying this, I am not suggesting that individual journalists and news workers are to blame for this failure; as I have tried to show in preceding chapters, the political economy of news production is probably the primary factor in determining the culture of newsrooms and in guiding journalistic practice. A Pew Research Center for People and the Press survey of 552 news workers, for instance, revealed that most feel that the credibility of their work has been seriously compromised by the commercial pressures exerted by their organizations' executives (Morin 1999, 34), but nonmainstream journalists may not resist postfeminist common sense in their reporting either: alternative-news accounts of the Hill–Thomas hearings and the Year of the Woman, for example, were seldom better than those from the mainstream media (Vavrus 1997). Mostly these accounts propagated either postfeminism or antifeminism—particularly that characterized by suggestions of women being victimized by feminism. Journalistic reports from all sources typically obscure the importance of feminism as one of the most socially valuable social movements of the twentieth century, a movement that has problematized and attempted to remedy a variety of societal ills directed at women and indirectly affecting men and children.

Public journalism promises a paradigm shift in how news workers conceive of their role in reporting meaningfully on issues that significantly affect the public. Still in its experimental stages, public journalism arose from a perceived need among journalists, their publics, and critics for more ethical, public-centered political journalism. Jay Rosen (1996), one of public journalism's most vocal academic advocates, argues that this perceived need was catalyzed by the 1988 presidential campaign, in which journalists and their audiences complained of having been manipulated by the sophisticated tactics of well-paid campaign consultants.[7] Since the 1988 campaign, journalism scholars, journalists, editors, and other news workers have been working together to create a better system of reporting, not only for politics but for the production of news generally. Under the auspices of the Poynter Institute and the Freedom Forum First Amendment Center, these public journalism groups actively seek to redefine journalism, reshape the culture that guides the practices of news production, and initiate an ongoing, substantial dialogic relationship between the press and the publics for whom they produce their work.

Public journalism "invites people to *become* a public." To that end, it "calls on the press to help revive civic life and improve public dialogue—and to fashion a coherent response to the deepening troubles in our civic climate, most of which implicate journalists" (J. Rosen 1996, 1, emphasis in original). A need for such activity has merit among a wide group of citizens: A survey of 1,765 people (roughly one-third journalists, one-third politicians, and one-third news consumers), conducted by Beverly Kees and Bill Phillips (1994) of the Freedom Forum, showed that participants voiced an urgent need for public journalism. Kees and Phillips argue that the

> best way to re-establish the public's trust in the political process and to avoid news restrictions is for the news media themselves to put community interests ahead of the interests of stock analysts or personal ambition—and to be seen doing it. The remedies are fair and accurate reporting instead of innuendo and speculation, a sense of proportion in presenting the news and the good sense to move on once the story has been told. (107)

The main idea that informs public journalism is that news workers can and should use their work to foster democratic practice by involving publics as participative citizens. Advocates of public journalism argue that the news industry has failed its publics by becoming lapdogs to the powerful rather than watchdogs over them. This is not a new complaint, however, the move to create a program for improvement and to implement it in different communities is a departure from the norm. The idea of a dialogic relationship between communities as publics and news workers—active, flexible, and based on good-faith efforts by both parties to understand the needs of one another—is at the heart of public journalism.

What is probably the most foundational practice in the public journalism movement is what J. Rosen refers to as "proactive neutrality" (1996, 13). Proactive neutrality is a conceptual replacement for objectivity, long assailed by media studies scholars as at best a dubious goal, at worst a destructive delusion both for its impossibility and disadvantage to audiences and media workers alike (see, e.g., Bagdikian 2000; Turow 1997). As an alternative, proactive neutrality is "neutral because it prescribes no chosen solution and favors no particular party of interest. It is proactive in its belief that journalism can in certain cases intervene in the service of broad public values without compromising its integrity" (J. Rosen 1996, 13).

Proactive neutrality encourages journalists to become active members of their communities so that they can enhance public trust and their own understanding of their publics. In this view, news editors who refuse to vote in local and national elections because it would compromise their objectivity would move from a place of reverence to ignominy, their detachment no longer a desirable condition. Proactive neutrality also encourages journalists to foster the overall health of their communities during their work time and off-hours. J. Rosen argues that the "force of . . . reporting will originate not in the distance [journalists] keep but in the connection they make to the real aspirations and daily struggles of the people they report to" (1996, 63).[8]

To activate publics through journalism, a number of different news organizations have experimented with addressing and learning to satisfy the stated needs of their communities. For example, Davis Merritt, editor of the *Wichita Eagle* newspaper, began in 1990 a program called "Where They Stand" to cover the gubernatorial election; the point of the new program was to remove the power from campaign workers to spin the campaign's messages and to look instead to citizens to tell the *Eagle* what they wanted journalists to cover in the campaign. The power to define the issues and the media's focus on them thus came from citizens rather than poll takers or campaign consultants. The campaigns were covered in terms of the ten issues that emerged as those most important to the community. Reporters analyzed each issue for its impact on the community and then summarized candidates' positions on each of the issues. Finally, reporters described "what, if anything, was said regarding those issues by the campaigns that week" (J. Rosen 1996, 36). Readers of the paper reported that they found this section of the paper the most helpful in making up their minds about the candidates.

Such a scenario sounds almost too good to be true, and Jay Rosen recognizes this. He tempers his discussion with a cautionary note that public journalists not be overly optimistic in what they convey to their audiences. Specifically, "the idea that citizens can 'take back control' of institutional structures . . . can lead to a kind of mythmaking, where the realities of power and influence are obscured by the charged rhetoric of 'empowerment'" (40). In other words, public journalists must walk a line between being overly sanguine about the potential to take on City Hall and being overly pessimistic about the possibilities to change the workings of power. Citing James Carey, J. Rosen notes that public journalists need to work from a different narrative—one constructed out of cautious optimism and a genuine desire to make publics in the United States more egalitarian and participative. Peter Parisi (1997) has criticized some examples of public journalism (which he distinguishes from the more locally focused civic journalism) for their myopia and excessively vague prescriptions for progress. What can prevent these problems, he argues, is an approach that comprises both local issues and their related structural elements. That is, in addition to allowing public good and community need to dictate topics and approaches to issues, news reports must include "authoritative discussion" of the larger "social and economic factors" to which local issues are necessarily linked. This can challenge even the most industrious, well-intentioned investigative reporters, because it asks them to adopt principles that contradict much of what they learned in school and through professional socialization. Most difficult to contend with for journalists may be the likelihood that "exploration of the public good can strain dominant ideology and fundamental journalistic narrative assumptions" (Parisi 1997, 681).

Acting out of a concern for communities is viewed by public journalism advocates as an ethical stance with a fringe benefit: it challenges the power monopoly that results from media organizations' control over important information, according to Everette Dennis, director of the Freedom Forum (in Kees and Phillips 1994, 80–81). In this paradigm, news organizations base their news decisions on the needs of the public and are charged with satisfying those rather than the needs of corporate owners. Forcing attention to the needs of communities helps combat the lack of attention to local/community issues that chain-owned newspapers, for example, typically demonstrate (Bagdikian 1997).

Kees and Phillips (1994) argue that in addition to acting for the greater good, public journalism can be an economically sound practice, because it visibly places "public service over profits," a route that is "the way to profits" (99) for its community enrichment. They cite former *Atlanta Journal Constitution* editor and media researcher Bill Kovach, who concluded that "just as American consumers want cars that will make them safely and efficiently mobile, American citizens want a press that will make them fully and effectively aware" (ibid.). Equating media audiences to car buyers is a problematic move that naturalizes a seller-consumer relationship between journalists and their audiences, thus restricting the ways in which to imagine this relationship. However, it does encourage a sense of accountability—both for news workers and publics—for the *results* of the work they do together. In his book *Doing Public Journalism*, author and journalist Arthur Charity (1995) makes a similar argument, noting that public journalism offers communities something that they cannot get from shorter *USA Today* or tabloid-type approaches to news: in-depth analyses and strong connections to particular community needs and concerns. He includes examples of newspapers whose turn to public journalism improved their relationships with their readers, along with other positive results: declines in accusations of bias, good attendance and response from newspaper-sponsored events, and, in some cases, increased circulation (156–57). However, Charity warns that because public journalism is still in the early stages of development, it is difficult to gauge other effects or long-term benefits.

A collaboration between public journalism and feminism could offer a challenge to the Gramscian common sense that I argue has emerged in the news coverage of political women during the 1990s and into 2000. Public journalism efforts could be enriched with insights from feminism about the ways in which institutional power is meted out, reproduced, and legitimated differentially through discursive practices that ascribe meaning to identity. Feminism would likely benefit from public journalism's intimate knowledge of how to frame and publicize important issues strategically, and from its experience with transforming expressed public needs into meaningful, community-specific analyses. Such a collaboration could focus attention on the omissions and limitations of postfeminist common sense.

One of the criticisms that Charity (1995) makes about conventional journalism is that it tends to depict issues in terms of polarized positions or factions. My reading substantiates Charity's assertion: polarity characterized the discourse surrounding the Hill–Thomas hearings and the Year of the Woman, for example, leading me to conclude that mainstream journalists and editors must gain something—perhaps professional respectability—when they frame these events in terms of a battle between the sexes (as cliché as that particular metaphor is, journalists have used it abundantly). A feminist public journalism sensitive to how gender, race, sexual orientation, and class can be deployed to polarize issues and communities would move us one step further toward avoiding this discursive trap, and this challenge to binary framing would be in keeping with both feminism and the principles of public journalism. A public journalism that analyzed and then responded meaningfully to the ways in which power works through a nexus of gender-race-class-sexual orientation would be better suited to dealing with the needs of any community that it was charged to serve.

CONCLUSION

This book has traced the discursive construction of women's relationship to electoral politics as it was embodied in high-profile media events during the final decade of the twentieth century. Media texts that focus on political women are full of contradictory elements that suggest a far-from-settled place for women in politics, and in culture generally. Some of the events in this coverage were activist in character and thus exemplified what politically motivated women and men could accomplish in increasing public support for their political positions. Their constructions in the media appear to signify a general acceptance of some first- and second-wave feminist principles, but the mainstream media's take on political women also, and importantly, produces a postfeminist hegemony. Postfeminism represents a direction for feminism that emphasizes the positionality and class interests of a relatively small group of women. Its "post" prefix signifies that it is a position "beyond" feminism; postfeminist texts are those that assume that second-wave feminist politics has accomplished all that it set out to and outlived its usefulness. The material realities of a majority of women's lives suggest otherwise, however. That is, the conditions in which many women in the United States live out their lives point to a need for political intervention rather than the apolitical consumerism and domesticity touted by media postfeminism. Postfeminism offers little or nothing to women who are not well situated materially and socially. It fails to address the needs and concerns of a majority of women, yet it significantly informs news discourse of women in politics. The hegemonic subject constructed in such discourse is not one who embodies or even speaks to the concerns of most women in this country.

A postfeminist hegemony may discourage or even obviate political activism or collective political work around feminist issues—or perhaps just that beyond the narrow band relevant to sustaining the lifestyles of elite women, commercial television's prime target. In this sense it could be considered antidemocratic in the same way that McChesney (1999) argues that media institutions today are anti-democratic: A small minority of relatively privileged women are those anointed by news workers to represent the political needs and goals of women as a whole. The life complexities of and great variations among women simply do not appear in mainstream reports of women in politics or of women living everyday lives. The ideal female subject in the news tends to be the apolitical soccer-mom consumer or the relatively well-heeled, well-financed postfeminist candidate. This ideal subject arises out of the media oligopoly's political economy and also serves to validate it: She is not especially threatening to the practices of corporate executives—often she is a corporate executive herself (e.g., former corporate attorney and Wal-Mart board member Hillary Rodham Clinton and former banking executive Dianne Feinstein). This female subject is an integral component in the media's contribution to postfeminist hegemony and in the commercial imperative that drives her construction in mainstream media texts.

Reading the representational politics of contemporary media reveals a consistent deference to neoliberal principles and suggests that the gender politics of media executives tend to postfeminism. This is a convergence which, if it were independent of reports on electoral politics, would warrant close study, but when these particular converged ideologies appear in news coverage of electoral politics, their likely influence on imagining democratic practice warrants strategies for resistance. In the current climate of media deregulation and consolidation, strategies for resisting the anti-democratic representational politics that result from corporate influence on news will most likely have to be found in us—media consumers—and perhaps in public journalism. To reiterate a point from chapter 1, this necessitates a kind of literacy that pushes us to consider two dimensions of the representational process: first, the stories about gender, race, class, and sexual orientation that are privileged in media texts along with those that *are not*, for the latters' absences can be particularly illustrative of news-industry common sense; and, second, the relations of production that exert direct and indirect influences on the stories told and not told, as well as on the attributes of the characters who populate them. The commercial imperative of the news business has become the all-important arbiter of the tales told in the news.

These dimensions have particular importance for electoral politics, which constitutes what is probably the single most important site for effecting major social change today. For women, the realm of electoral politics could be especially significant for its ability to politicize the personal and codify structural improvements to lives that could use some relief, but neoliberal postfeminism's dominance in the news distracts from the kind of collective activism that appears necessary for structural changes to come about. It is worth remembering that this converged ideology is only one of many different constructions that could shape reporting on electoral politics. Its naturalized authority makes it difficult to consider other ways to frame news reports, but this is precisely what is necessary to refashion political reporting into something that "invites people to *become* a public" (J. Rosen 1996, 1, emphasis in original). Self-constituted publics, such as those J. Rosen has envisioned forming in conjunction with public journalism, offer hope to challenge the hegemony of neoliberal postfeminism and the public consent to its dominance that it assumes. In the process, they could redirect media attention away from its exclusive focus on glass ceilings and move it down, onto floors—a more apt metaphor for the many U.S. women whose incomes hover at this level and whose job descriptions quite literally place them there. The need for universal political empowerment is great, and savvy publics, in their ability to work with and on the media system, could help bring it about and make the twenty-first century one in which the needs of the majority—and not an elite minority—form the centerpiece of our electoral system.

Notes

Introduction

1. I place "real world" in quotation marks not because I doubt the existence of a material world, but because I want to point to the contested nature of the term. Media studies researchers—and I am no exception—are typically loath to draw a line that determines where the media world ends and the "real" world begins. Given the saturation of the "real" with media-generated images, narratives, textual fragments, and so on, it becomes an impossible—and ultimately an unproductive—task to demarcate their separation point. But this is not to claim that "nothing exists outside of discourse." Instead, I follow Stuart Hall (1997) in refuting this claim with the following: "nothing which is meaningful exists outside of discourse" (44). In other words, the meanings that media consumers make with the texts that proliferate and circulate endlessly play a role in determining very real behaviors toward and policies about the people and circumstances featured in media texts. Although media corporations promote specific meanings in their representations, what readers and viewers will do with these meanings is never guaranteed.

2. In her campaigns—in 1992 and then for reelection in 1998—Patty Murray relied upon the "mom in tennis shoes" label to signify one very important aspect of her identity: that of being a typical parent. An opponent had directed the term at Murray when she was a state legislator, and it had been intended as an epithet. Murray, however, seized the term and used it herself as a means of establishing common ground between her and other moms—especially middle-class working mothers.

3. Yeakel's opponent was incumbent Arlen Specter, one of Anita Hill's most strident interrogators on the Senate Judiciary Committee.

4. Feminism should more accurately be considered a plural term, both as a philosophy and as a social movement. In using "feminism" as a singular term, I am not denying this, however, I would argue that the goal I have described is central to all of the feminisms with which I am familiar. While different feminisms may take issue with one another about how best to achieve this goal, its centrality as a goal seems indisputable.

Chapter 1

1. I use the term *political women* to denote women who, either consciously or inadvertently, appear in the media in formal, electoral political contexts. Thus although political woman Anita Hill was not campaigning for an office or working for someone else's campaign, she was part of a process of formal politics—the nomination hearings of Clarence Thomas, by the Senate Judiciary Committee, a group composed of elected officials.

2. To study this relationship, I draw from feminist media studies, cultural studies, and political economy, and I employ qualitative textual analysis—close readings—to theorize the means by which media ascribe meaning to women's presence in the mediated public sphere. I examine the terrain created by the interplay between the discourses of mainstream media and their cultural, material effects, their "effective materiality" (Fiske 1994, 77). These can be understood only in their historical context—a context constituted by symbolic and material conditions.

3. Bush Sr.'s son, George W. Bush, also signed a Gag Ruling—the same prohibition on discussing abortions, but limited to international family planning clinics—the day after he was inaugurated in January 2001.

4. 59.3 percent of women ages eighteen and over were married, 19.3 percent had never been married, and the rest were either widowed or divorced (U.S. Bureau of the Census 1992, 43).

5. The sources I used did not attribute a cause to this disparity, but given the difficulties that many poor, inner-city, and rural women have with obtaining access to family planning and women's health clinics, these differences are not altogether unexpected. According to the Alan Guttmacher Institute, Title X funding was cut by 66 percent between 1980 and 1990. This is crucial: 1 in 5 women relies on Title X family-planning clinics, which have sliding scales for low-income women; many of these are women of color (Women's Action Coalition 1993, 8). Overall, federal funding for maternal and child care decreased by 23.4 percent between 1982 and 1992 (ibid., 40).

6. Despite the similarity of its prefix to other contemporary "posts," such as poststructuralism and postmodernism, postfeminism is not a new term. As far back as 1919, the term was used in conjunction with a move among "female literary radicals in Greenwich Village" to decenter analyses of sex—popularized during the suffrage era— and to broaden social criticism so as to be "'pro-woman without being anti-man'" (Cott 1987, 282).

7. This naturalized discourse was class and race specific; that is, only a minority of women—mostly white and middle class to elite—could opt out of workforce labor. Because of low wages and race discrimination, the economic needs of many families required that women work for pay (Coontz 1992). Their material conditions thus prevented an articulation to hearth and home to supplant that to wage labor.

8. I am grateful to Lisa Disch for illuminating this point.

9. In this sense, it fits well with Gramsci's conception of hegemony as a process by which the subaltern capitulate to power, even in cases in which it does not benefit them to do so. Stacey (1993) notes, for example, that many of the postfeminist women she spoke with were clearly experiencing economic difficulties—many of which could be traced to a lack of a feminist critique of particular practices and issues (e.g., employers' lack of concern about the impact of scheduling on family responsibilities, such as child care).

10. Bagdikian has coined the term "media-industrial complex" in his research on media conglomerates. An obvious riff on Eisenhower's "military-industrial complex," Bagdikian's term is a similar sort of warning, but it is a warning about the undemocratic ramifications of collusion between media institutions and commercial interests.

11. I am not confident assuming that news consumers are totally duped by what the news pretends to be. Without an analysis of media audiences in the context of news viewing/reading, an assumption of how audiences read news texts falls prey to what John Thompson (1990) calls the "fallacy of internalism": using texts alone to speculate about their consequences on audiences (105).

12. Since 1984—when Bagdikian published the first edition of his book *The Media Monopoly*—the number of corporations that control almost all mainstream media outlets in the United States has dropped steadily from fifty corporations to just six today, but while the numbers of these corporations decrease, their size (reach, power, and profitability) increases.

13. In a dramatic illustration of one consequence of this increase in corporate control, Rupert Murdoch, CEO of News Corp. (one of the six parent companies that Bagdikian [2000] names and that Robert McChesney [1999] refers to as one of the "Holy Trinity" media corporations that dominate global media), told his stockholders the following in 1999:

> Our reach is unmatched around the world. We're reaching people from the moment they wake up until they fall asleep. We give them their morning weather and traffic reports through our television outlets around the world. We enlighten and entertain them with such newspapers as the *New York Post* and the *Times* [of London] as they have breakfast, or take the train to work. We update their stock prices and give them the world's biggest news stories every day through such news channels as Fox or Sky News. . . . And when they get home in the evening, we're there to entertain them with compelling first-run entertainment on Fox. . . . Before going to bed, we give them the latest news, and then they can crawl into bed with one of our best-selling novels from HarperCollins. ("Murdoch Round the Clock" 2000, 5)

14. From these I selected the majority (at least 75 percent) of the stories. To examine the Hill–Thomas hearings, I used only television news accounts; I focused

on television because other analyses of the hearings (such as Morrison 1992 and Hill and Jordan 1995) used print media almost exclusively. I looked at television news instead to see if meaningful differences between the two existed, and because I believed that television's representations of these events perhaps bore greater responsibility for the intensely affective context of the hearings. I analyzed all of the evening news broadcasts, special reports, and talk shows that invoked Anita Hill's or Clarence Thomas's name (for more than five seconds to eliminate teasers and other promotional devices), aired on ABC, CBS, and NBC from October 6–October 16, 1991. I also analyzed CNN's almost uninterrupted coverage of the hearings and its special reports on the hearings.

The Year of the Woman coverage came from ABC, NBC, CNN, and a variety of newspapers: the *New York Times*, for national coverage, and local newspapers, such as the *Chicago Tribune* (Carol Moseley Braun), the *Los Angeles Times* (which covered both Barbara Boxer and Dianne Feinstein), the *Philadelphia Inquirer* (Lynn Yeakel), and the *Seattle Times* (Patty Murray). (CBS was absent from this analysis, because it was unavailable from the Vanderbilt Television News Archives, the source from which I obtained most of the television news footage from chapters 2 and 3 in this book.) Soccer mom coverage was from CBS, NBC, and various newspapers available from the First Search index. I focused on television coverage of Hillary Rodham Clinton, analyzing fifty-five of the 418 stories about her candidacy: I chose all of those stories that were not repetitions of one another and that were composed of fifty words or more. These stories were from ABC, CBS, NBC, FOX, CNN, and several independent stations. I selected the texts for the afterword not to get a sense of how feminism was represented in a wide range of outlets but by those from a selected range—specifically, texts published or aired during the period 1998–1999, which had gained some amount of notoriety for their stance on feminism in women's lives.

15. This cartel behavior was illustrated in a story from the *New York Times* business section that described a first-time joint effort between two news programs from two different networks: ABC's *Nightline* and PBS's *Frontline*. In this particular venture, *Frontline* paid *Nightline* to report and produce an episode of *Frontline* scheduled to appear in January 2001, hosted by *Nightline's* Ted Koppel. This was an effort to share resources and "deal with the fallout from the continued dispersion of the broadcast audience to cable television." Broadcast news producers have been forced to become "video entrepreneurs" to compete with their cable counterparts (Rutenberg 2000, 1).

Chapter 2

1. Such stereotypes were particularly inappropriate, since Hill had worked in two federal departments, attended an Ivy League law school, and had practiced law in a prestigious Washington law firm. If anything, these were strong indicators of her insider status.

2. A November 2000 wire story showed that even nine years after the hearings, Anita Hill was still speaking out about white masculine bias in politics. She has reportedly turned her experiences into a "pulpit from which to speak about the plight of women and minorities in America." As a lecturer, an author, and now a professor at Brandeis University, Hill has increased her cultural capital and credibility to such an extent that Senator Alan Simpson (a *very* vocal critic of Hill on the Senate Judiciary Committee) invited her to speak at a Harvard University seminar that he had organized (Madigan 2000). This illustrates well Stuart Hall's argument about the impossibility of guaranteeing meaning; closure or fixity in cultural meanings is virtually impossible to achieve. Even a powerful effort to discredit her ultimately failed to fix Anita Hill's signification.

3. This was an inaccurate depiction of their ideological positions. As many critics have noted (see, e.g., Morrison 1992; Hill and Jordan 1995), Hill and Thomas shared many similarities—more with each other than with many of their supporters.

4. The decision to delay Thomas's nomination vote in order to hear Anita Hill's testimony was not made until October 9. Coverage up until that time was thus full of speculation about whether the Senate would permit Hill's testimony.

5. At one point, Simpson referred to Hill's charges as "this sexual harassment crap" (NBC 1991c), and Hill herself noted that Simpson "threatened me with 'plain old Washington variety harassment' for raising the issue of sexual harassment, and as the senators struggled to regain the control and power they perceived they had lost during the events that led to the second round of hearings" (Hill 1995, 280–81).

6. Much of the discussion in this section is a result of conversations with Mike Greco, Ginna Husting, and Steve Wiley, to whom I am indebted.

7. Thomas's use of the lynching metaphor is considered historically inaccurate, because lynching was reserved for African-American men who were accused of giving attention to or raping *white* women. Historical accounts of lynching reveal incidents of African-American men being lynched, because they were accused of raping—or just looking at—white women, not African-American women.

8. Thomas's nomination had been challenged by a number of groups, including practicing African-American attorneys and judges, for his judicial mediocrity and silence on important issues such as abortion.

9. Nancy Fraser's (1992) essay on the Hill–Thomas hearings points out that much of the criticism of Anita Hill can be understood in terms of its class bias, in addition to its gender and racial bias.

10. A "no" vote meant that the confirmation vote would not go on as scheduled but would be delayed in order to hear from Anita Hill.

11. Anita Hill's name was leaked to the press from an FBI report of her charges against Thomas.

12. This "diagnosis" was subsequently found to be suspect, not only because a psychiatrist who had never met Anita Hill had made it but because the pathology was not accepted by the psychiatric and counseling communities as a legitimate disorder (Phelps and Winternitz 1992).

13. This is a legal term used to denote evidence that comes from a questionable, possibly disreputable, source. Thanks to Pam Cox-Otto for pointing this out.

14. I am not suggesting that this use of dirt metaphors is exclusive to these accounts of the hearings. These terms are used routinely in reports of political wrangling, but here, in a context in which they are used in conjunction with many other metaphors of abjection, they work as integral parts of the stories that TV told about Anita Hill and sexual harassment vis-à-vis electoral politics.

15. The norm in this case was overwhelmingly in favor of Clarence Thomas's confirmation and credibility.

16. For questions concerning gender issues, the networks used "person-on-the-street" polls, along with polls based on much larger, and presumably representative, samples. Of the three polls that used reported data during the period I analyzed, two broke down the findings by sex (ABC/*Washington Post* and CBS/*New York Times*), perhaps leaving the impression that sex was the only variable that might confound the results of these survey questions—or of a full understanding of the phenomenon under consideration.

17. The image that concluded this program was that of the Capitol dome, captured in the reflecting pool beneath it. The water in the pool gyrated with concentric rings, projecting an image of a Capitol institution beset by agitation and shakiness.

CHAPTER 3

1. Even elite working women (with an average income of $248,000) reported that they were exhausted and overworked by the excessive demands placed upon them by a combination of paying jobs and domestic labor. In a poll of 1,250 women, "identified as high-ranking company officials in Fortune 100 companies," reported in the *Washington Post Weekly*, the majority of respondents reported that they routinely sacrificed sleep and time to fulfill their myriad obligations (Grimsley 1996, 37).

2. Although second-wave feminism has been critiqued for its white, middle-class bias and for its single-minded focus on gender as the preeminent basis of oppression—to the extent that movement adherents often *did not* work with other protest groups—its collective activist base, along with its woman-centered agenda, still have merit; indeed, some of the contemporary sociopolitical and material conditions in the United States make these all the more urgently needed.

3. For example, Murray's opponent, Rod Chandler, responded to her in one of their debates with a nonsequitor rendering of an old song, *Dang Me:* "Dang me, dang

me, they ought to take a rope and hang me—hang me from the highest tree. Woman would you weep for me?" (Matassa 1992b, B-1). Reports of this incident were without any sort of stereotypic or arch commentary (although journalists did report being confused by the reference).

4. A fourth frame, that composed of the horse-race aspects of each campaign, existed in the local coverage, however, I will not discuss it here.

5. However, McManus (1995) argues that journalists' and news workers' professional behavior is almost always subject to their bosses' deference to the "principal norm of business," which is "to maximize profit over an indefinite period" (308). See also the essays in chapter 4 of *Censored 2000* (Phillips 2000) for numerous examples of parent corporation and advertiser influence on reporters and the news.

6. My thanks to Ginna Husting for pointing this out.

7. Not "getting it" was a notion—almost always directed at men—that male politicians not only did not understand the rudimentary aspects of women's struggles with sexual harassment but were incapable of comprehending women's issues writ large. The use of the phrase gained popularity after Geraldine Ferraro's comment that on the subject of sexual harassment, the Senate Judiciary Committee "just didn't get it." The phrase spawned a newsletter (printed on pink paper) that circulated in women's groups during the Year of the Woman: *The Getting It Gazette*.

8. Political commentator Anthony Lewis (1992) titled his *New York Times* column "Women: They Are the Change" just after the Democratic National Convention. He observed that the respect shown to women at the convention indicated a major shift in thinking about women's roles and power in partisan politics.

CHAPTER 4

1. Political scientist Susan Carroll (1988) lists specific changes as increased numbers of single women and women as heads of households, increased divorce rates, increased acceptability of egalitarian relationships, and broadened opportunities for women during the preceding decade (255).

2. According to Bonk, the mere fact that the voting data of 1980 were cross-tabulated by sex was a measure of success for liberal feminists; up until that time, sex was a variable not considered important enough to include in poll evaluations (1988, 84).

3. Reagan's attempts to improve his standings with women voters might be termed poorly placed at best and insincere at worst. For instance, one of the stories meant to ameliorate the "woman problem" was written by rabid antifeminist Patrick Buchanan in the extremely conservative *Washington Times*. It was titled "Should Reagan Try to Tame the Shrews?" Another of these stories appeared in *USA Today*. It was titled "Reagan Is Wooing Women" (Bonk 1988, 96–97).

4. This is not altogether surprising. As Karlyn Kohrs Campbell has pointed out (personal communication; 1998), this sort of playful tone, combined with reports of election events as games, is consistent with the way in which news media cover elections as horse races. This kind of reporting tends to be woefully short on historical contextual information and long on discussions of the competitive aspects of campaigns.

5. Thanks to an anonymous *Political Communication* reviewer for illuminating this point.

6. Thanks to an anonymous reviewer for pointing out this reference's connection to soccer moms.

7. Assumptions about the apolitical nature of soccer moms were reinforced in news reports about Sara Jane Olson (a.k.a. Kathleen Soliah)—allegedly a former Symbionese Liberation Army (SLA) "soldier"—arrested in St. Paul, Minnesota, in June 1999. Olson had been quietly ensconced in a middle-class neighborhood in St. Paul for almost twenty-five years since becoming a fugitive from charges that she had conspired to kill Los Angeles police officers with pipe bombs. After her arrest, local news reports and a call-in radio talk show repeatedly referred to her as a soccer mom and expressed shock that Olson, a pillar of the St. Paul community, could have been an SLA member. Callers and journalists were dismayed that a *soccer mom* might be capable of radical politics—and perhaps urban terrorism; their statements implied that soccer moms were supposed to be disinterested in politics and therefore immune to such taint.

8. I am grateful to Pat Kovel-Jarboe for providing me with a copy of this advertisement.

9. Today, the target age of women consumers has been expanded to include women between ages eighteen and forty-nine (Dow 1996, xx).

10. According to the U. S. Census Bureau, 70 percent of married women in the U. S. labor force had children under age eighteen at this time (U.S. Bureau of the Census 1997, 404). Of the total number of women in the U.S. labor force, 82.6 percent were between ages twenty and fifty-four, falling roughly into the "age of acquisition" category (ibid., 397).

Chapter 5

1. The Lexis–Nexis database shows that a total of fifty-one TV news programs mentioned any of the other six female Senate candidates, whereas Hillary Clinton's name was mentioned in 418 of them between January 1 and November 7, 2000.

2. Senate candidates were Maria Cantwell (D-WA), Jean Carnahan (D-MO), Hillary Rodham Clinton (D-NY), Dianne Feinstein (D-CA), Kay Bailey Hutchison (R-TX), Olympia Snowe (R-ME), and Debbie Stabenow (D-MI). Feinstein, Hutchison, and Snowe were running as incumbents. Carnahan's situation was unusual, in that

her husband, Governor Mel Carnahan, was the Democratic nominee; however, Mel Carnahan was killed in a plane crash as he was campaigning in October. Jean took over his campaign and won election to the Senate. All of the other female Senate candidates won as well. In House races, 122 women ran, and fifty-nine won seats. The House of Representatives and the Senate now have a record number of women members: thirteen in the Senate and fifty-nine in the House (Center for American Women and Politics 2001, 1).

3. Since 1961, Roper Organization polls have shown that respondents believe television to be the most credible medium for news reports (Head, Sterling, and Schofeld 1994). Television is also ubiquitous: As of 1999, 98.4 percent of U.S. homes had televisions, and these homes average about two televisions each (U. S. Bureau of the Census 1999).

4. This sort of treatment fulfills a significant professional imperative for news workers: to cover those stories characterized by their deviance from accepted social and institutional norms. News accounts of feminists reveal that adherence to feminist principles is enough to mark feminists *and* feminism as being deviant; this aspect thus characterizes news coverage of feminism (Karlyn Kohrs Campbell, personal communication, June 2001).

5. See Kathleen Hall Jamieson (1995, 24–30) for a discussion of how reporters decontextualized these remarks, leading to a widespread public perception of Hillary as being a feminist insensitive to stay-at-home mothers.

6. Such polarized choices can be found elsewhere in coverage of Hillary, such as *Newsweek*'s January 15, 1996, cover which, under a photograph of Hillary's face, posed the question, "Saint or Sinner?" Jamieson (1995) demonstrates the prevalence of these dichotomies, or double binds, in discussions of women in mainstream media.

7. Adherence to this provision is one of the conditions that broadcasters must demonstrate in order to receive or to renew a license to broadcast. Although the terms "public interest," "convenience," or "necessity" may be ambiguous or difficult to interpret, I would argue that in electoral politics there can be no clearer application than to the issues, candidates, and events of political candidates in an election year.

8. Shawn J. Parry-Giles (2000) demonstrates that television news organizations have tended to rely on a few archival images of Hillary Clinton, and that they then recycle these images, repeatedly, in different stories. This recycling occurs even in contexts in which the image is out of sync with the text.

9. Events that took on panic proportions between January and November 2000 included Mayor Giuliani's handling of NYPD officers shooting unarmed black men; allegations of Bill and Hillary Clinton improperly raising money for Democrats by trading donations for Lincoln bedroom overnight stays; allegations of Hillary's use of Air Force One, free of charge, for campaign trips; Mayor Giuliani's announcement of beginning divorce proceedings with his wife, Donna Hanover, while simultaneously admit-

ting to having an affair; Mayor Giuliani's announcement that he had prostate cancer, and, later, that he would be leaving the race; an accusation that Hillary had called a campaign staffer from Bill's failed gubernatorial campaign a "Jew bastard"; and the announcement of Giuliani's replacement, Representative Rick Lazio. As is typical of mass mediated panics such as those described in chapter 2, these were short lived and affect infused.

10. Patterson (2001) argues that the sacrifice of hard news for soft news has contributed to an erosion of trust in government and a loss of interest in politics overall.

11. Senator Russ Feingold of Wisconsin, for example, ran his 1996 campaign with a policy that prohibited campaign donations of more than $100.

12. Two of the candidates, Maria Cantwell of Washington and Jean Carnahan of Missouri, received more media attention than their compatriots. The events surrounding Carnahan's husband's death and the novelty of her running in his place are what news reports featured. The bulk of Cantwell's coverage came *after* election night, when her race was considered too close to call because of the large numbers of absentee ballots received after November 7. The vacuum that Hillary left after she had won her race was partially filled with Cantwell coverage, although Cantwell did not generate the extent of coverage that Hillary received.

13. This accusation was made by a campaign manager for Bill Clinton in his second gubernatorial campaign, who claimed that Hillary had angrily referred to him as a "Jew bastard" after Clinton lost the race. The accusation was published in a book, *State of a Union,* by *National Enquirer* reporter Jerry Oppenheimer.

Afterword

1. This identity reflects the findings of sociologist Arlie Hochschild (1989) in *The Second Shift*: women who work for pay are typically responsible for most of the unpaid work inside of their homes, even when they are coupled with working men, a situation that forces another daily shift of labor onto already tired women. This is an important explanation for the exhaustion, overwork, and enormous stress that working women today report experiencing. "Women's move into the economy is the basic social revolution of our time," Hochschild reports (239). However, the material practices—public or private—that would alleviate women's having to shoulder household work almost exclusively, did not follow from this revolution.

2. This comment is in reference to an issue that has dogged Calista Flockhart in the "real world." That is, tabloid and nontabloid reporters have pointed out how very thin she is, and they have asked her repeatedly if she suffers from anorexia or bulimia. Flockhart has denied that she suffers from either of these disorders and has dismissed any suggestion that she has a problem with her weight.

3. One of *Ally McBeal*'s standard narrative techniques is the catfight—usually between Ally and her former boyfriend's spouse, Georgia. In a number of scenes, Ally and Georgia duke it out either metaphorically—in a fantasy scene with cat heads—or literally—in a kick-boxing ring. Susan Douglas (1994) has noted that the depiction of female relationships is an important indicator of a producer's/director's stance on feminism. Competition between women—and particularly competition for the attention of men—is often used as a subtle suggestion that women exist oppositionally to one another more often than cooperatively, or with mutually agreed upon goals. The "catfight," Douglas argues, is a "staple of American pop culture" (1994, 221), and it is a particularly effective means of signifying a schism between women.

4. That Crittenden uses quotation marks around the term *date rape* is revealing. Elsewhere in the book, she relies upon a Katie Roiphe-like argument about feminism and a cult of victimhood that she claims feminism produces. This is much like Roiphe's argument in *The Morning After: Sex, Fear, and Feminism on Campus* (1993), that the concept of date rape was concocted by feminists who needed one more issue that would make women feel like victims and prey to men and patriarchal practices.

5. The IWF has made itself quite available to policy makers as well as to media personnel. According to the *Washington Post*, members of the IWF are poised to exert influence in the George W. Bush administration: one member is in Bush's cabinet (Labor Secretary Elaine Chao), one is married to the vice president (Lynne Cheney), and one was nominated to be labor secretary (Bush's first labor secretary nominee, Linda Chavez). Other members are in, or are being nominated for, slightly less prestigious positions, and the IWF briefs nominees on gender issues before their Senate confirmation hearings (Morin and Deane 2001, 12).

6. I am grateful to Bonnie J. Dow for illuminating this point.

7. Arguably the most expert of these was George Bush Sr.'s chief consultant, Michael Deaver. In an interview with Bill Moyers as part of a program called "Illusions of News," Deaver stated, with no chagrin whatsoever, that he and the Bush campaign had bamboozled reporters time and again into playing promotional video news releases that cast George Bush and Ronald Reagan in a consistently positive light. Deaver described this process as a game that reporters played because, "while they won't admit it, they're not in the news business. They're in the entertainment business." Deaver gleefully recounted how he and his staff would sit back and watch this footage as it appeared on the evening news without critical comment, saying, "Ha ha! We did it again!"

8 This scenario seems to presume that the parent corporation of a news organization will be amenable to public journalism, but this is an unlikely scenario in today's consolidated, advertising-saturated media environment. As Peter Parisi concludes, public journalism's charter to follow the "public good can call for levels of journalistic aggressiveness not easily mustered within corporate-owned news outlets" (1997, 680).

References

100 leading media companies. 1999. *Advertising Age* (August 16): S1–S10.

A woman's place: In the Senate. 1992b. *New York Times*, June 4, p. A-22.

ABC. 1991a. *Nightline.* (October 7). New York: American Broadcasting Companies.

ABC. 1991b. *Good morning America.* (October 9). New York: American Broadcasting Companies.

ABC. 1991c. *World news tonight.* (October 10). New York: American Broadcasting Companies.

ABC. 1991d. *Nightline.* (October 11). New York: American Broadcasting Companies.

ABC. 1991e. *This week with David Brinkley.* (October 13). New York: American Broadcasting Companies.

ABC. 1992a. *World news tonight.* (April 17). New York: American Broadcasting Companies.

ABC. 1992b. *Nightline.* (May 29). New York: American Broadcasting Companies.

ABC. 1992d. *Good morning America.* (August 6). New York: American Broadcasting Companies.

ABC. 2000a. *Good morning America.* (February 7). New York: American Broadcasting Companies.

ABC. 2000b. *Good morning America.* (August 15). New York: American Broadcasting Companies.

ABC. 2000c. *This week.* (September 17). New York: American Broadcasting Companies.

ABC. 2000d. *Good morning America.* (October 26). New York: American Broadcasting Companies.

Acland, C. 1995. *Youth, murder, spectacle: The cultural politics of "youth in crisis."* Boulder: Westview Press.

Albiniak, P. 2001. Free time, front burner: Two bills are in the works to require broadcasters to give time to candidates. *Broadcasting & Cable* (March 12): 16.

Alexander, A. L. 1995. "She's no lady, she's a nigger": Abuses, stereotypes, and realities from the Middle Passage to Capitol (and Anita) Hill. Pp. 3–25 in *Race, gender, and power in America: The legacy of the Hill–Thomas hearings*, ed. A. F. Hill and E. C. Jordan. New York: Oxford.

Alliance for Better Campaigns 2001. *Gouging democracy: How the television industry profiteered on campaign 2000*. Available on-line: http://bettercampaigns.org/Doldisc/gouging.htm.

Andersen, R. 1995. *Consumer culture and TV programming*. Boulder: Westview Press.

Apple, R. W., Jr. 1992a. Sisterhood is political: Steady local gains by women fuel more runs for high office. *New York Times*, May 24, pp. IV-1, IV-5.

Apple, R. W., Jr. 1992b. Primary victories bring Year of the Woman closer. *New York Times*, June 9, p. A-24.

Argetsinger, A. 1996. Politics provides few kicks for suburban "soccer moms." *Washington Post*, October 27, pp. B-1, B-6.

Aufderheide, P. 2000. *The daily planet: A critic on the capitalist culture beat*. Minneapolis: University of Minnesota Press.

Ayres, B. D., Jr. 1992. Women's issues draw attention in two contests: Two female Democrats run well in California. *New York Times*, May 25, p. A-9.

Bagdikian, B. 1992. *The media monopoly*, 4th ed. Boston: Beacon Press.

Bagdikian, B. 1997. *The media monopoly*, 5th ed. Boston: Beacon Press.

Bagdikian, B. 2000. *The media monopoly*, 6th ed. Boston: Beacon Press.

Bayer, A. 1999. Elizabeth Dole tapping women for campaign funds/fuel (August 20). Copley News Service.

Bellafante, G. 1998. Feminism: It's all about me. *Time* (June 29): 54–60.

Bellah, R. N., R. Madsen, W. M. Sullivan, A. Swidler, and S. M. Tipton. 1991. *The good society*. New York: Alfred A. Knopf.

Berke, R. 1991a. Women accusing Democrats of betrayal. *New York Times*, October 17, pp. A-1, A-22.

Berke, R. 1991b. Thomas hearings may be over, but senators find a war looming. *New York Times*, October 25, p. A-14.

Black, E. 2001. Few willing to defend journalism of today. *Minneapolis Star Tribune*, May 18, p. A-16.

Bonk, K. 1988. The selling of the "gender gap": the role of organized feminism. Pp. 82–101 in *The politics of the gender gap: The social construction of political influence*, ed. C. M. Mueller. Newbury Park, Calif.: Sage.

Boyd, B. M. 2000. Run for her life. *Ms.* (August–September): 48–53.

Brenner, J. 1993. The best of times, the worst of times: U.S. feminism today. *New Left Review* 200: 101–59.

Broder, D. S. 2001. Where the money goes. *Washington Post Weekly* (March 26–April 1): 4.

Burnham, M. 1992. The Supreme Court appointment process and the politics of race and sex. Pp. 290–322 in *Race-ing justice, en-gendering power: Essays on Anita Hill, Clarence Thomas, and the construction of social reality*, ed. T. Morrison. New York: Pantheon Books.

Burrell, B. 1997. *Public opinion, the First Ladyship, and Hillary Rodham Clinton*. New York: Garland Publishing.

Byerly, C., and C. A. Warren. 1996. At the margins of center: Organized protest in the newsroom. *Critical Studies in Mass Communication* 13:1:1–23.

Campaign record. 2001. *Broadcasting and Cable* (February 19): 4.

Campbell, K. K. 1998. The discursive performance of femininity: Hating Hillary. *Rhetoric & Public Affairs* 1:1–19.

Carey, J. W. 1989. *Communication as culture*. Boston: Unwin Hyman.

Carlson, M. 1992. All eyes on Hillary. *Time* (September 14): 28–33.

Carroll, S. 1988. Women's autonomy and the gender gap: 1980 and 1982. Pp. 236–57 in *The politics of the gender gap: The social construction of political influence*, ed. C. M. Mueller. Newbury Park, Calif.: Sage.

CBS. 1991a. *CBS evening news*. (October 6). New York: Central Broadcasting System.

CBS. 1991b. *CBS evening news*. (October 8). New York: Central Broadcasting System.

CBS. 1991c. *CBS evening news*. (October 10). New York: Central Broadcasting System.

CBS. 1991d. *CBS evening news*. (October 11). New York: Central Broadcasting System.

CBS. 1991e. *CBS evening news*. (October 12). New York: Central Broadcasting System.

CBS. 1991f. *CBS evening news*. (October 14). New York: Central Broadcasting System.

CBS. 1991g. *CBS evening news*. (October 15). New York: Central Broadcasting System.

CBS. 1992. *CBS evening news*. (July 14). New York: Central Broadcasting System.

CBS. 1996. *CBS evening news*. (August 29). New York: Central Broadcasting System.

CBS. 2000a. *The early show*. (January 12). New York: Central Broadcasting System.

CBS. 2000b. *The early show*. (June 28). New York: Central Broadcasting System.

Center for American Women and Politics. 2001. *Election 2000: Summary of results for women*. Available on-line: http://www.rci.rutgers.edu/~cawp/facts/Smmary2000.html.

Center for Responsive Politics. 2000. *Lobbyist spending by industry*. Available on-line: http://www.opensecrets.org/lobbyists/98industry.htm.

Charity, A. 1995. *Doing public journalism*. New York: Guilford Press.

Clair, R. P. 1994. Hegemony and harassment: A discursive practice. Pp. 59–70 in *Conceptualizing sexual harassment as discursive practice*, ed. S. Bingham. Westport, Conn.: Praeger.

Clymer, A. 1992. This year, all sure bets are off. *New York Times*, September 20, p. IV-3.

CNBC. 2000a. *Tim Russert*. (May 20). New York: National Broadcast Company.

CNBC. 2000b. *Early today*. (August 15). New York: National Broadcast Company.

CNN. 1991a. *Crossfire*. (October 8). Atlanta: Cable News Network.

CNN. 1991b. *Larry King live*. (October 8). Atlanta: Cable News Network.

CNN. 1991c. *Larry King live*. (October 10). Atlanta: Cable News Network.

CNN. 1991d. *Larry King live*. (October 14). Atlanta: Cable News Network.

CNN. 1991e. *Larry King live*. (October 15). Atlanta: Cable News Network.

CNN. 1991f. *Larry King live*. (October 16). Atlanta: Cable News Network.

CNN. 1992a. *Inside politics*. (September 16). Atlanta: Cable News Network.

CNN. 1992b. *Inside politics*. (October 21). Atlanta: Cable News Network.

CNN. 1992c. *Inside politics*. (November 4). Atlanta: Cable News Network.

CNN. 2000a. *CNN morning news*. (January 6). Atlanta: Cable News Network.

CNN. 2000b. *CNN talkback live*. (January 20). Atlanta: Cable News Network.

CNN. 2000c. *CNN Saturday*. (February 5). Atlanta: Cable News Network.

CNN. 2000d. *CNN Sunday morning*. (February 6). Atlanta: Cable News Network.

CNN. 2000e. *Larry King Live*. (February 7). Atlanta: Cable News Network

CNN. 2000f. *CNN newsroom*. (February 7). Atlanta: Cable News Network.

CNN. 2000g. *CNN talkback live*. (February 7). Atlanta: Cable News Network.

CNN. 2000h. *CNN Sunday*. (May 7). Atlanta: Cable News Network.

CNN. 2000i. *The world today*. (August 15). Atlanta: Cable News Network.

CNN. 2000j. *Early edition*. (September 14). Atlanta: Cable News Network.

Cocco, M. 1999. For women, 2000 race is not a sorority run. *The Des Moines Register*, August 30, p. 7.

Consalvo, M. 1999. Introducing the issues: An interview with Eileen Meehan. *Journal of Communication Inquiry* 23:4:321–26.

Coontz, S. 1992. *The way we never were: American families and the nostalgia trap*. New York: Basic Books.

Coppock, V., D. Haydon, and I. Richter. 1995. *The illusions of "post-feminism": New women, old myths*. London: Taylor & Francis.

Corcoran, K. 1993. Pilloried Clinton. *American Journalism Review* (January–February): 27–29.

Costello, C. B., S. E. Miles, and A. J. Stone, eds. 1998. *The American woman, 1999–2000: A century of change—what's next?* New York: Norton.

Costello, C. B., and A. J. Stone, eds. 2001. *The American woman, 2001–2002.* New York: Norton.

Cott, N. 1987. *The grounding of modern feminism.* New Haven and London: Yale University Press.

Creedon, P., ed. 1993. *Women in mass communication,* 2d ed. Newbury Park, Calif.: Sage.

Crenshaw, K. 1992. Whose story is it, anyway? Feminist and antiracist appropriations of Anita Hill. Pp. 402–40 in *Race-ing justice, en-gendering power: Essays on Anita Hill, Clarence Thomas, and the construction of social reality,* ed. T. Morrison. New York: Pantheon Books.

Crittenden, D. 1999. *What our mothers didn't tell us: Why happiness eludes the modern woman.* New York: Simon and Schuster.

Darnovsky, M. 1991. The New Traditionalism: Repackaging Ms. Consumer. *Social Text* 29:72–95.

Davis, F. 1991. *Moving the mountain: The women's movement in American since 1960.* New York: Simon and Schuster.

Deem, M. 1999. Scandal, heteronormative culture, and the disciplining of feminism. *Critical Studies in Mass Communication* 16:1:86–93.

Deetz, S. A. 1992. *Democracy in an age of corporate colonization: Developments in communication and the politics of everyday life.* Albany: State University of New York Press.

Department of Health and Human Services. 1990. *Health: United States 1989* (DHHS Publication No. PHS 90–1232). Hyattsville, Md.: U.S. Department of Health and Human Services.

Donovan, J. 1992. *Feminist theory: The intellectual traditions of American feminism.* New York: Continuum.

Douglas, S. 1994. *Where the girls are: Growing up female with the mass media.* New York: Times Books.

Dow, B. 1996. *Prime-time feminism: Television, media culture, and the women's movement since 1970.* Philadelphia: University of Pennsylvania Press.

Dowd, M. 1991. Vote on Thomas is put off as Senate backing erodes over harassment charge. *New York Times,* October 9, pp. A-1, A-19.

Dowd, M. 2000. Bush does tactical penance, while McCain plays with TNT. *Minneapolis Star Tribune,* March 2, p. A-21.

Duffy, M., and J. M. Gotcher. 1996. Crucial advice on how to get the guy: The rhetorical vision of power and seduction in the teen magazine *YM*. *Journal of Communication Inquiry* 20:1:32–48.

Duke, L. L., and P. J. Kreshel. 1998. Negotiating femininity: Girls in early adolescence read teen magazines. *Journal of Communication Inquiry* 22:1:48–71.

Dyson, M. E. 1993. *Reflecting black: African-American cultural criticism*. Minneapolis: University of Minnesota Press.

Echols, A. 1989. *Daring to be bad: Radical feminism in America 1967–1975*. Minneapolis: University of Minnesota Press.

Eisenstein, Z. 1994. *The color of gender: Reimaging democracy*. Berkeley: University of California Press.

Elliott, S. 1997. Advertising: Maidenform aims for soccer moms and just about everyone else. *New York Times*, March 12, p. D-2.

Evans, S. 1989. *Born for liberty: A history of women in America*. New York: Free Press.

Fairness and Accuracy in Reporting. 1999a. *Why does Larry King think Hillary Clinton's hair, legs, smile, and figure are "news"*? (June 14). Available on-line: http://www.fair.org.

Fairness and Accuracy in Reporting. 1999b. *Women have not "taken over the news."* (October 12). Available on-line: //www.fair.org.

Fairness and Accuracy in Reporting. 2001. Man of the year. *EXTRA! Update* (February 2): 2.

Faludi, S. 1991. *Backlash: The undeclared war against American women*. New York: Crown.

Feldman, L. 1996. GOP spoke of soccer moms, Democrats spoke to them. *The Christian Science Monitor*, November 13, p. 3.

Ferguson, M. 1990. Images of power and the feminist fallacy. *Critical Studies in Mass Communication* 7:3:215–30.

Fiske, J. 1994. *Media matters: Everyday culture and political change*. Minneapolis: University of Minnesota Press.

Flanders, L. 1994. The "stolen feminism" hoax: Anti-feminist attack based on error-filled anecdotes. *EXTRA!* (September–October). Available on-line: http://www.fair.org.

Folbre, N. 1994. *Who pays for the kids? Gender and the structures of constraint*. London: Routledge.

Foulger, S. M. 1996. Confessions of a soccer mom. *Washington Post*, November 19, p. A-21.

Four sites account for half of Web surfing. 2001. Available on-line: http://www.cnn.com/2001/TECH/internet/06/05/internet.consolidatoin/index.html.

FOX. 2000a. *The O'Reilly factor*. (July 20). New York: FOX News Network.

FOX. 2000b. *Special report with Brit Hume*. (August 14). New York: FOX News Network.

FOX. 2000c. *Special report with Brit Hume*. (August 30). New York: FOX News Network.

FOX. 2000d. *Hannity and Colmes*. (September 27). New York: FOX News Network.

Frank, T. 2000. *One market under God: Extreme capitalism, market populism, and the end of economic democracy*. New York: Doubleday.

Frankovic, K. 1988. The Ferraro factor: The women's movement, the polls, and the press. Pp. 102–23 in *The politics of the gender gap: The social construction of political influence*, ed. C. M. Mueller. Newbury Park, Calif.: Sage.

Fraser, N. 1989. *Unruly practices: Power, discourse and gender in contemporary social theory*. Minneapolis: University of Minnesota Press.

Fraser, N. 1990. Rethinking the public sphere: A contribution to the critique of actually existing democracy. *Social Text* 25/26:56–80.

Fraser, N. 1992. Sex, lies, and the public sphere: Some reflections on the confirmation of Clarence Thomas. *Critical Inquiry* 18:3:595–612.

Gallagher, M. 1992. Women and men in the media. *Communication Research Trends* 12:1:1–36.

Garcia, K. J. 1996. Soccer moms to the rescue and other snippets of election lore. *San Francisco Chronicle*, October 12, p. A-5.

Garner, A., H. M. Sterk, and S. Adams. 1998. Narrative analysis of sexual etiquette in teenage magazines. *Journal of Communication* 48:4:59–78.

Garnham, N. 1993. The media and the public sphere. Pp. 359–76 in *Habermas and the public sphere*, ed. C. Calhoun. Cambridge: MIT Press.

Gilligan, C. 1982. *In a different voice: Psychological theory and women's development*. Cambridge: Harvard University Press.

Gilman, S. J. 2000. Lunching with the enemy. *Ms.* (October–November): 61–69.

Gist, M. 1993. Through the looking glass: Diversity and reflected appraisals of the self in mass media. Pp. 104–17 in *Women in mass communication*, 2d ed., ed. P. Creedon. Newbury Park, Calif.: Sage.

Gitlin, T. 1987. Television's screens: Hegemony in transition. Pp. 240–65 in *American media and mass culture: Left perspectives*, ed. D. Lazere. Berkeley: University of California Press.

Goldberg, C. 1996. Suburbs' soccer moms fleeing the G.O.P., are much sought. *New York Times*, October 6, pp. A-1, A-24.

Goldman, R., D. Heath, and S. Smith. 1991. Commodity feminism. *Critical Studies in Mass Communication* 8:3:333–51.

Goldman, R., and A. Rajagopal. 1991. *Mapping hegemony: Television news coverage of industrial conflict*. Norwood, N.J.: Ablex.

Gramsci, A. 1971. *Selections from the prison notebooks of Antonio Gramsci*. Translated and edited by Q. Hoare and G. N. Smith. New York: International Publishers.

Grimsley, K. D. 1996. No easy path to the top: A new survey shows women who have advanced in corporate America have paid a price. *Washington Post Weekly* (March 4–10): 37.

Grossberg, L. 1992. *We gotta get out of this place: Popular conservatism and postmodern culture*. London and New York: Routledge.

Habermas, J. 1989. *The structural transformation of the public sphere: An inquiry into a category of bourgeois society*. Translated by Thomas Burger and Frederick Lawrence. Cambridge: MIT Press.

Hall, S. 1982. The rediscovery of "ideology": Return of the repressed in media studies. Pp. 56–90 in *Society, culture, and the media*, ed. M. Gurevitch, T. Bennett, and J. Curran. London: Methuen.

Hall, S. 1986. On postmodernism and articulation: An interview with Stuart Hall. *Journal of Communication Inquiry* 10:2:45–60.

Hall, S. 1993. Encoding/decoding. Pp. 90–103 in *The cultural studies reader*, ed. S. During. London and New York: Routledge.

Hall, S. 1997. *Representation: Cultural representation and signifying practices*. London: Sage.

Hall, S., C. Critcher, T. Jefferson, J. Clarke, and B. Roberts. 1978. *Policing the crisis: Mugging, the state, and law and order*. New York: Holmes & Meier.

Hallin, D. 1994. *We keep America on top of the world: Television journalism and the public sphere*. London: Routledge.

Hansen, S. B. 1994. Lynn Yeakel versus Arlen Specter in Pennsylvania: Why she lost. Pp. 87–108 in *The Year of the Woman: Myths and realities*, ed. E. A. Cook, S. Thomas, and C. Wilcox. Boulder: Westview Press.

Head, S. W., C. H. Sterling, and L. B. Schofeld. 1994. *Broadcasting in America*, 7th ed. Boston: Houghton Mifflin.

Here come the women candidates. 1992. *New York Times*, April 30, p. A-22.

Herman, E. S., and N. Chomsky. 1988. *Manufacturing consent: The political economy of the mass media*. New York: Pantheon Books.

Higginbotham, L. A., Jr. 1992. An open letter to Justice Clarence Thomas from a federal judicial colleague. Pp. 3–39 in *Race-ing justice, en-gendering power: Essays on Anita Hill, Clarence Thomas, and the construction of social reality*, ed. T. Morrison. New York: Pantheon Books.

Higginbotham, L. A., Jr. 1995. The Hill–Thomas hearings—what took place and what happened: White male domination, black male domination, and the denigration of black women. Pp. 26–36 in *Race, gender, and power in America: The legacy of the Hill–Thomas hearings*, ed. A. F. Hill and E. C. Jordan. New York: Oxford.

Hill, A. F. 1995. Marriage and patronage in the empowerment and disempowerment of African-American women. Pp. 271–92 in *Race, gender, and power in America: The legacy of the Hill–Thomas hearings*, ed. A. F. Hill and E. C. Jordan. New York: Oxford.

Hill, A. F., and E. C. Jordan, eds. 1995. *Race, gender, and power in America: The legacy of the Hill–Thomas hearings*. New York: Oxford.

Hinds, M. D. 1992. Skillful political novice: Lynn Hardy Yeakel. *New York Times*, April 29, p. A-19.

Hochschild, A. 1989. *The second shift: Working parents and the revolution at home*. New York: Viking.

hooks, b. 1990. *Yearning: Race, gender, and cultural politics*. Boston: South End Press.

hooks, b. 1992. Democracy, Inc. *Artforum* 30:5:13–16.

Jameson, F. 1991. *Postmodernism, or the cultural logic of late capitalism*. Durham, N.C.: Duke University Press.

Jamieson, K. H. 1995. *Beyond the double bind: Women and leadership*. New York: Oxford University Press.

Jhally, S., producer and director. 1996. *Race, the floating signifier*. [film]. Northampton, Mass.: Media Education Foundation.

Johnson, S., and F. James. 1992. How Braun's campaign overcame the odds. *Chicago Tribune*, March 22, p. A-1.

Kalb, M. 2000. Can we trust TV? *Washington Post*, November 29, p. A-39.

Kamen, A. 1996. Is a father figure what America's women want? A recent recruit to the Clinton campaign effort pushes her metaphors. *Washington Post Weekly* (January 29–February 4): 15.

Kamen, P. 1991. *Feminist fatale: Voices from the "twentysomething" generation explore the future of the "Women's Movement."* New York: Donald Fine.

Katzenstein, M. F. 1990. Feminism within American institutions: Unobtrusive mobilization in the 1980s. *Signs* 16:1:27–54.

Kees, B., and B. Phillips. 1994. *Nothing sacred: Journalism, politics, and public trust in a tell-all age*. Nashville: The Freedom Forum First Amendment Center.

Kelley, C. E. 2001. *The rhetoric of Hillary Rodham Clinton: Crisis management discourse*. Westport, Conn.: Praeger.

Kellner, D. 1992. *The Persian Gulf TV War*. Boulder: Westview Press.

Kellner, D. 1995. *Media culture: Cultural studies, identity and politics between the modern and the postmodern*. London and New York: Routledge.

Kelly, M. 1993. Hillary Rodham Clinton and the politics of virtue. *New York Times Sunday Magazine*, May 23, pp. 22–25, 63–66.

King, P. H. 1996. Soccer moms: An abridged field guide. *Los Angeles Times*, October 16, p. A-3.

Kirshenbaum, G. 1996. Why all but one woman senator voted against welfare. *Ms. Magazine* (March–April): 16–19.

Klein, E. 1984. *Gender politics: From consciousness to mass politics*. Cambridge: Harvard University Press.

Klemesrud, J. 1972. Do women want equality? A poll says most now do. *New York Times*, March 24, p. 36.

Kolbert, E. 1991. Most in national survey say judge is the more believable. *New York Times*, October 15, pp. A-1, A-20.

Kuczynski, A. 2001. Newsweeklies turn a cold shoulder to hard news. *New York Times on the Web*, May 14. Available on-line: http://www.nytimes.com/2001/05/14/ business/14MAG.html.

Laclau, E., and C. Mouffe. 1985. *Hegemony and socialist strategy: Towards a radical democratic politics*. London: Verso.

Lacour, C. B. 1992. Doing things with words: "Racism" as speech act and the undoing of justice. Pp. 127–58 in *Race-ing justice, en-gendering power: Essays on Anita Hill, Clarence Thomas, and the construction of social reality*, ed. T. Morrison. New York: Pantheon Books.

Lafky, S. A. 1993. The progress of women and people of color in the U.S. journalistic workforce: A long, slow journey. Pp. 87–103 in *Women in mass communication*, 2d ed., ed. P. J. Creedon. Newbury Park, Calif.: Sage.

Lake, C. 1992. Women won on the merits. *New York Times*, November 7, p. A-21.

Lakoff, G., and M. Johnson. 1980. *Metaphors we live by*. Chicago: University of Chicago Press.

Landy, M. 1994. *Film, politics, and Gramsci*. Minneapolis: University of Minnesota Press.

Lauzen, M. M., and D. M. Dozier. 1999a. Making a difference in prime time: Women on screen and behind the scenes in the 1995–96 television season. *Journal of Broadcasting and Electronic Media* 43:1:1–19.

Lauzen, M. M., and D. M. Dozier. 1999b. The role of women on screen and behind the scenes in the television and film industries: Review of a program of research. *Journal of Communication Inquiry* 23:4:355–73.

Lawrence, C. R. 1995. The message of the verdict: A three-act morality play starring Clarence Thomas, Willie Smith, and Mike Tyson. Pp. 105–28 in *Race, gender, and power in America: The legacy of the Hill–Thomas hearings*, ed. A. F. Hill and E. C. Jordan. New York: Oxford.

Lemons, S. 1973. *The woman citizen: Social feminism in the 1920s*. Urbana: University of Illinois Press.

Lewis, A. 1992. Jumpers and doers. *New York Times*, July 17, p. A-27.

Lewis, J. 1999. Reproducing political hegemony in the United States. *Critical Studies in Mass Communication* 16:3:251–67.

Lubiano, W. 1992. Black ladies, welfare queens, and state minstrels: Ideological war by narrative means. Pp. 323–63 in *Race-ing justice, en-gendering power: Essays on Anita Hill, Clarence Thomas, and the construction of social reality*, ed. T. Morrison. New York: Pantheon Books.

MacFarquhar, N. 1996. What's a soccer mom anyway? *New York Times*, October 20, pp. IV-1, IV-6.

Madigan, T. 2000. Nine years later, Anita Hill is at peace—but she won't forget. (November 22). Knight Ridder/Tribune News Service. Retrieved December 8, 2000, from the World Wide Web: http://www.star-telegram.com.

Malveaux, J. 1995. Foreword. Pp. xi–xvii in *Race, gender, and power in America: The legacy of the Hill–Thomas hearings*, ed. A. F. Hill and E. C. Jordan. New York: Oxford University Press.

Manegold, C. S. 1992a. The battle over choice obscures other vital concerns of women. *New York Times*, August 2, p. IV-1.

Manegold, C. S. 1992b. Women advance in politics by evolution, not revolution. *New York Times*, October 21, pp. A-1, D-21.

Mann, P. S. 1995. On the postfeminist frontier. *Socialist Review* 24:1,2: 223–41.

Manther, L. V. 1998. Voters' choice. [Letter to the editor]. *Minneapolis Star Tribune*, August 23, p. A-28.

Marable, M. 1992. Clarence Thomas and the crisis of black political culture. Pp. 61–87 in *Race-ing justice, en-gendering power: Essays on Anita Hill, Clarence Thomas, and the construction of social reality*, ed. T. Morrison. New York: Pantheon Books.

Marshall, W., and M. Schram, eds. 1993. *Mandate for change*. New York: Berkley Books.

Martin, N. 1993. Who is she? A case study of the enigmatic First Lady. *Mother Jones* (November–December): 34–38, 43.

Matassa, M. 1992a. Murray sharing in glory given to women nominees. *Seattle Times*, July 14, p. A-5.

Matassa, M. 1992b. Chandler goes on the attack in debate. *Seattle Times*, October 16, pp. B-1, B-2.

McAllister, M. 1999. *The new face of television plugola*. Media Forum presentation, National Communication Association annual conference, November.

McChesney, R. 1997. *Corporate media and the threat to democracy*. New York: Seven Stories Press.

McChesney, R. 1999. *Rich media, poor democracy: Communication politics in dubious times*. Urbana: University of Illinois Press.

McConnell, B. 2001. Add news or ad time? Critics contend TV cuts political reporting to generate more ads. *Broadcasting & Cable* (March 19): 11.

McKay, N. 1992. Remembering Anita Hill and Clarence Thomas: What really happened when one black woman spoke out. Pp. 269–89 in *Race-ing justice, en-gendering power: Essays on Anita Hill, Clarence Thomas, and the construction of social reality*, ed. T. Morrison. New York: Pantheon Books.

McLaughlin, L. 1995. Feminist communication scholarship and "the women question" in the academy. *Communication Theory* 5:2:144–61.

McManus, J. 1995. A market-based model of news production. *Communication Theory* 5:4:301–38.

McMillan, J. J., and G. Cheney. 1996. The student as consumer: The implications and limitations of a metaphor. *Communication Education* 45:1:1–15.

Meyers, M. 1997. *News coverage of violence against women: Engendering blame*. Newbury Park, Calif.: Sage.

Modleski, T. 1991. *Feminism without women: Culture and criticism in a "postfeminist" age*. New York: Routledge.

Morin, R. 1999. What's dumbing down journalism? *Washington Post Weekly Edition*, April 5, p. 34.

Morin, R., and C. Deane. 2001. The administration's right-hand women. *Washington Post Weekly Edition* (May 7–13): 12.

Morrison, T., ed. 1992. *Race-ing justice, en-gendering power: Essays on Anita Hill, Clarence Thomas, and the construction of social reality*. New York: Pantheon Books.

Mouffe, C. 1992. Feminism, citizenship, and radical democratic politics. Pp. 369–84 in *Feminists theorize the political*, ed. J. Butler and J. Scott. New York: Routledge.

Mueller, C. M. 1988. The empowerment of women: Polling and the women's voting bloc. Pp. 16–36 in *The politics of the gender gap: The social construction of political influence*, ed. C. M. Mueller. Newbury Park, Calif.: Sage.

Murdoch Round the Clock. 2000. *Extra!* (November–December): 5.

Murphy, M. 1999. How women took over the news. *TV Guide* (October 9–15): 16–23.

NBC. 1991a. *NBC nightly news*. (October 8). New York: National Broadcasting Company.

NBC. 1991b. *NBC nightly news*. (October 10). New York: National Broadcasting Company.

NBC. 1991c. *NBC nightly news*. (October 12). New York: National Broadcasting Company.

NBC. 1991d. *NBC nightly news*. (October 14). New York: National Broadcasting Company.

NBC. 1991e. *NBC nightly news.* (October 15). New York: National Broadcasting Company.

NBC. 1992a. *NBC nightly news.* (April 6). New York: National Broadcasting Company.

NBC. 1992b. *NBC nightly news.* (April 25). New York: National Broadcasting Company.

NBC. 1992c. *NBC nightly news.* (June 3). New York: National Broadcasting Company.

NBC. 1992d. *NBC nightly news.* (July 14). New York: National Broadcasting Company.

NBC. 1996a. *NBC nightly news.* (March 5). National Broadcasting Company.

NBC. 1996b. *NBC nightly news.* (July 13). National Broadcasting Company.

NBC. 1996c. *NBC nightly news.* (October 15). National Broadcasting Company.

NBC. 2000a. *The today show.* (January 7). New York: National Broadcasting Company.

NBC. 2000b. *Later today.* (February 7). New York: National Broadcasting Company.

NBC. 2000c. *The today show.* (June 28). New York: National Broadcasting Company.

NBC. 2000d. *Nightly news.* (August 14). New York: National Broadcasting Company.

Ness, S. 2000. Women in media: Why so few at the top? (August 28). Available on-line: http://www.fcc.gov.

Nichols, J. 1999. Will any woman do? The candidacy of Elizabeth Dole. *The Progressive* (July): 31–33.

Nightingale, V. 1990. Women as audiences. Pp. 25–36 in *Television and women's culture: The politics of the popular,* ed. M. E. Brown. London: Sage.

Noble, B. P. 1992. The missing issue in Campaign '92. *New York Times,* November 8, p. III-23.

Norton, E. H. 1995. Anita Hill and the Year of the Woman. Pp. 242–47 in *Race, gender, and power in America: The legacy of the Hill–Thomas hearings,* ed. A. F. Hill and E. C. Jordan. New York: Oxford.

Now the word is balance. 1998. *USA Weekend* (October 23–25): 4–6.

Nyhan, D. 1996. Move over, men; soccer moms rule. *The Boston Globe,* November 1, p. A-27.

Paglia, C. 1990. *Sexual personae: Art and decadence from Nefertiti to Emily Dickinson.* New Haven: Yale University Press.

Paglia, C. 1994. *Vamps and tramps: New essays.* New York: Vintage Books.

Painter, N. I. 1992. Hill, Thomas, and the use of racial stereotype. Pp. 200–14 in *Race-ing justice, en-gendering power: Essays on Anita Hill, Clarence Thomas, and the construction of social reality,* ed. T. Morrison. New York: Pantheon Books.

Parisi, P. 1997. Toward a "philosophy of framing": News narratives for public journalism. *Journalism and Mass Communication Quarterly* 74:4:673–86.

Parry-Giles, S. J. 2000. Mediating Hillary Rodham Clinton: Television news practices and image-making in the postmodern age. *Critical Studies in Media Communication* 17:2:205–26.

Patterson, O. 1995. The crisis of gender relations among African Americans. Pp. 56–104 in *Race, gender, and power in America: The legacy of the Hill–Thomas hearings*, ed. A. F. Hill and E. C. Jordan. New York: Oxford.

Patterson, T. E. 2001. *Doing well and doing good: How soft news and critical journalism are shrinking the news audience and weakening democracy—and what news outlets can do about it.* Boston: Joan Shorenstein Center on the Press, Politics and Public Policy, John F. Kennedy School of Government, Harvard University.

Peck, R. 1996. Confessions of a soccer mom. *New Orleans Times Picayune*, October 22, pp. F-1,2.

Phelps, T., and H. Winternitz. 1992. *Capitol games: Clarence Thomas, Anita Hill, and the story of a Supreme Court nomination.* New York: Hyperion.

Phillips, P. 2000. *Censored 2000: The year's top 25 censored stories.* New York: Seven Stories Press.

Pollitt, K. 1993. The male media's Hillary problem. *The Nation*, May 17, pp. 657–60.

Pollitt, K. 1994. *Reasonable creatures: Essays on women and feminism.* New York: Vintage Books.

Pozner, J. L. 2001. Cosmetic coverage: Media obsessed with cutting political women down to size. *Extra!* (March–April): 8–10.

Quayle, M. 1992. Workers, wives and mothers. *New York Times*, September 11, p. A-35.

Quindlen, A. 1992a. Little big woman. *New York Times*, February 2, p. IV-17.

Quindlen, A. 1992b. Gender contender. *New York Times*, April 26, p. IV-19.

Rakow, L., and K. Kranich. 1991. Woman as sign in television news. *Journal of Communication* 41:1:8–23.

Rapp, R. 1987. Is the legacy of second-wave feminism postfeminism? *Socialist Review* 18:1:31–37.

Rapping, E. 1994. *Media-tions: Forays into the culture and gender wars.* Boston: South End Press.

Reinhold, R. 1992. Two women win nomination in California Senate races. *New York Times*, June 3, pp. A-1, A-17.

Resnick, J. 1995. From the Senate Judiciary Committee to the country courthouse: The relevance of gender, race, and ethnicity to adjudication. Pp. 177–227 in *Race, gender, and power in America: The legacy of the Hill–Thomas hearings*, ed. A. F. Hill and E. C. Jordan. New York: Oxford.

Rhodes, J. 1993. "Falling through the cracks": Studying women of color in mass communication. Pp. 24–31 in *Women in mass communication*, 2d ed., ed. P. Creedon. Newbury Park, Calif.: Sage.

Rich, A. 1979. *On lies, secrets, and silence*. New York: Norton.

Rivers, C. 1996. *Slick spins and fractured facts: How cultural myths distort the news*. New York: Columbia University Press.

Roberts, J. L. 2001. Chances are, you've only surfed a few sites today: Media consolidation comes to the Internet. (June 4). Available on-line: http://www.msnbc. com/news/582461.asp?pne=msn&cp1=1.

Roberts, C., and S. Roberts. 2000. Swaying the swing voter. *USA Weekend* (September 1–3): 6–8.

Roiphe, K. 1993. *The morning after: Sex, fear, and feminism on campus*. Boston: Little Brown and Co.

Rosen, J. 1996. *Getting the connections right: Public journalism and the troubles in the press*. New York: The Twentieth Century Fund.

Rosen, R. 1996. Clinton jilted poor sisters for soccer moms. *Los Angeles Times*, November 8, p. B-9.

Ross, A. 1992. The private parts of justice. Pp. 40–60 in *Race-ing justice, en-gendering power: Essays on Anita Hill, Clarence Thomas, and the construction of social reality*, ed. T. Morrison. New York: Pantheon Books.

Rubenstein, S. 1996. Political debate doesn't interest busy soccer moms. *San Francisco Chronicle*, October 17, pp. A-15, A-26.

Ruggiero, J. A., and L. C. Weston. 1985. Work options for women in women's magazines: The medium *and* the message. *Sex Roles* 12:5-6:535–47.

Russo, M. 1994. *The female grotesque: Risk, excess and modernity*. New York: Routledge.

Rutenberg, J. 2000. Media: To stay afloat, unlikely ties in TV news. *The New York Times on the Web*, November 27. Retrieved November 27, 2000, from the World Wide Web: http://www.nytimes.com/2000/11/27/business.

Sanders, M. 1993. Television: The face of the network news is male. Pp. 167–71 in *Women in mass communication*, 2d ed., ed. P. Creedon. Newbury Park, Calif.: Sage.

Satran, P. R. 1996. Might you be the coveted Soccer Mom? *Chicago Tribune*, November 4, p. 5-1.

Scheer, R. 1996. A new low: Pandering to "soccer moms." *Los Angeles Times*, October 8, p. B-7.

Scheuer, J. 1999. *The sound bite society: Television and the American mind*. New York: Four Walls Eight Windows.

Shalit, R. 1998. Canny and Lacy: Ally, Dharma, Ronnie, and the betrayal of postfeminism. *The New Republic,* April 6, pp. 27–32.

Slack, J. D. 1989. Contextualizing technology. Pp. 329–45 in *Rethinking communication: Volume 2, paradigm exemplars,* ed. B. Dervin et al. Newbury Park, Calif.: Sage.

Smith-Rosenberg, C. 1985. *Disorderly conduct: Visions of gender in Victorian America.* New York: Alfred A. Knopf.

Sobieraj, S. 1999. Is Bush eyeing Dole and her female support? (August 19). The Associated Press.

Solomon, N. 1994. *False hope: The politics of illusion in the Clinton era.* Monroe, Maine: Common Courage Press.

Sommers, C. H. 1995. *Who stole feminism? How women have betrayed women.* New York: Simon and Schuster.

Spelman, E. V. 1988. *Inessential woman: Problems of exclusion in feminist thought.* Boston: Beacon Press.

Spigel, L. 1992. *Make room for TV: Television and the family in postwar America.* Chicago: University of Chicago Press.

Stabile, C. 1992. Shooting the mother: Fetal photography and the politics of disappearance. *Camera Obscura* 28:179–205.

Stacey, J. 1991. *Brave new families: Stories of domestic upheaval in late twentieth century America.* New York: Basic Books.

Stacey, J. 1993. Sexism by a subtler name? Postindustrial conditions and postfeminist consciousness in the Silicon Valley. Pp. 322–38 in *Gendered domains,* ed. S. Reverby and D. Helly. Ithaca, N.Y.: Cornell University Press.

Stall, B. 1992. Battle with Wilson left Feinstein tougher, quicker. *Los Angeles Times,* April 28, pp. A-1, A-20.

Stansell, C. 1992. White feminists and black realities: The politics of authenticity. Pp. 251–68 in *Race-ing justice, en-gendering power: Essays on Anita Hill, Clarence Thomas, and the construction of social reality,* ed. T. Morrison. New York: Pantheon Books.

Steeves, H. L. 1997. *Gender violence and the press: The St. Kizito story.* Athens, Ohio: The University Center for International Studies.

Steinem, G. 1999. Sex, lies, and advertising. Pp. 137–53 in *Common culture: Reading and writing about American Popular Culture,* 2d ed., ed. M. Petracca and M. Sorapure. Upper Saddle River, N.J.: Prentice Hall.

Suarez, R. 1998. A matter of (no) trust. *Minneapolis Star Tribune,* July 27, p. A-6.

Tackett, M. 1996. "Soccer moms" tell why Clinton gets backing. *Chicago Tribune,* September 15, p. I-7.

Taeuber, C. M., ed. 1996. *Statistical handbook of women in America.* Phoenix: Oryx Press.

Tavris, C. 1996. Misreading the gender gap. *New York Times*, September 17, p. A-15.

Thelwell, M. 1992. False, fleeting, perjured Clarence: Yale's brightest and blackest go to Washington. Pp. 86–126 in *Race-ing justice, en-gendering power: Essays on Anita Hill, Clarence Thomas, and the construction of social reality*, ed. T. Morrison. New York: Pantheon Books.

Thompson, J. B. 1990. *Ideology and modern culture: Critical social theory in the era of mass communication*. Cambridge: Polity Press.

Tomasky, M. 2001. *Hillary's turn: Inside her improbable, victorious Senate campaign*. New York: Free Press.

Treichler, P. A. 1999. *How to have theory in an epidemic: Cultural chronicles of AIDS*. Durham, N.C.: Duke University Press.

Tronto, J. 1995. Changing goals and changing strategies: Varieties of women's political activities. Pp. 396–414 in *U.S. women in struggle: A Feminist Studies anthology*, ed. C. Moses and H. Hartmann. Champaign: University of Illinois Press.

Turow, J. 1997. *Media systems in society: Understanding industries, strategies, and power*, 2d ed. New York: Longman.

Underwood, D. 1995. *When MBAs rule the newsroom: How the marketers and managers are reshaping today's media*. New York: Columbia University Press.

United States Bureau of the Census. 1992. *Statistical abstract of the United States: 1992*. Washington, D.C.: Author.

United States Bureau of the Census. 1997. *Statistical abstract of the United States: 1997*. Washington, D.C.: Author.

United States Bureau of the Census. 1999. *Statistical abstract of the United States: 1999*. Washington, D.C.: Author.

van Zoonen, L. 1994. *Feminist media studies*. London: Sage.

Vavrus, M. 1997. Alternative news and Others in the Year of the Woman. Unpublished manuscript.

Vavrus, M. D. Forthcoming. Domesticating patriarchy: Hegemonic masculinity and television's "Mr. Mom." *Critical Studies in Media Communication*.

West, C. 1992. Black leadership and the pitfalls of racial reasoning. Pp. 390–401 in *Race-ing justice, en-gendering power: Essays on Anita Hill, Clarence Thomas, and the construction of social reality*, ed. T. Morrison. New York: Pantheon Books.

Wilcox, C. 1994. Why was 1992 the "Year of the Woman"? Explaining women's gains in 1992. Pp. 1–24 in *The Year of the Woman: Myths and realities*, ed. E. A. Cook, S. Thomas, and C. Wilcox. Boulder: Westview Press.

Wilkerson, I. 1992a. Illinois senator is defeated by county politician. *New York Times*, March 18, p. A-19.

Wilkerson, I. 1992b. Storming the Senate "club." *New York Times*, March 19, p. A-20.

Wilkerson, I. 1992c. Black woman's Senate race is acquiring a celebrity aura. *New York Times*, July 29, pp. A-1, A-13.

Wilkerson, I. 1992d. Where Anita Hill is the silent third candidate. *New York Times*, August 31, pp. A-1, A-12.

Willis, S. 1991. *A primer for daily life*. London and New York: Routledge.

Wines, M. 1992. Women need free markets, not government, Bush says. *New York Times*, September 19, p. A-7.

Winfield, B. H. 1997. The First Lady, political power, and the media: Who elected her anyway? Pp. 166–80 in *Women, media and politics*, ed. P. Norris. New York: Oxford University Press.

Witt, L., K. M. Paget, and G. Matthews. 1994. *Running as a woman: Gender and power in American politics*. New York: Free Press.

WLNY-TV. 2000. *News 55 at 11*. (November 3). West Palm Beach: Paxson Communications.

WNBC. 2000. *News Forum*. (February 6). New York: National Broadcasting Company.

Wolf, N. 1992. *The beauty myth: How images of beauty are used against women*. New York: Anchor Books.

Women's Action Coalition. 1993. *WAC stats: The facts about women*. New York: The New Press.

Year of the woman and the odd couple. 1992. *New York Times*, October 17, p. A-20.

INDEX